IAIN WATSON is a BBC Political Correspondent who works across TV, radio and online. He reports regularly for Radio 4's *Today* programme and previously for BBC2's *Newsnight* and the flagship BBC1 political show *On the Record*. He extensively covered both the 2010 and 2015 general elections, spending the entire campaigns 'on the road'. He also covered the Scottish referendum. Despite being Westminster editor of the *Sunday Herald*, he was delighted to decamp to Edinburgh to cover the first elections to the Scottish parliament in 1999. He lives in London with his wife and son.

Some of the book's lessons are just as applicable to the Conservatives as to Labour.
CONSERVATIVE HOME

The real – if guilty – pleasure of Watson's book is his bird's-eye view of a campaign that combined bad optics with terrible symbolism.
THE NATIONAL

Luath Press is an independently owned and managed book publishing company based in Scotland and ⟨…⟩ ty or grouping.

Five Million Conversations

How Labour lost an election and rediscovered its roots

IAIN WATSON

Luath Press Limited
EDINBURGH
www.luath.co.uk

First published 2015

ISBN: 978-1-910745-26-7

The paper used in this book is recyclable. It is made from
low chlorine pulps produced in a low energy, low emissions manner
from renewable forests.

Printed and bound by
Bell & Bain Ltd., Glasgow

Typeset in 11 point Sabon
by 3btype.com

The author's right to be identified as author of this work under the
Copyright, Designs and Patents Act 1988 has been asserted.

To Rachel and Alexander Watson
And for Agnes Watson (1932–2014)

Contents

Acknowledgements

Thanks to the government ministers, shadow ministers, senior politicians, special advisers, strategists – and voters – who gave me their accounts of a fascinating election, and its unexpected aftermath. Many of you are quoted. But this book wouldn't have been possible without the assistance of those who are not. You know who you are – and I'm not telling! I, of course, take responsibility for all errors in a publication which was necessarily swiftly produced. So a special mention, too, for the publishers who made it possible.

My gratitude to all my BBC colleagues who remained on a relatively even keel despite spending so much time covering an intense election – especially the 'core team' of Dave 'renaissance man' Bull and Dan Grant. Thanks are due to Maxine Collins, Jack Evans, Peter Hunt, Sarah Kirby, Simon Lister, Lucy Manning, Callum May, Richard Perry, John Prendergast, Sam Smith and Paul Twinn. Let's not do it again soon though...

And above all thanks to Rachel for reading this – and to Alexander for not disrupting it too much!

Preface

At the start of this campaign I said that we wanted to have four million conversations in four months. And I am so proud that today, on the final day of campaigning, we will top five million conversations. This race is going to be the closest we have ever seen. It is going to go down to the wire.

ED MILIBAND, 6 May 2015

THIS BOOK TRIES to solve a mystery. How could Labour's activists talk to a record number of voters – and end up with fewer seats than at the previous election? What was the nature of those conversations? Was there any way to report – and react to – the scepticism campaigners were hearing on the doorsteps? Why did all this apparent activity bequeath the next leader greater challenges than the last? From Cardiff to Colne, Glasgow to Gloucester, Leeds to London, I followed Labour's election campaign around Britain. As this book reveals, those around Ed Miliband never expected him to lead a majority government. But they did assume he would do enough to deprive the Conservatives of outright victory and 'lock out' David Cameron from Downing Street, without the need for a formal deal with the SNP. How could Labour get it so wrong? And how will the party's next leader avoid the same mistakes?

This book covers all the significant moments in Labour's campaign. The day-by-day approach is designed to offer an insight into how political parties try to control their message, their messengers – and those who try to report on both. It also offers you a front-row seat at the daily dramas of the most closely fought election in two decades.

But this is a lot more than a campaign diary. It examines what one senior politician called 'failures of policy, personnel and organisation' – and looks forward to the challenges Jeremy Corbyn will face. With access to some of the party's most revealing private polling, this book explores how Labour failed to reassure voters on the two policy issues which concerned them most – its record on spending and its stance on immigration. And it charts how big ideas were boiled down to what one frontbencher called 'small bribes'. Through the prism of the much-mocked Edstone, it shines a light on the party's personnel – and the behind-the-scenes battles which hampered the quality and speed of decision making. As for organisation, it discovers that what the Conservatives and the SNP got right can be as instructive as what Labour got wrong.

A large, if not decisive, contribution to Labour's defeat was the loss of

40 of the 41 seats the party had held in Scotland. The book provides new information on the divisions and lack of decisiveness at the very top of the party over how to handle the SNP threat – and how to counter the Conservative charge that a weak Labour government would be at the mercy of Alex Salmond and Nicola Sturgeon.

Above all, it concludes that when parties have millions of conversations with voters, they can learn more from listening than talking.

The Accidental Leader

12 September

- Jeremy Corbyn is elected Labour leader.
- He gets the support of nearly 60 per cent of his party's members and supporters.
- He is the most left wing leader of his party since Michael Foot in 1983.
- Can he now change the party as well as its leadership?

HIS HEAD SHOOK in disbelief. The full-time official of the Labour Party must have seen the result coming, but he couldn't help utter the phrase: 'How the f*** did that happen?'

To be fair, it was probably the sheer scale of Jeremy Corbyn's victory that shocked him.

251,417 Labour members and supporters had backed Corbyn, and he had beaten all three of his rivals – Andy Burnham, Yvette Cooper and Liz Kendall – by more votes than they had between them. He gained nearly 60 per cent of the ballot – coming 40 points ahead of second placed Burnham, the former frontrunner who had garnered a little less than one in five of the votes cast. While Corbyn smiled as though he had just heard he had won £25 on the premium bonds, his nearest rival sat stiff as a statue, apparently hoping his tear ducts would be just as immobile.

The venue for the announcement was close to the ultimate prize. Jeremy Corbyn, a republican, was declared Labour's new leader on Saturday 12 September at the Queen Elizabeth Conference Centre – just a mere tilt of the head and glance of the eye away from Downing Street and the Houses of Parliament. Yet for many Labour stalwarts in the audience these centres of power might as well have existed in a parallel universe. Jeremy Corbyn's politics are to the left of Michael Foot and he is supported by only one in ten of his MPs. But he has the biggest mandate of any of his party's leaders, ever.

I had 'tweeted' that Corbyn had won before it was officially announced because a member of Labour's ruling National Executive Committee told me the result – but they hadn't told me the extent of it. And as the NEC chairman Jim Kennedy – who would probably be quite good at drawing raffles – benevolently but rather underwhelmingly delivered the news officially from the conference stage, the atmosphere in the room was like a moving image that had just been paused. There was a stunned silence which lasted just a few seconds, but it felt like everyone had needed a little time to suspend disbelief, take a sharp breath, then move on. Normal service was resumed relatively swiftly when a member of Labour's staff – and not a Corbyn supporter – began the applause from the back of the hall. Soon, there was an ovation. That was a signal for the 'snappers' – who had maintained almost a dignified distance from the row of seats where the candidates had been uncomfortably juxtaposed – to rush like greyhounds from their traps and surround the new leader. Liz Kendall's vote – just 4.5 per cent of the total – hadn't even been announced at that point. Her result was quickly dispensed with, and a besieged but becalmed Corbyn took to the stage with the diminutive but determined press officer Anna Wright – who had been a mainstay of Labour's election campaign – almost single-handedly trying to part the sea of photographers to let the new leader deliver his victory speech.

The old method of electing a Labour leader – with special privileges for MPs and trade unions – had been swept aside by his predecessor Ed Miliband in favour of a system which gave each of the party's members – and a new franchise of supporters – an equal say in choosing who leads them. Corbyn had not been the first choice of the small Socialist Campaign Group of MPs to stand for leader – but Diane Abbott, who had failed to win in 2010, was concentrating on her ultimately unsuccessful bid to be her party's candidate for London Mayor. John McDonnell, the Group's chair, had failed to get enough support from fellow MPs to get on the ballot in 2007 – when Tony Blair had stood down – and in 2010 when Gordon Brown resigned. He had had a heart attack since then and had persuaded his long-standing political ally to lead the charge this time.

And now here was Jeremy Corbyn, ready and willing to throw open the door of his party as leader. In his first remarks on being elected, he also extended his hand of friendship to those who had drifted away from Labour in recent years. He declared:

> Our party has changed. We have grown enormously because of the hopes of so many ordinary people for a different Britain, a better Britain, a more equal Britain, a more decent Britain. They are fed up with the inequality, the injustice, the unnecessary poverty, all those issues have brought people in in a spirit of hope and optimism. So I say to the new members of the party, or those that have joined in as registered supporters or affiliated supporters: welcome, welcome to our party, welcome to our movement. And I say to those returning to the party who were in it before and felt disillusioned and went away: welcome back, welcome back to your party, welcome home.

I dashed out to broadcast the result from a nearby radio car. However weird the atmosphere had been in a room full of long-standing Labour Party members and politicians, outside there was jubilation as his newer supporters – some rather grizzled, but many of them young and vibrant – were waiting to catch a glimpse of him. Many were sporting red and white Corbyn T-shirts or displaying other memorabilia. Some had placards as they prepared to join a pro-refugee demonstration, which the new leader had announced he would address that afternoon, in Parliament Square. He may have acquired new powers, but his first act on assuming the mantle of leadership would be to join a protest, and climb aboard a makeshift stage where he was subsequently joined by veteran singer/songwriter Billy Bragg, who led an impromptu rendition of the 'Red Flag'. Until then some of his admirers whiled away the time by selling far left newspapers to each other. The *Labour Briefing* vendor was declaring to all and sundry 'we have our party back'. The publication had been influential when Ken Livingstone had led the Greater London Council in the '80s and Corbyn had been on its editorial board. It had championed social causes – including an equal age of consent for all – which had once been marginal but had now become mainstream, though the economic policies it advocated had been as unpopular with Tony Blair as they were with the Tories.

To keep any well-wishers congregating outside the conference centre at bay, three burly but polite security staff were blocking the entrance and tried to prevent me going back in to gain reaction to the result. After a stand-off, good sense prevailed and, once back inside, I gathered a wide range of views.

The Tottenham MP David Lammy had nominated Corbyn for leader to encourage a wide ranging debate on Labour's future after its election failure but hadn't expected or wanted him to win. Nonetheless he told me he didn't regret his decision:

> Absolutely not. He didn't get my vote, but you know we now have a movement. Under Bill Clinton, the Democrats were very top-down and I saw Obama change that. We have a renewal now and we have a different party now and we must deal with members as they are, not as we would like them to be. Under Ed Miliband's leadership people who had left over Iraq were already coming back. So were the Greens, and of course former Lib Dems. So we were in the process of changing. I have always been sceptical that a pure left-wing offer would work in England – it might work in Scotland and maybe even London, but not in England as a whole. But Jeremy's authenticity really struck home. This is the end of the spin-doctor-policy-wonk-go-to-Oxford-become-a-researcher-then-an-MP kind of politics.

Angela Eagle had chaired Labour's NEC when the new rules for electing a Labour leader had been adopted. Again not a Corbyn supporter, she told me she would serve in his shadow cabinet. 'I am a feminist and we need women at the top echelons of the party'. She was to be appointed Shadow Business Secretary and Shadow First Secretary of State.

Fellow NEC member Jonathan Ashworth said he was prepared, for now, to take the new leader at his word: 'Jeremy Corbyn said he wants to move forward inclusively and have democratic decision making. Let's see how that develops.'

But John Woodcock – the Blairite MP who had been a leading figure in the Liz Kendall campaign – had no intention of sitting on the Labour front bench alongside someone who he felt would take the party back to an unelectable past. He represented Barrow-in-Furness, where Britain's nuclear submarines were constructed. He had pledged at the election to resign as an MP if Labour resiled on a commitment to renew the nuclear deterrent, but had just seen a unilateralist become his party's leader for the first time in three decades…

Days before he had been elected so decisively, I had asked Jeremy Corbyn himself what his priorities would be as leader – and some of those sceptical stalwarts perhaps do have grounds for feeling nervous, not just about Labour's electoral prospects – that is already concerning them – but about the scale of changes that might be necessary to bring the party more in to line with his own policies. He is out of step not with Labour's aims – even the Tony Blair-revised Clause IV describes the party as 'democratic socialist' – but with many existing Labour positions, from nuclear weapons to renationalisation, and existing Labour MPs' views. It will take something of a grassroots revolution to move those policies closer to the leader's own, but this is how he summed up his approach:

> I want people to come in and have an influence – and not wait for an all seeing, all knowing leader at some point in five years' time to send the policies down the food chain for the footsoldiers to knock on doors and deliver – get the people involved in the policies in the first place, and people will have a real strength and real feeling and real passion behind what they do.

His other immediate priorities, he told me, were 'a strong absolute opposition to the welfare reform bill. And the brutality behind it' – his leadership rivals had initially abstained on this – and 'an opposition to the sale of public assets'. But above all he would 'challenge this agenda of the Conservatives of greater inequality, where the most vulnerable are being asked to pay the price of the banking crisis of 2008'.

Ed Miliband moved his party, in his words, 'beyond New Labour.'

Jeremy Corbyn is likely to move it so far beyond that it will be over the current political horizon. But he believes he has every right to do so: 'the mandate for the new leader comes from the biggest democratic process that any political party in Britain has ever undertaken'

Celebrating victory on 12 September was Corbyn supporter Stuart Watkin, who had worked for Katy Clark when she was MP for North Ayrshire and Arran. She had been defeated by the SNP at the general election. He said:

> His campaign has really sparked something off. Over the years members have been seen as voting and leafleting fodder by party leaders. Now there will be a debate – and I am sure if 400,000 of our 500,000 members want to keep nuclear weapons Jeremy will listen. But if they think Trident's a waste of money well, the MPs need to get in line with the party members who put them there. If they ignore them, that's the up to their local Labour parties but I think when the dust settles people will realise the strength of the mandate Jeremy has won.

* * *

So how has a 66-year-old who has languished on Labour's backbenches for half his life – since he was first elected for Islington North in 1983 – become leader of what is now Britain's largest political party?

His views came under far greater scrutiny than ever before during the leadership contest but there is a sense in which he is still something of an unknown quantity – during that political battle Ed Miliband's former deputy chief of staff Lucy Powell said she had never spoken to him. So one of her first conversations must have been on 13 September, when he offered – and she accepted – the role of Shadow Education Secretary.

Perhaps his lack of contact with some fellow MPs at Westminster was part of the attraction for a wider group of voters – he didn't look or sound like a conventional, modern-day politician.

A couple of weeks before his elevation to his party's leadership I went to meet him to try to find out more about what influenced him, and what motivated him and his recent admirers.

* * *

The capacity crowd were keen to get inside the venue. If they had been queueing to see the latest cinema blockbuster there would have been popcorn vendors at hand to offer sustenance. If this had been a football crowd, there would have been purveyors of hot pies. But the 500 people on the streets of Chelmsford were eager to attend Jeremy Corbyn's 87th rally of his leadership campaign and all that was on offer to them was food for thought. Paper sellers on – and to – the left of Labour were pushing copies of *Socialist Worker* and *Socialist Appeal*, the organ of a Trotskyist group which had splintered from the Militant Tendency.

For Corbyn there were now no no-go areas. He was attracting more people to his meetings in Conservative-held seats than the former leader of his party managed to pull out to most well-organised rallies in marginal constituencies during the most closely fought election in recent years. The Conservative MP for Chelmsford – Hillary Clinton-supporting Simon Burns – has a majority of more than 18,000 and the small Essex city hasn't returned a Labour MP to Westminster since the dying days of the post-war Attlee government, when the party won a by-election. So what the media dubbed Corbyn-mania was indeed rather manic and a phenomenon people wanted to experience for themselves. Some had clearly come out of their homes on the cusp of September – just as the weather was turning autumnal – in order to bask in the rekindled warm glow of fellow-feeling.

Sasha McLoughlin was very much younger than Jeremy Corbyn but had nonetheless waited a long time for someone who shares her politics to be in such a prominent position: 'It's the first time a Labour leader has represented me in years. You vote Labour because that's what you do but it's so exciting to have a left-wing leader, not a Tory in disguise.'

A local teacher, Helen Davenport, had been attracted back from the Greens. She was a personification of the problem Labour had in policing their leadership rules – more of that later! Although she had backed another party, she was genuinely being swayed back to her old allegiances because Corbyn was on the ballot: 'I'd given up hope. But now there's an alternative. I like his ideas on renationalising rail and he has a more sympathetic policy on immigration. He has the wisdom of Tony Benn.'

'I am a lifelong socialist and appalled that we have a government that is using austerity in my view for ideological reasons,' said Brian Little-child, a former Communist Party member. Despite the surname, he is of Jeremy Corbyn's generation. 'The other candidates, even Andy Burnham, are too close to Blair and what he stood for – we looked like pink Tories.' But hadn't Tony Blair fought three election winning campaigns for Labour?, I ventured. For Brian, winning elections wasn't everything: 'The chances are Jeremy won't get elected in 2020. But what we need is a good opposition to keep the Tories in check. And look, maybe this is where to start the change.'

For Sue Millman – of a similar age to most of Corbyn's leadership rivals: 'I have been a member of the Labour party in the past, I never joined another party. I was disillusioned. I am an active trade union member and he is the most relevant Labour leadership candidate there is.' But her attitude was 'I won't get fooled again.' He was not quite relevant enough yet for her rejoin Labour and vote for him as leader. She would only return to the fold once she saw him in action and if 'there are sufficient changes that make me feel enthusiastic again'.

Gerard D'Arcy, on the other hand, was solidly Labour, and a recent Corbyn convert. 'He is straight-talking, There's no artifice. No spin. The other candidates are preened, moulded. He looks like a '70s sociology lecturer but people are now into the issues, not the image – no one cares about what his smile looks like.' He said Andy Burnham would have been 'excellent' but had now been relegated to his second choice.

But it wasn't just the people of Chelmsford who had turned out to see Jeremy Corbyn. An internationalist from an early age, he was nonplussed to be surrounded as soon as he himself set foot in the venue by Finnish television, a reporter from France's *Le Monde* and a German journalist. He calmly restored order from chaos and politely took questions from each. He was asked to dispense advice to Finland's social democrats – 'I am impressed with education and the level of public services in Finland – I wish them well in expanding the socialist traditions of Finland.' He gave his assessment of Socialist François Hollande's rocky record as French President: 'He hasn't been able to sufficiently challenge austerity and has imposed quite a lot of it himself. I do hope the reforms of previous socialist governments such as the [shorter] working week are safe.'

There has been a lot of speculation about – and a small amount of evidence of – 'entryism'. That is, people mostly to the left of Labour – Trotskyists in particular – joining or becoming supporters in order to change the party and use it the means of conveying a more radical, even revolutionary, message to voters. Corbyn seemed more concerned about 'exitism' – people who had left the party because it wasn't radical enough. Asked to comment on whether he felt close to Syriza and Podemos – the Greek and Spanish movements to the left of Labour's sister parties in those countries – he said:

> Labour's the mass party broadly of the centre left in Britain. Parties to its left haven't done particularly well partly because of the electoral system. The election for Labour leader has provided the space and opportunity for people to get involved in a political discussion. I want the Labour Party to be an open door.

*   *   *

Unlike his Oxbridge educated opponents, Jeremy Corbyn hadn't gone to university. He dropped out of a course on trade union studies at what was then North London Poly in the '70s after a row about the syllabus. He told me:

> I have got very few qualifications but I have a fascination of reading and read a lot. I spent a lot of time in the school library and the local library and I have this view that everyone I meet knows something I don't know and we can learn from each other.

His father David was an electrical engineer. His mother Naomi, a teacher at girls' grammar school, weaned him on socialist literature. His parents had met demonstrating against Franco's Spain. So not for Jeremy the capers of the Famous Five, but the conversations held between painters and decorators in 'Mugsborough' – or Hastings – more than a century ago: 'My mother gave me the *Ragged Trousered Philanthropists* to read.'

The main character, Frank Owen, rails against his workmates, who seem all too content to donate their 'surplus value' to their bosses:

> As Owen thought of his child's future, there sprang up within him a feeling of hatred and fury against his fellow workmen. They were the enemy – those ragged-trousered philanthropists, who not only quietly submitted like so many cattle to their miserable slavery for the benefit of others, but defended it and opposed and ridiculed any suggestion of reform. They were the real oppressors – the men who spoke of themselves as 'the likes of us' who, having lived in poverty all their lives, considered that what had been good enough for them was good enough for their children.

The book was written by Robert Tressell, himself a painter and signwriter, and published posthumously after he succumbed to TB in his early 40s. Corbyn was also influenced by George Orwell's writings and said he joined Labour because of the 'the injustice I saw in society'.

With the help of BBC producer Tom Edgington, I had interviewed his astrophysicist brother Piers for Radio 4's PM programme on the day that Jeremy Corbyn made the ballot for Labour leader. The family had moved from Wiltshire to a large house, formerly a B&B, in Shropshire when Jeremy was seven. Piers said their home had been 'alive with political discussion' and that Jeremy had been actively involved in debating at school. He had, however, been trounced in a school election in 1964 when he stood as a Labour candidate. That was the prestigious Adams' Grammar School in Newport, near Telford, where Jeremy had been a prefect. But he had challenged those in authority in other ways at this boys' school – which dates from the 1600s – by campaigning against older pupils being dragooned into the army cadets. The school's Combined Cadet Force, though, exists to this day. Sometimes protests don't lead to change. Corbyn's opposition to selective schooling has remained constant. Outside of school hours, Piers told me his brother had been the leading light in the Wrekin Young Socialists, Labour's youth wing. So I asked Jeremy Corbyn about his earliest political activities. Many of the issues he campaigned on then, he still campaigns on now:

> We formed the Young Socialists in the early '60s. I became the secretary of it and was extremely active. We had what we thought were massive meetings of 40 or 50 people every Sunday night in various pubs and produced a local magazine. We got involved in campaigning against the then Conservative government's immigration bill because we thought it was trying to divide families. We also campaigned against nuclear weapons and on the war.

That was, of course the Vietnam war. 'Yes I was against, obviously,' he said with a smile.

On one issue, though, there is no longer any need for him to campaign. He was a staunch anti-apartheid campaigner, opposing – like another leading Labour figure, then a Liberal, Peter Hain – the Springbok rugby tour of England in 1970. He is therefore used to digging in for the long haul. And of course he continues to oppose 'global injustice' and argues for debt relief and cancellation for third world economies.

While his three leadership rivals had been advisers to MPs before becoming MPs themselves, he had been a researcher to the National Union of Tailor and Garment Makers in the early '70s before working as an organiser for NUPE, the public service union. It has now been subsumed into UNISON, one of the big backers of his leadership bid.

His political career began on Haringey council in north London in 1974. He chaired the public works, and then planning, committees. Labour peer Toby Harris was a fellow councillor at the time. He confirmed that Corbyn took a close interest in planning and the built environment as well as housing but his focus had always been global as much as local:

> I have known him for more than 40 years and his political position on most issues has hardly shifted. He feels passionately about what are called 'national liberation struggles' – issues around Palestine and Ireland. When I first met him he was a trade union organiser – very passionate in opposing public sector cuts. It'd be very much the same sort of thing that he is saying now.

While his views have been nothing if not consistent, his relationships have been more fluid. He married his fellow councillor Jane Chapman but they split in 1979. She told the *Mail on Sunday* she would vote for him but that they had had an austere existence in the '70s, which mostly involved meetings rather than nights out – and she had sought a better work/life balance.

Corbyn very much likes to keep his private life private, and he used his first speech as Labour leader to denounce an intrusive press:

> I say a huge thank you to all of my widest family, all of them, because they have been through the most appalling levels of abuse from some of our media over the past three months. It has been intrusive, it has been abusive, it's been simply wrong. And I say to journalists: attack public political figures, make criticisms of them, that's okay, that is what politics is about. But please don't attack people who didn't ask to be put in the limelight, and merely want to get on with their lives. Leave them alone, leave them alone in all circumstances.

But his private and political lives became intertwined as his second marriage broke up towards the end of the last century. A member of Amnesty International, Corbyn had been a prominent critic of Augusto Pinochet's military dictatorship in Chile. The left of centre democratically elected government had been ousted in 1973 by a military junta, which tortured and imprisoned opponents who were in most cases probably slightly less left-wing than Corbyn himself. In 1987 he married Chilean exile Claudia Bracchitta, whose family had brought her to Britain in the '70s aged 11. They had three sons. In 1998 she wanted to send the eldest, Ben – now a football coach – to a selective grammar school in the outer London borough of Barnet, because the local Islington comprehensive was deemed a 'failing school'. This was portrayed in the tabloids as Corbyn – despite being a grammar school boy himself – being prepared to sacrifice his marriage for his political principles. Ben was already at the grammar school when the story broke. Although the couple subsequently divorced, it wasn't entirely due to the issue of their son's education. Corbyn's brother Piers told me it seemed apparent the marriage had problems well before this incident, and that Ben's parents had been drifting 'amicably apart'. Andy McSmith reported in the *Observer* in 1999 that while they had been living under the same roof, they had been pursuing separate lives for the preceding two years. Corbyn at the time had called for greater regulation of the press: 'I wish we had the French system, where public figures have genuinely private lives and there is no *Daily Mail*.'

In 2015 Jeremy Corbyn married his third wife, Laura Alvarez, who imports Fairtrade coffee. The relationship has attracted little media interest but he is no longer a backbencher so it would be unsurprising if he doesn't return to the theme of privacy and intrusion.

Peter Gruner, who until recently was a journalist on Corbyn's local·paper, the *Islington Tribune,* did however give me a little peek in to the new Labour leader's hinterland: 'He is a member of the parliamentary cheese committee. And he once told me he likes his stilton hard, mature and a little mouldy. And he'll only have it on bread he bakes himself.'

While he had an appetite for bread and cheese, he confided to Gruner he had no hunger for power:

A rumour went around a few years ago that he wanted to stand as deputy leader of the party and he told me 'No, that's a load of old rubbish! Why would I want to that? I couldn't criticise the party – I couldn't look myself in the mirror.' And now look at him!

Corbyn is a teetotal vegetarian who eschews cars in favour of public transport. He even refused to be interviewed in an electric vehicle by BBC colleague Chris Mason. He can often be seen travelling into Westminster from his north London home on his pushbike – though he has recently admitted to a guilty secret. Just as John Prescott was known as 'two Jags', Corbyn, it transpires, has two bikes.

And though political plotting might be unavoidable in a three-decade career at Westminster he is just as fascinated with a plot of land – his allotment. But he isn't a Tom Good of the Labour Party. The relatively soft image conceals a hard core of beliefs.

* * *

Jeremy Corbyn was elected for Islington North in 1983 and proudly stood on the manifesto ridiculed by another Labour MP – Gerald Kaufman – as the longest suicide note in history. It called for unilateral disarmament and withdrawal from the EU. I asked him what he had learned from that experience. He blames splits, rather than socialism, for Labour's worst post-war result:

'It taught me the formation of the SDP was catastrophic to the electoral chances of Labour. The Conservative so-called triumph in 1983 owed more to the division of the opposition vote than a move to the left.'

So, as leader, within days he had extensive meetings with those to his right to try to avoid a similar scenario. Nonetheless, many of Ed Miliband's shadow cabinet refused to serve under him, or in some cases weren't offered attractive enough roles. The refuseniks included leadership contenders Yvette Cooper and Liz Kendall, the former Shadow Work and Pensions Secretary Rachel Reeves, the former Shadow Education Secretary Tristram Hunt – and after an extensive meeting – the former Shadow Business Secretary Chuka Umunna. None, though, have signalled they intend to split away.

But the SDP was far from catastrophic for Corbyn's career. Now, it might be a bit of stretch to blame or praise (depending on your view) those former Labour ministers in the Gang of Four – Shirley Williams, David Owen, Bill Rodgers and Roy Jenkins – for Jeremy Corbyn's political ascent, but if they hadn't split from their former party it's possible his parliamentary career wouldn't have begun when it did. The incumbent Islington North MP — Michael O'Halloran – joined the newly-formed Social Democrats, taking many on the right of his local party with him, thereby clearing the way for an already active left-wing to select Corbyn as the Labour candidate in 1982.

Martyn Sloman was a member of Islington North at the time and recounts his experiences in a recently published memoir – *Labour's Failure and My Small Part In It* – which paints a vivid but ghastly vision of life in London Labour at the time, as the 'new left' battled with the old order:

> No one ever looked forward to going to a meeting of the North Islington Labour Party.
>
> There was a running fight between two hostile factions that frequently spilled over into aggression: on one occasion police were summoned to calm a situation that had arisen at the Annual General Meeting of the Women's Section. The Labour Party always held power in Islington and there was a lot at stake. The North Islington factions represented the worst of the Labour Party at the time. The 'old Right', to pick a convenient label, and the 'new Left', a wide coalition of traditional left-of-centre Labour Party members, Trotskyist entryists, and others who had lost confidence and patience with O'Halloran. In the1970s and early 1980s the Party meetings were a pitched battle; there were contests for every position, however trivial.

Now it's not impossible that Corbyn may have unseated O'Halloran in any case as the left had pushed through the policy of mandatory re-selection of MPs. This was subsequently watered-down and there has to be unhappiness with an MP's performance to 'trigger' a ballot of all local members rather than having open contests during each parliament. The Campaign For Labour Party Democracy intended to push again for mandatory re-selection of MPs at the 2015 Labour conference, but the move was ruled out of order.

Martyn Sloman very much saw Jeremy Corbyn as a campaigning MP but one who was – irrespective of his politics – perhaps too thin-skinned to be his party's leader. He told me:

> He was never rude. And never aggressive. But this was his weakness – he didn't like criticism at all. He bridled at it. I can remember during the miners' strike challenging him about how he was behaving towards a

Labour MP from Notttinghamshire [where many NUM members were refusing to strike without a national ballot] and he was very resentful.

Certainly, when first elected, Corbyn was more in tune with the party's policies then than he is now. But five years later Neil Kinnock abandoned Labour's support for unilateral disarmament. The party ditched promises to renationalise privatised industries. And then Tony Blair excised the commitment to 'common ownership of the means of production, distribution and exchange' from Clause IV of the party's constitution in 1995.

For parties that nominally advocated co-operation over competition there were no shortage of left-wing alternatives to Labour so when Corbyn's politics were swept away, especially by the Blairite wind of change, I wondered why he hadn't joined an organisation more in touch with his own views?

'I want to see a more equal, more just society and the Labour Party has always been the vehicle to achieve that, especially with its organic link to the trade unions. I have argued my case on lots of issues and I think things are changing.'

That organic link with the trade unions had stood him in good stead now. While Andy Burnham said he wouldn't accept union cash for his leadership campaign – the better to defend Labour's union link – Corbyn had no such concerns. He was supported by the leadership of UNITE – who signed up far more of its members as 'affiliated supporters', with a vote in the leadership contest, than any other union. But he also received the backing of unions with left-wing leaderships which had severed their formal connections with the Labour Party, such as the rail workers union the RMT and the FBU, representing firefighters.

And although he had been marginalised by successive Labour leaderships, as an MP he had a national platform for his views. One he was not afraid of using. It has meant that his opponents – in the press, in parliament and yes, in his own party – have an arsenal of ammunition to use against him. But as he was elected as a very different leader, perhaps some of the new members of the Labour Party won't be as shocked as the media assumes they'll be.

* * *

Jeremy Corbyn has rebelled against his own party 533 times since Tony Blair was elected in 1997, and even rebelled in one in four votes when Labour was in opposition between 2010 and 2015. Some of his political positions have been seen by successive leaderships as mildly irritating. For example in 1988 he signed an Early Day Motion – a kind of parliamentary petition with no standing in law – calling for then Soviet Union to 'give complete rehabilitation to Leon Trotsky' – the Russian revolutionary killed in Mexico, it is assumed, on Stalin's orders using an object more suited to his homeland: an icepick.

The first of his predecessors as leader that he really upset was Neil Kinnock in 1984. Just weeks after the Brighton bomb Jeremy Corbyn invited two IRA supporters convicted of terrorist offences – Linda Quigley and Gerard MacLochlainn (or McLaughlin) to a meeting in the House of Commons. MacLochlainn – later a Sinn Fein councillor in his home city of (London) Derry – had been arrested in Wales and convicted of conspiracy to cause explosions and possession of explosives four years earlier. He had been imprisoned in England and on his release became Sinn Fein's representative in London. He says he helped with 'back-channel' contacts between Gerry Adams and the British government. He also met members of Labour's front bench team a decade later in 1994, so Corbyn could argue that he was simply ahead of the curve in fostering the peace process. That wasn't how it was seen by many of his Labour colleagues at the time,

The *Glasgow Herald* in 1984 contained an account of Corbyn's dressing down by Labour's then chief whip Michael Cocks who described him as 'highly irresponsible'. But Corbyn had been unapologetic. He had said: 'I felt it important than any MP who wishes to meet anyone from anywhere should have the right to do so.'

He added that he had wanted to discuss prison conditions, and the meeting had been arranged before the Brighton bombing. But the following year he opposed the Anglo-Irish agreement, making these remarks in the House of Commons debate:

'We believe that the agreement strengthens rather than weakens the border between the six and the 26 counties, and those of us who wish to see a united Ireland oppose the agreement for that reason.'

In 1987 Jeremy Corbyn took part in a minute's silence for the eight IRA men and one civilian killed by the British army in an ambush at Loughgall – though his allies say the gesture was a protest against what he regarded as a 'shoot to kill' policy of extra-judicial execution.

On his election as Labour leader, he was congratulated by Sinn Fein's Gerry Adams. When he heard this, a senior staffer to a member of the shadow cabinet was spitting blood that Corbyn was, in his view, 'supporting the IRA while my Dad was risking his life serving in in Northern Ireland.'

Nonetheless, Corbyn gained admiration rather than approbation for campaigning for the release of the 'Birmingham Six' and 'Guildford Four', wrongly convicted of terrorist offences. He never worried if a cause was popular – he was prepared to be the 'Islington One' if necessary.

More recently Jeremy Corbyn's 'promotion of dialogue' with groups associated with violence or extremism has come under far greater scrutiny. And his own dialogue with a TV presenter wasn't too diplomatic.

He demonstrated his exasperation when asked on *Channel 4 News* why he referred to Hamas and Hezbollah as 'friends'.

Remarks he made at a Palestine Solidarity meeting in 2009 had surfaced. He had said:

> Tomorrow evening it will be my pleasure and my honour to host an event in parliament where our friends from Hezbollah will be speaking. And I've also invited friends from Hamas to come and speak as well. Unfortunately the Israelis would not allow them to travel here.

He explained his use of the term 'friend' on Channel 4:

> I'm saying that people I talk to, I use it in a collective way, saying our friends are prepared to talk. Does it mean I agree with Hamas and what it does? No. Does it mean I agree with Hezbollah and what they do? No. What it means is that I think to bring about a peace process, you have to talk to people with whom you may profoundly disagree.

But he didn't welcome being interrupted by presenter Krishnan Guru-Murthy, and snapped: 'Can I finish?' Then, quite literally finger-wagging, he went-on 'you are not prepared to discuss the wider issue of the Middle East' and accused the presenter of 'trivialising' those issues and of 'tabloid journalism'.

He had asked afterwards if he could do the interview again, but it had been broadcast live. Since then he mostly kept any irritation in check but on 19 August he was asked by Martha Kearney on Radio 4's *World At One* if he had met Dyab Abou Jahjah – who had been denied entry to Britain by the then Labour Home Secretary Jacqui Smith. He replied: 'Sorry, who? I saw the name this morning and asked somebody, who is he?' Photographs appeared on social media of Jeremy Corbyn sitting beside Abou Jahjah at an anti-war meeting in the House of Commons before his ban in 2009. Abou Jahjah was controversial because he reportedly told a Flemish magazine in 2004 that he considered every dead American, British and Dutch soldier 'a victory' – though, writing on his blog, Jahjah said this was a misrepresentation of his long-held belief that the Iraq war had been illegal and 'every soldier taking part in an illegal occupation is a legitimate target for resistance.'

Jeremy Corbyn's campaign issued a clarification that afternoon on his behalf: 'My staff have researched this and told me that I did meet this man.'

But he added he met 'thousands of people as an MP' and 'I meet a lot people on all sides in the Middle East and it does not mean I agree with their views.'

As Jeremy Corbyn has spent three decades or more backing national liberation movements – some of which are or have been involved in 'armed struggle' – it is likely that he will come under continued political fire as Labour leader for past associations.

But while says he promotes peace, he actually doesn't talk to just anyone. He does draw the line at speaking to ISIS. While he would not support British involvement in a bombing campaign on their positions in Syria, he told me: 'I don't see any organisation there that at this stage anyone can talk to. Obviously the killing and violence has to stop.'

It's clear, though that he means killing and violence by all concerned should cease, and he has doubts about the legality of western drone strikes as well as the activities of those prosecuting Syria's civil war.

*   *   *

Although he holds controversial views on international issues, Jeremy Corbyn's first major challenges are likely to be on domestic policy. His campaign wanted to promote ideas and discussion and he issued 13 policy documents which even included proposals for rural areas and for arts funding. The trouble is, on major policy areas, his position and his party's are separated more by a canyon than a gap.

He is against any 'arbitrary timetable' for moving the current account deficit into surplus, while Labour in its election manifesto was committed to eliminating it by 2020. But it's his plans to boost the economy which have attracted attention – and drawn criticism from many in his own party. These were set out in his document of 22 July entitled *The Economy in 2020*. At their core is his proposal for 'People's Quantitative Easing':

> One option would be for the Bank of England to be given a new mandate to upgrade our economy to invest in new large scale housing, energy, transport and digital projects: Quantitative easing for people instead of banks... Another option would be to strip out some of the huge tax reliefs and subsidies on offer to the corporate sector. These amount to £93 billion a year – money which would be better used in direct public investment... These funds could be used to establish a 'National Invest-ment Bank' to invest in the new infrastructure we need and in the hi-tech and innovative industries of the future.

At his Chelmsford rally he defended these schemes as practical, not radical: 'If you said to people in Germany I have a radical new idea of a National Investment Bank they would just shrug their shoulders and say we are doing that already. What's extreme about that?'

But increasing the supply of money in the economy when it is already growing would – say his critics – push up inflation and interest rates, leading to an erosion in living standards. And those sceptics include not only Yvette Cooper but Chris Leslie, the man who took over from her husband Ed Balls as shadow Chancellor over the summer and who refused to serve in a Corbyn shadow cabinet.

He also wants to renationalise the big six energy companies which his leadership opponents have suggested would be a waste of money which could be better used on, for example, expanding child care or social care.

There is likely to be more unity on his benches in opposing the welfare bill and possibly fewer arguments than anticipated on bringing rail back in to public ownership, so long as Jeremy Corbyn was willing to do this incrementally as franchises expire.

On nuclear weapons, though, Labour can't fudge their position until the election. The party could face a decision as early as spring 2016 on whether to back the renewal of Trident. He will argue that his mandate as leader trumps the mandate Labour MPs got from the electorate as recently as May to retain the deterrent. He told me:

> The elected leader will have a very large mandate from the members and the Parliamentary Labour Party – important as it is – I hope will recognise there is at the very least a mandate for a full debate within the party. I feel strongly about nuclear weapons. We have to have that debate fairly soon as the government might reach a decision in 2016.

He wants Labour to undertake its own strategic defence review – and he stands by his three-decade old policy of setting up a defence diversification agency, which would use skills people have gained in the nuclear and armaments industry and put them to what he would see as more productive use. He has written on his website:

> The cost of Trident replacement has met with huge public disquiet ... Apart from the astronomical cost, the moral case and the dangers of encouraging proliferation, the UK's weapons are not ours, nor are they independent. We are part of the US defence network, and they can only be fired with US approval...Security does not come from threats but from understanding and wellbeing.

So this doesn't appear to be an issue on which he can compromise. The trouble is, existing Labour policy – on which the party's MPs were collectively elected by more than nine million voters, not the quarter of a million that made Corbyn leader – is for a like-for-like replacement of Trident. The party was committed to continuous 'at sea' deterrence, and during the election, Ed Miliband clarified that this, just as the Conservatives were advocating, would mean support for four new submarines.

* * *

Late at night on Sunday 13 September, locked away in a commons office
with Rosie Winterton – who had agreed to continue as Labour's chief whip
– Corbyn tried to construct his shadow cabinet. Three journalists – including
my colleague Eleanor Garnier, had perched outside. A voice from inside was
overheard saying they had 'a problem with defence'. The then Shadow
Culture Secretary Chris Bryant had refused to take the portfolio due to his
fundamental disagreements in this area – and concerns over policy on
Russia – with Corbyn. He became Shadow Leader of the House instead.

Corbyn proceeded cautiously, however, and the following day
appointed Angela Eagle's twin sister Maria to the defence brief – despite
the fact that she favoured the renewal of the nuclear deterrent.

Len McCluskey – the general secretary of the UNITE union which
backed Corbyn's leadership bid – wasn't pushing for an early resolution
of the problem, pointing out that though he himself was a unilateralist,
his union took a different position and he accepted that policy. And for
Maria Eagle's part, she was willing to undertake a review of policy on
Corbyn's behalf.

So an early row over nuclear weapons had been defused – or rather
delayed, but with the detonator set to 2016. But some of Jeremy Corbyn's
other policy positions came under scrutiny, not from the media but from
his MPs. At his first meeting as leader with his Parliamentary Labour Party
on 14 September, Corbyn was asked to provide clarity on his view of NATO.
He had previously called for the western alliance to be wound up in 1990,
after the collapse of the Warsaw Pact. Again he tried to avoid confronta-
tion and talked of the need to review policies. But this peace campaigner
was facing a more hostile inquisition from his parliamentary colleagues
than the press – largely because some were seeking clarity, but for many
others they were anticipating the questions he was likely to be asked
publicly not as a candidate for the party leadership, but as the leader.

Amongst the barrage of 20 questions, he was also interrogated on his
attitude to another multi-national institution – the EU. He had re-ap-
pointed Hilary Benn – the son of one his late political soulmates Tony – as
Shadow Foreign Secretary. On the *Today* programme that morning Benn
had said Labour would campaign in the forthcoming referendum to stay
in the EU 'under all circumstances'. But that's not what the former Shadow
Business Secretary Chuka Umunna had heard direct from his new boss.
He said Corbyn's ambivalence to EU membership meant he couldn't serve
in the shadow cabinet. Corbyn's allies say that while Umunna left the front
bench 'by mutual agreement', he hadn't been offered a specific post in any
case. But Umunna gave this reason for returning to the backbenches:

> It is my view that we should support the UK remaining a member of the EU... and I cannot envisage any circumstances where I would be campaigning alongside those who would argue for us to leave – Jeremy has made it clear to me that he does not wholeheartedly share this view.

Some of those present at that first parliamentary meeting were dismayed at Corbyn's negative tone on the EU, once seen by those on the left as a 'capitalist market.' He refused to endorse Hilary Benn's view and said he wouldn't give Cameron 'a blank cheque'. In 2005 Corbyn had supported a 'non' vote in the French referendum on the EU constitution, writing in the *Morning Star* of 'the dangers to workers' rights and living standards if this Trojan horse for neoliberal economics is imposed on Europe'.

An MP who listened to Corbyn said the logic of the position was to come out of the EU if Cameron negotiated a watering down of workers' rights – so 'we could let a majority Tory government dilute them even more – it's mad'. But Corbyn's allies – including the Shadow Chancellor John McDonnell – said he was simply proposing that Labour needs now to make the case for the Europe it wants to see, and not be regarded as defenders of the status quo. They also argued that David Cameron must not be given a 'free pass'. If the Prime Minister came back from negotiations with a package which excluded the UK from employment rights enjoyed by those in other member states while signing up to a new transatlantic trade agreement that could see more public services put out to tender, then the option of the exit door shouldn't be entirely closed. Corbyn, after all, had been a founder member – with Hilary Benn's father, Tony – of the People's Assembly Against Austerity which took the view that 'all the US and EU agreements that force open public services to private gain' must be repudiated. But the emphasis and default position would be on staying in the EU, and arguing for change – not leaving.

The new Chief Secretary to the Treasury Seema Malhotra later admitted, however, that while she wanted to 'stay and fight for a better Europe', that this – with nuclear weapons – was another debate still to be had under Corbyn's leadership.

He was also asked about Syria and Northern Ireland and while he set out his views, some of those present said they didn't discern how he was going to reconcile them with existing policy.

The Luton MP Gavin Shuker asked his new leader he would support Labour councils that were making cuts. In the past Corbyn had been willing to defy the law on the poll tax but even earlier, in the '80s, had been on the side of an argument amongst the left that suggested it was better for local authorities not to set a rate than to agree budgets that 'slashed' public services. Here he had moderated his tone over the years and said he understood the difficult choices councils had to make. But the fact the question was asked showed how little some MPs knew of his views – and how so few shared them.

But one of the main concerns of the MPs had been – well, themselves. Some were worried that in order to bring policy and leader in to closer alignment, he and his new supporters – who were inundating some constituencies – would be prepared to turf them out of their seats and select someone else. After all, in the 48 hours since Corbyn's election 28,000 more people had joined the Labour Party – many likely to have been inspired by him rather than their sitting MP.

On this they did receive reassurance. The new leader said there would be 'no need to change the party selection of candidates.' He said he wanted 'unity' and would fight Conservative moves to change constituency boundaries and reduce seats – a process some Corbyn-sceptics see as leading to their own demise.

The party's new deputy, Tom Watson – who had seen off Stella Creasy, Caroline Flint, Angela Eagle and Ben Bradshaw to take the post – was physically positioned on Corbyn's left throughout the meeting but will now be trying to push him, relatively gently initially, at least a little to the right. He has a huge mandate of his own – getting around twice as many votes as his nearest rival (though 90,000 fewer than Corbyn amassed for leader) and has called for co-operation with the top team from his fellow MPs. But in a speech just before his election he spoke out against the mandatory re-selection of MPs, and also restated his own support for NATO and nuclear weapons within 24 hours of assuming his new role. He had destabilised Tony Blair before Gordon Brown took over so although he can be a force for unity, he can also be, well, a force – and if Corbyn crosses any of his red lines he could be pivotal in deciding on the longevity of the leadership. But his emphasis will be on trying to make the will of the members work, as Corbyn didn't exactly just scrape home on the ballot.

Also at the meeting – but remaining silent – was Peter Mandelson. He had failed before the election to wield the knife on Ed Miliband, who was in attendance to greet his successor, and he is unlikely to be a successful assassin this time as few MP s would risk the early wrath of an enthused and expanded membership.

But in an email to colleagues, the secretary of the 'Blairite' Labour First Group, Luke Akehurst, described Corbyn's victory as 'the biggest reverse modernisers in this party have ever suffered' and added: 'absolutely nothing has changed since May about the way ordinary voters – 98 per cent of whom did not participate in the leadership election – view the world.'

* * *

So how did a leader who only gained the positive support of ten per cent of his MPs get elected?

Clearly new leadership rules were vital. But so too were their astute use.

For someone who is nearly two decades older than his nearest leadership rival – and whose politics in essence haven't fundamentally altered since his election to parliament three decades ago – his campaign methods have, to paraphrase John Prescott, placed his traditional values in a modern setting. He was the internet insurgent, fighting the Labour establishment to get on the leadership ballot, battling the British establishment once he got there. The hashtag – channelling Obama's first presidential campaign – '#Jezwecan' was being seen every 25 seconds once he became officially a candidate. His Facebook page was the most popular of the four contenders. As will be revealed later, Labour hasn't quite matched its opponents' social media skills in recent years, but the Corbyn campaign was best prepared to exploit a powerful tool to create 'a buzz' around his candidacy.

The aim in part initially was to put pressure on MPs to nominate him for fear of appearing anti-democratic and out of touch.

But Corbyn, more than the other candidates, also seemed more suited to being a social media sensation – soon there were spoof accounts, some poking fun at his seriousness of purpose, such as #corbynjokes, which gained more than 20,000 followers – for example: 'What's black and white and red all over? The blood on the hands of the US military and their lapdog Blairite allies'. Or, 'What is heard but never seen? The Chilcot Report'.

Others had him photoshopped as everything from revolutionary Che Guevara – or was it the BBC's '70s sitcom character Wolfie Smith of the Tooting Popular Front? – to James Bond. But as we will show, a similar level of affectionate attention on the internet didn't bolster his predecessor's electoral chances.

What it did, though, for Corbyn, was give the left-winger a significantly higher profile just as the Labour Party was in effect publicly advertising votes for its new leader. For £3 anyone professing to share the party's values could sign up as a supporter at a cut price rate and choose Ed Miliband's successor. And, astutely, Corbyn's campaign was the first to put up a 'how to become a registered supporter' link on its website. Even after the August deadline passed, the link stayed up taking those who were interested to this Labour Party message: 'New members who joined after 3pm on Wednesday 12 August will be able to vote in future elections – and you will be able to shape the Labour Party locally and nationally.'

That too is sensible – while supporters can vote for the Labour leader they have very limited rights when it comes to participation in the day to day running of the party – they can't stand as council candidates, for example. So if Jeremy Corbyn wants to shape the party more in the image of his own politics, supporters will have to be enticed into becoming full members. It's also possible that supporters will be transformed in to members despite paying a reduced rate – or that they will be given a year's 'trial membership' without paying the full whack of £46.50 But in any case, he did better than his opponents at encouraging or enthusing people to take that first step.

The website of the Stop the War coalition – set up after 9/11, and of which Jeremy Corbyn was founder member and chair – also pointed out how its activists could sign up to be Labour supporters:

> We can all help to build Jeremy's campaign, to make sure that a strong alternative voice to war and austerity gets the hearing it deserves. His candidacy for the Labour leadership can only make the movements for peace and social justice stronger.

Then it set out the simple steps to turn ideas into actions:

> **How to vote for Jeremy Corbyn as Labour leader.** Anyone can vote in the Labour Party leadership election, which is now run on the basis of one-person-one vote. The election is not restricted to Labour Party members but open to the new category of Labour supporter. Registration as a supporter costs just £3. Register here.

The anti-war coalition includes many people active in other left-wing parties – and none.

'It was a perfect storm', a shadow cabinet member privately admitted. Corbyn 'spoke to' those disillusioned with politics and/or austerity and who wanted to 'hit out' at a majority Conservative government.

His social media profile – portraying him as an interesting outsider – also helped fund his campaign. In July with 50 days of the contest to go, his team set a 'crowdfunding' target of £50,000 – '50 for 50', they called it. The target was exceeded in not 50 days but in just 15. Going into the last week of the campaign, he had raised just shy of £200,000 in small donations. Oh, and the 'Jeremy Corbyn for leader' badges usually available via his website had all sold out. His new-found supporters will have to hope he doesn't do the same.

It would be easy to portray the Corbyn takeover as a clever coup but he has clearly tapped in to a feeling that extends well beyond Britain's small band of ultra-leftists. His hastily-appointed press officer Carmel Nolan rejects the idea that a smart, well-organised coterie have hijacked the Labour Party. She told me of a 17 year old campaign volunteer whom she had taken to see Corbyn speak at a commemoration of Hiroshima in

London in August. The teenager pointed at the object adorning the speakers' stage and exclaimed: 'what's that thing?' It was the CND symbol. Nolan said:

> Some commentators portray Jeremy as a relic. But he is attracting new people who like his green credentials, his bike, his straight answers rather than his position on Trident. He's tapped in to unease by young people. They didn't know a world where their boss couldn't contact them at all hours on their smart phones, or when tution was free, or you didn't have to live with your parents until you were 30. So to them what he is saying is new – they are thinking that things don't have to be like this.'

As part of a new way of doing politics, Corbyn invited members of the public to send him the questions they wanted put to David Cameron at his first-ever PMQs. He received more than 40,000 responses. That's not a sign that people are disillusioned with politics – they just want their politics done differently. And, for now, it seems an ageing, unassuming but unflinching man with no great oratorical skill is their vehicle. He asked those questions more in the manner of a local radio DJ than a leader of the opposition – name-checking Marie, Steve, Paul, Claire, Gail and Angela, but while he gave those away from Westminster a voice right at the heart of the Commons chamber, there was no sustained pressure put on David Cameron. He was asked by my colleague Carolyn Quinn if he really wanted to be Prime Minister – and he advised her that the best form of leader was 'the reluctant leader'.

* * *

Sometimes, though, people are judged by the company they keep.

A massive mandate as Labour leader, you would assume, might be accompanied by a honeymoon. Instead, attempts to form a new 'inclusive' shadow cabinet proved to be an immediate challenge, with pressure on him to abandon one of the longest running relationships in British politics. He has been a long-standing political ally of his campaign agent, John McDonnell, and was determined to appoint him as Shadow Chancellor. He came under some pressure from some of his union backers to put McDonnell elsewhere as he was seen as a divisive and abrasive figure.

There was also some suspicion that McDonnell would be the power behind the throne. Two weeks before Corbyn declared his candidacy, his now shadow chancellor had been arguing for a broader debate and set up the *Radical-Labour* website with this mission statement:

> So far neither the political range of candidates for the Labour leadership nor the ideas they have voiced have set the world of progressive politics alight. If we want to use the selection of a new leader to excite people about the potential of socialist politics, then it's up to us to get this debate going.

A former colleague once said McDonnell was a bit like life in medieval times – 'nasty, brutish and short'. McDonnell is certainly more personally pugnacious than the new Labour leader but is not without charm and certainly not without intelligence. And Corbyn seemed to take the view that it was better for a leader and his Shadow Chancellor to be on the same page politically and economically. Now, I wonder where he got that idea.

McDonnell, like Corbyn, had formed a kind of unofficial opposition to the Blair administration when the Hayes and Harlington MP joined his Islington North counterpart in 1997. Together they had rebelled over Iraq and many of the flagship policies of the administration – from foundation hospitals to tuition fees in England.

McDonnell had represented the same area of west London on the Greater London Council between 1981 and its abolition by Mrs Thatcher's government five years later, serving as finance chair then deputy leader to Ken Livingstone, but disagreeing over whether to – in effect – refuse to implement government-imposed cuts. He had described himself as 'London's chancellor' – and Livingstone praised him recently for handing a £3bn budget at the GLC 'while always balancing the books.' He – unlike some on the left – has widespread experience of running things. He was chief executive of the Association of London Authorities and its successor body, the Association of London Government and has experience of working with wider movements outside the Labour Party – including the People's Assembly Against Austerity, the umbrella group which also encompasses activists from the Greens, and parties to the left of Labour. But it's McDonnell's politics even more than his economics which is causing concern amongst some of Corbyn's parliamentary colleagues.

He, like his leader, is a long-standing supporter of a United Ireland. In 2003 at a commemoration of the late IRA hunger striker Bobby Sands he said: 'It's about time we started honouring those people involved in the armed struggle. It was bombs and bullets and sacrifice made by the likes of Bobby Sands that brought Britain to the negotiating table.'

He later explained his rationale – that he was a supporter of the peace process, that he wanted all republican groups to 'stand down' and by paying tribute to them he was signalling they could do so with dignity. His motivation was to save, not sacrifice, lives, he argued.

In 2010, speaking to a trade union audience in Southport, McDonnell recounted that he had been asked what he would do if – like the main character in the BBC series Ashes to Ashes – he could go back to the '80s. He mused that as a former member of the GLC which she abolished, and a researcher for the mineworkers union the NUM, which her government had battled, he would probably 'assassinate Thatcher'. He provoked laughter at the time but later apologised.

Earlier this year, when he rebelled against the Labour leadership's position of abstention on the Welfare Reform and Work Bill, he proved he had a vivid turn of phrase when he said: 'I would swim through vomit to vote against this bill. And listening to some of the nauseating speeches in support of it, I might have to.'

Another member of the Ken Livingstone coterie – though more recently – is also an ally of Corbyn's and will play a pivotal role in his leadership team. Simon Fletcher was close to members of Socialist Action – a Trotskyite grouping – in the past but went on join Ed Miliband's team a couple of years ago – so he knows all about the inner workings of an opposition leader's office. He had been Livingstone's resourceful chief of staff when he was London Mayor, during his first term of office in 2000. Livingstone had failed to win the Labour nomination and stood as an independent that year against the official party candidate, Frank Dobson. Fletcher helped mastermind the victory but also negotiated an early 're-entry' for his boss back into Labour before the 2004 election.

Labour peer Toby Harris served on the London Assembly when Simon Fletcher worked with Ken Livingstone and he chaired the Association of London Government when John McDonnell was its chief executive. He told me:

> Jeremy is nice enough but not very organised. Both Simon and John McDonnell are organised and effective. Simon Fletcher is very bright and able – he has a political ideology but he tends to think what's the best way of making things happen. John McDonnell was very effective and very competent.

Two 'Cats' will be influential in the new leadership, team too – Cat Smith, who used to work in Jeremy Corbyn's office and who is now MP for Lancaster and Fleetwood, and Islington councillor Kat Fletcher – the London borough's deputy mayor – who co-ordinated the work of 16,000 volunteers in the Corbyn campaign.

And then there's the veteran, if that's the right word, of the Stop the War coalition, Carmel Nolan – a former radio producer who had the unenviable task of handling the growing press interest in the person who was until recently an unfashionable 66-year-old backbencher. She wanted a temporary role but was persuaded to stay on amid unprecedented interest in a new leader. She has a turn of phrase every bit as colourful as John McDonnell's and likened her recent experience to being 'at the reins of a runaway horse'. She was certainly there when things went from a trot to a gallop.

But while Corbyn had prominent, competent women on the team that got him elected, one of the earliest self-inflicted wounds was to have what are usually regarded as the top jobs in the shadow cabinet – Home, Foreign, and Treasury – all filled by men.

To soften this Angela Eagle – in addition to shadowing Business – was told she would be 'Shadow First Secretary of State.'

The usually spin-free Corbyn then argued critics were living in the '18th century' when the so-called great offices of state mattered more. He regarded the education portfolio, which had gone to ex-Miliband aide Lucy Powell, and Health – with Heidi Alexander, who had campaigned against the downgrading of a hospital in her south London constituency – as being as more important.

But the new MP for Birmingham Yardley, Jess Phillips, challenged him at his first meeting of the Parliamentary Party – and said 'ok, if these jobs are so unimportant, why not do a swap?' He declined to move McDonnell away from the apparently peripheral position of Shadow Chancellor.

He declared that a majority of seats at his top table would be filled by women – 16 out of 31 – but critics note that he has devised jobs which don't actually shadow any cabinet-level minister, such as a post of 'Young People and Voter Registration' minister – which, out of loyalty to her party, Blairite Gloria De Piero accepted.

But it's policies at least as much as personnel that will determine the new leader's success or failure.

* * *

The new Labour deputy leader Tom Watson has described Corbyn as a different type of politician and while it is impossible to predict what would be in the party's next election manifesto 'he will want to have some arguments.' If Jeremy Corbyn successfully transforms Labour's policy positions so they become closer to his own, does that mean he will make his party less electable?

Conventional wisdom says yes. Loudly. When Labour last stood on a platform that leant as far to the left, it got 27.6 per cent of the vote under Michael Foot in 1983, and Mrs Thatcher enjoyed a majority of 144. But the Left argues that things have changed – there is no SDP to split the opposition to the Conservatives, and no Falklands War to boost an incumbent Prime Minister – but there is austerity, which has gone unchallenged by all the major parties and a change of approach could provide an opportunity to win power.

But research from Labour's former policy chief Jon Cruddas into why his party lost the last election – shared with the *Labour List* website on 5 August – came up with this finding:

Voters did not reject Labour because they saw it as austerity lite. Voters rejected Labour because they perceived the Party as anti-austerity lite. 58 per cent agree that 'we must live within our means so cutting the deficit is the top priority'. Just 16 per cent disagree. Almost all Tories and a majority of Lib Dems and UKIP voters agree. Amongst working class C2DE voters 54 per cent agree and 15 per cent disagree. Labour voters are evenly divided; 32 per cent agree compared to 34 per cent who disagree.

As I followed Labour's election campaign around the country, I had discovered lack of clarity on the deficit was almost certainly damaging, too.

But writing on his website, John McDonnell addresses this and provides a clue as to why Corbyn was insistent he should be Shadow Chancellor. Labour's own private polling suggests the party won't get a hearing unless it faces up to the deficit. So McDonnell deftly argues the difference with the Conservatives – and undoubtedly with some of his colleagues inside Labour – won't be over whether to eliminate the deficit, but when and how:

> It is unarguable that no modern party leader can win an election if behind in the polls on economic competence. Ed Miliband, sadly, was proof of this truism. Deficit denial is a non-starter for anyone to have any economic credibility with the electorate. This was a key finding of the poll recently published by Jon Cruddas, examining why Labour lost the election. So let me make it absolutely clear that Labour under Jeremy Corbyn is committed to eliminating the deficit and creating an economy in which we live within our means... We accept that cuts in public spending will help eliminate the deficit, but our cuts won't be to the middle-and low-income earners and certainly not to the poor.

* * *

So how did it come to this? Even Jeremy Corbyn's team believe Labour's lack of economic credibility cost them the election.

In fact the scale of the defeat isn't as straightforward to explain. Those who work closely with Ed Miliband would have heard him describe the reasons why Labour ended up with fewer seats than in 2010 as 'over-determined' – in other words, multi-faceted.

In a sense Miliband's election campaign – and the leadership contest that was a consequence of it – begat Corbyn-mania, as a section of the electorate clearly wanted to campaign against a majority Conservative government which had been made possible in part by Labour's failures. Their motivation was perhaps similar in nature to the mixture of disappointment, and a desire for difference, which fuelled the post-referendum SNP surge.

They favoured a candidate with a simple message to succeed Ed

Miliband, who often floundered between reassurance and radicalism. But could a campaign full of clarity and conviction, rather than compromise, really have made Corbyn unnecessary?

Labour has a new leader but he will face many of the same challenges that were exposed at election time – from improving the party's organisation and polling to winning back at least some seats in Scotland, where Corbyn will now spend at least a day every month.

Labour has new footsoldiers but an impressive ground war didn't win enough votes in 2015.

What might make things different next time? Join me on a journey around the country as we go back to the Ed Miliband era and experience the campaign which changed British politics – in an unpredictable way – as it unfolds.

There may be Trouble Ahead: The Election in Microcosm

14 March

- Ed Miliband reveals his election pledges before the start of the official election campaign.
- Labour appear to miss warning signs of how their opponents will fight that campaign.
- The lack of consultation and engagement with some Shadow Cabinet members becomes obvious when not all of them know how many election pledges will be unveiled.
- Those around Ed Miliband seem to be in denial about his lack of popularity.

IT COULD HAVE been called the *Shadow Cabinet Express*. Bleary eyed, I stumbled on to the 7.37am from Euston and looked for a quiet coach in the hope of catching a nap. Labour would issue their election pledge card in Birmingham today, a city where a Labour administration had seen off a Conservative–Lib Dem coalition. The vast majority of voters hadn't yet engaged with election issues, parliament was a fortnight away from being dissolved, but for many of us in the media it felt like the campaign had been underway in earnest at least since the start of the year, and our enthusiasm was tempered with a degree of exhaustion.

In the same railway carriage, also seeking peace and quiet was the cerebral Jon Cruddas, Labour's policy supremo. He was using the downtime to read a book on Irish history. But as peckishness began to trump the desire to narrow my sleep deficit, I made my way to what was once called a buffet but is now rebranded as the train 'shop' to pick up a bacon sandwich. Unlike Ed Miliband the previous year, I assumed I might have the luxury of consuming it minus the glare of publicity. But I put my breakfast plans on hold when I discovered that Cruddas was not a lone representative of Labour's upper echelons.

There was something of the spirit of a Sunday school trip in the next coach which was jammed packed with relatively gleeful members of Labour's top table and their advisers, no doubt full of anticipation at the unveiling of the fifth – and what was assumed would be the final pledge: Higher Living Standards for Working Families.

The small print repeated Labour's promise to freeze energy bills – this had made the political weather when it became the centre point of Ed Miliband's conference speech in 2013. But, oops – since then the 'Big Six' energy companies had been bringing prices down, partly aided by a concerned coalition government which had lifted some environmental burdens from their shoulders. Labour had to explain that their 'freeze' would now allow prices to fall, although not rise. This recalibration hadn't been widely understood. So the pledge card didn't just do the 'vision thing' – it included a new promise: lower fuel bills in time for the next winter, just so long as the regulator agreed. Cruddas would describe such initiatives – which were often politely referred to as 'retail offers' – in blunt terms as 'small money bribes'.

* * *

Back on the *Shadow Cabinet Express* on a crisp clear day in mid-March, most of Labour's front rank politicians appeared to be travelling hopefully. With such an emphasis on living costs, I asked the Shadow Transport Secretary, Michael Dugher if there was an edict to travel standard class at all times. He confided that he usually takes the car. Rather more significantly, and embarrassingly, one of his colleagues was wondering out loud just how many pledges Labour had. 'Seriously how many? Is it three? Is it more than five?'

Perhaps someone hadn't been paying attention. Or hadn't been adequately briefed or involved. To maximise and elongate their impact, the preceding four pledges had been drip-fed to the media since January – starting with a commitment to balance the books. Much the same approach was adopted during the election campaign itself, when the party launched a series of topic-based 'mini-manifestos'. Some of these might well have had an impact, but not necessarily the one envisaged by Labour's strategists. But all that was in the near future. Labour's more immediate challenge would be how to handle a pre-election budget.

So I stopped at the table occupied by Ed Balls and Yvette Cooper, who were discussing whether an announcement on the NHS should be brought forward if George Osborne attempted to occupy Labour's territory by devoting more money to the health service. Deep in conversation, I was unaware of an approaching fellow passenger. 'Excuse me!' the middle-aged woman exclaimed. At first I assumed – or indeed feared – she had overheard the conversation and wanted to add her political tuppence worth. But it was much, much worse than that.

She was intimating that she wanted to pass down the corridor so I beckoned her on. 'I can't get past', she said tersely, glancing briefly and disapprovingly in the direction of my expanding girth. I threw in the towel, pressed myself against an empty seat a little further away from the Balls/Cooper table and the frustrated traveller went on her way. I tried to resume a serious conversation until a few moments later history repeated as farce when the train guard – whose BMI made me look like a greyhound to his bull terrier – also exclaimed that I was blocking the passage. Ed Balls and myself broke in to laughter with the then Shadow Chancellor – whose waistline was on a similar trajectory, despite his regular and occasionally robust encounters on the football pitch – observing how there is often a gap between the perception we have of ourselves and reality. And this gap was to become a chasm for Labour during the campaign proper.

On arrival in the second city, I hitched a lift on the double decker bus that was laid on to take the Shadow Cabinet – minus Ed Miliband, who was arriving separately – the short distance to the international conference centre where the pledge card would be unveiled. I used the opportunity to discuss Labour's prospects.

The consensus seemed to be that while Labour politicians weren't receiving a hostile reception – at least in England – on the doorstep, there was a problem in motivating traditional supporters. This appeared to be symbolised by the turnout for the pre-election rally at which the pledge card would be highlighted on a huge screen, and its physical representation distributed to members and media alike.

1,500 activists had been expected to cram in to the hall but there was some consternation amongst officials when it became clear the venue wouldn't be filled to capacity. Empty spaces were deftly consigned to an upper circle that was so high above the stage and the cameras that it was almost in orbit while some prominent politicians leaned against the walls of the stalls to give the impression that it was standing room only.

The atmosphere was upbeat. The event was hosted by Carrie and David Grant, stars of children's TV series *Pop Shop*. That's pretty much the only time my young offspring has been jealous of my job. But by far the best contribution came from actor Shaun Dooley. Star of Cold War thriller *The Game* and ITV's dark drama *Broadchurch*, he was unexpectedly good at comic one liners.

He said he would hope that in the forthcoming campaign Ed Miliband would throw not just the kitchen sink, but both kitchen sinks, at David Cameron. This followed the not very helpful revelation that the party leader's north London home – expensive enough to qualify for Labour's proposed mansion tax on properties worth more than £2 million – had not one, but two, kitchens.

Ed Miliband and his wife Justine had been filmed for one in a series of BBC profiles of the party leaders. For reasons no more sinister than that of available light, and convenience for the camera crew, both sides had decided a little family kitchenette was the very place to conduct the chat. This room was apparently so poorly appointed that Sarah Vine – the *Daily Mail* columnist married to Michael Gove – denounced it as 'forlorn' and something that would be found in a communist housing project. Ed Miliband's friend – and *Times* columnist – Jenni Russell leapt in to defend his middle-class honour, revealing on Twitter the existence of a 'lovely' kitchen elsewhere in the spacious Miliband home. Tabloid charges of hypocrisy and champagne socialism flowed, so Ms Russell had to clarify that you couldn't even sit in the other, unfilmed kitchen – it was apparently a bit like the area where reporters made their tea at her newspaper – and she and the Milibands agreed the little, filmed kitchenette was the one they used regularly.

Now Ed Miliband was trying hard to motivate those voters who might well take great pride in fitting a new kitchen – but certainly couldn't afford a couple of them, or whose houses simply wouldn't be large enough to accommodate two cooking areas. So in a late addition to his speech, he stressed how all parties are not the same. He wanted to counter an anti-politics mood. But while the Conservatives were well aware of the dangers an incoming Labour government may pose to their traditional supporters, the potential beneficiaries of a change in power appeared to be taking some convincing.

But events outside the Birmingham venue were more significant than those taking place inside. And these should have rung alarm bells for the Labour leadership. First, a lone *Sun* reporter turned up wearing an Alex Salmond mask. He retreated following a minor and swift scuffle with an official. But one swallow doesn't make a political storm. Soon, around 15 Conservative activists appeared with their faces covered by the image of the SNP's former leader and carrying placards warning of higher taxes and spending if a Labour government needed propping up by a party which was campaigning against austerity, and a longer timetable for clearing the deficit. Unlike the loquacious Mr Salmond they remained silent and apparently impervious to any jibes thrown at them as they posed for the cameras.

This wasn't any old stunt. Accompanying them was none other than the Conservative chief whip Michael Gove – a sure sign that this message that a weak Labour government could be pulled to the left by the Scottish Nationalists was going to feature prominently in the English campaign. Yet the reaction of Labour officials was largely to ignore this. One said he was 'flattered' Michael Gove had turned up: 'He must take us seriously.' There were to be regular appearances by the Salmond – and then Sturgeon – mask-wearers outside Labour events as the Conservatives found their attack resonated in the English marginals. The drip, drip, drip of this toxic message was never successfully stemmed, and in the campaign proper a torrent would flow. But something else was going on in the streets of Birmingham.

* * *

I was struck by the lack of Ed Miliband on his party pledge card. Labour's first such device – back in 1997 – had a beaming Tony Blair all over it. Yet the 2015 version had just an unobtrusive signature in the bottom corner from Ed Miliband. BBC producer Sean Clare enlarged and laminated both cards and we went to test the reaction in the nearby marginal seat of Birmingham Yardley. Labour would win here as the seat was Lib Dem held and Nick Clegg's party were on the verge of a near-total collapse, but would be less successful in the Midlands in those seats where the Conservatives were their main opponents. And the reaction to the pledge card didn't augur well for the campaign when we stopped to question voters at random. It may well have been that Labour was preferred to the Lib Dems, but the lack of enthusiasm was striking. 'God they are right to keep him off the pledge card – he is no Tony Blair', said a middle-aged woman accompanied by her young daughter, who wasn't interested in politics. Then a group of three women identified themselves as Labour voters. One of them felt a bit embarrassed to say she didn't take to Ed Miliband but would probably back the party after all. A gruff middle-aged man absolutely wouldn't vote for him no matter what.

As for the pledges, as a man in his 40s put it: 'I would vote for those policies, yes. If I thought they would do them. But I don't think any of them will.' He told me he was old enough to remember the Blair pledge card. 'Ah we were less cynical then,' he chuckled. Times had changed. So Ed Miliband was – as he recognised – up against apathy, cynicism, even *ennui* with politics and politicians. This would lead him in the campaign itself to the front door of perhaps Britain's most famous non-voter, Russell Brand.

But what of that other impediment to office – Ed Miliband himself?

Senior Shadow Cabinet members and advisers have said that the party's own polling on the leader was too often kept from them – but what was being picked up in our *vox pops* was pretty much reflected in the pollsters' findings. At this stage Labour had a target of talking to four million voters. If the activists on the phone banks and on the doorsteps weren't hearing doubts about leadership, then they were deliberately putting in earplugs.

There had been serious discussions about whether and how to remove the party leader the previous autumn. The party's unofficial in-house journal the *New Statesman* had featured an unflattering piece by its editor, Jason Cowley, which had been published – appropriately enough for something which lit a fuse on a plot – on 5 November. Cowley had talked about Miliband's 'appalling approval ratings and the lack of enthusiasm many of his MPs have for him' and that

> He doesn't really understand the lower middle class or material aspiration. He doesn't understand Essex Man or Woman. Politics for him must seem at times like an extended PPE seminar: elevated talk about political economy and the good society.

One former minister told me: 'it crystallised what everyone thought.' The former Labour leader Neil Kinnock spoke regularly to Miliband and on this occasion privately advised him to raise his game. Others thought the game was – or should be – up. At least two approaches were made to Alan Johnson to persuade him to stand if Miliband were ousted. Peter Mandelson had been approached by some backbench MPs to see if he could use his usually considerable powers of persuasion to change Johnson's mind. Johnson felt a coup would play badly with the public – some of his colleagues believed the very opposite, but he was adamant he wouldn't topple Miliband. And as no other viable candidate had been willing to put their name in the frame, putsch didn't come to shove.

At that time disaster wasn't absolutely certain. But the feeling was that much good work had been destroyed by Ed Miliband's failure to mention the deficit in his 'look, no notes' speech at the previous year's party conference.

Much has been written about this since – he had less time to rehearse as the conference took place so soon after the energy-sapping white-knuckle ride of the Scottish referendum. There had been a late addition to his speech on tackling ISIS. He himself had been mortified at his performance and had shut himself away in his hotel room.

And I know from the conversations I had, it wasn't just the passage on the deficit that had been missing – much of what he intended to say on immigration was overlooked, too. And while saving the health service had been a prominent theme of what he had remembered of his speech, the more innovative policy of integrating social care was afforded scant mention and had largely been pared down even before trying to commit the speech to memory. But it was the lack of the D-word which inflicted the most damage.

In the following month's private polling, the Conservatives had achieved 'crossover' – that is, they had now pulled away from Labour. And they would stay in the lead until March 2015. That same polling suggested that Miliband's personal ratings had fallen to what one insider described as 'near catastrophic levels'.

As one of his aides put it, the deficit hadn't run through the speech like the words on a stick of rock. It could so easily be forgotten because it was a 'bolt-on' paragraph or two. And if his own advisers had been disappointed, some closer to the Shadow Chancellor were furious. A speech devoted to the deficit would follow that December but their feeling was the damage had been done. At least one of Balls' allies had wanted Miliband ousted. But with no credible challenger, there was no challenge.

The perceptions of his leadership had improved by now, but from a very low base. So I had wondered if the lack of his image on the pledge card would be a sign that he wouldn't be front and centre of the campaign – that more focus would be on the Shadow Cabinet as a whole. I was told firmly that this wouldn't be the case. But another Shadow Cabinet adviser took the opposing view. 'I can't believe', he said to me, 'they are going to run this like a presidential campaign. Not only is he not a president – he is not a f***ing prime minister.'

Deal or No Deal

16 March

- Ed Miliband hopes to defuse speculation about the SNP before the campaign begins.
- He rules out a coalition with Nicola Sturgeon – on a visit to Yorkshire.
- The issue will come to dominate the campaign – and hasn't gone away for his successor.

ED MILIBAND LAID bare his divisions with Nicola Sturgeon, not in Paisley or Perth – but in Pudsey. The Labour leader had been limbering up for the election campaign with a 'People's Question Time' event in this marginal Yorkshire seat – though it was an appearance on the real *Question Time* that would prove even more controversial in the last week of the campaign. But under the cosh from what he would describe as the 'unholy alliance' of the Conservatives and SNP, he had decided to strike back.

These apparently public events are organised by local party activists and usually the 'people' are a select bunch of floating voters, not opponents. Policies tend to be explained, and not announced, in this type of forum. Today would be different.

The Conservatives had shown their hand. On the internet and at selected poster sites, the star of their campaign wasn't David Cameron – it was the SNP's Alex Salmond. Ed Miliband featured too, though only peeping out from Salmond's shirt pocket. Those masked activists in Birmingham had been a foretaste of what was to come. Clearly a key theme of the campaign would be that a weak minority Labour government would meekly cave in to left-wing SNP demands.

Ed Miliband's response would at least settle what had been a remarkably long stand off at the very heart of the Labour party – and which had been every bit as tense as the denouement of *Reservoir Dogs*.

He had faced competing but equally robust advice from the moment Jim Murphy had been elected as the leader of the Scottish Labour Party the previous December. Or as one insider put it, 'he was dragged into a massive argument'. Murphy's position was completely at odds with the stance taken by UK general election co-ordinator, Douglas Alexander. The two different approaches can best be summed up like this – metaphorically, Alexander wanted to shake former Labour voters until they came to their senses, and Murphy wanted gently to woo them until they became more pliable.

Alexander argued strongly that Miliband should rule out a coalition deal with the SNP early, and hard. If the key message was to be that the only way to guarantee a Labour government was to vote Labour – and an SNP vote risked letting Cameron in by the back door – then this hard fact had to be rammed home. No soft options.

As one strategist put it:

> Douglas's view was 'we need them to think they have to vote Labour... it's a fact we need to establish – if they don't like the fact that more Labour votes will reduce the chances of a Tory government, it's still a fact.

Miliband was being advised to do no such thing by the new leader in Scotland. Murphy's argument wasn't that there should be a deal – simply that now would be the wrong time to rule it out well before the formal – or 'short' – election campaign began. That's because he took the view that the starting point in winning back voters who had supported Labour in 2010 but had voted 'Yes' in the referendum was not, in effect, to tell them they had been wrong, or to deliver an ultimatum. Yes, a coalition would have to be ruled out in due course, but his view was to see how many people could be won over before doing so. After all, in the post-referendum landscape, polls were suggesting that Scottish voters liked the sound of an SNP–Labour coalition, however impossible that was going to be.

Jim Murphy had also obtained funding for focus groups which initially explored the views of 'soft' SNP supporters – that is, those who had backed the Nationalists at Holyrood but wanted a Labour government at Westminster. The views of these voters, however, soon suggested that ruling out working with Nicola Sturgeon's party would be counter-productive. As one insider described it:

> It felt to them like we were penning them up – we said if you vote SNP, you will get a Tory government. But that's because we won't work with the SNP. So in effect it seemed we were saying 'f*** you' and that made them more SNP and less Labour.

At this stage the sheer scale of Labour's defeat in Scotland hadn't seemed inevitable. John Curtice, Professor of Politics at Strathclyde University suggested that Labour could keep most of their seats if they could pin back the SNP lead to around five per cent. It was a tall order, but coming a good and not a distant second could bolster the prospects of Labour returning to power at Westminster. So it was decided to handle these potential defectors from the Labour-voting camp with care. Data from the vast, academic British Election Study had also distinguished between the attitudes of 2010 Labour voters who had voted 'Yes' in the referendum and who were likely to vote SNP, and those who were remaining loyal. The 'defectors' tended to be more left-wing – far more of them agreed with the phrase that 'cuts had gone too far', and also that they wanted to see more powers devolved to the Scottish parliament.

A record £2 million was spent on the campaign in Scotland, with some of the funding devoted to convening far more regular focus groups. At one stage there were as many as three or four a week. They were carried out by the party's UK pollsters Stan Greenberg, and, more often, James Morris. The latter had advised Ed Miliband on his leadership campaign nearly five years previously.

The pollsters registered that offers to extend the Holyrood parliament's welfare powers – along with a concentration on left-wing issues such as denouncing the need for more food banks and arguing for stronger employment rights – had helped to restore a Labour brand tarnished in the eyes of 'soft' SNP voters by a close association with the Conservatives during the referendum campaign. However, these same voters still felt Labour would 'put Westminster before Scotland'.

So initially Miliband had followed Murphy's advice, and when he was asked on the *Andrew Marr Show* in January about what would happen in the event of a hung parliament he responded with a rather bizarre and contorted formulation: 'I am not about deals' – which raised more questions than it answered.

But the disarray and disagreement over what to say about the SNP didn't end there. Lord Falconer, the eminent barrister who had been Lord Chancellor and Justice Secretary in Tony Blair's government, had been tasked with doing detailed work on the transition to power, particularly in the event of a hung parliament. He knew a formal coalition would not happen, but also didn't want it ruled out early on because it might then invite further questions about other deals short of a coalition – such as 'confidence and supply'. Under this scenario, the SNP might sustain a Labour government by voting for its budget in return for concessions, but not ministerial positions. He felt the door to informal pacts should be kept open as a minority Labour government might need them, certainly in the second half of a parliament.

Crucially, he believed there was another good reason for Labour to avoid being dragged in to saying 'no' to every permutation of a deal when in opposition. There was a grave danger that even any discussion of future legislation, or budget measures with SNP MPs when in government would be characterised, however inaccurately, by a hostile press as a 'deal'. If voters saw this the same way, then that could cause the party to suffer the catastrophic loss of trust which had beset the Liberal Democrats after making their pledge to scrap tuition fees in opposition – and then messily, divisively, abandoning it in power.

Then, there were those that argued quite simply that a day talking about the SNP was a day not spent talking about Labour's plans for government, so the best way to make a problem go away was not advertise its existence. In this camp were Bob Roberts, the head of communications, and Spencer Livermore who had been put in charge of the election campaign at Labour's head office.

So on Murphy's instructions, Miliband initially didn't rule out a coalition – and on Roberts's advice tried not to mention the elephant in the room.

By March it still wasn't quite clear that there would be a stampede of trumpeting elephants in that room, but it was obvious that the issue had transcended the question of Labour's prospects in Scotland. The senior aide to the Shadow Scottish Secretary, Martin McCluskey, recalls being driven in to central London after his flight from Glasgow had landed at Heathrow – and witnessing some of the most expensive advertising sites in the UK, bought up by the Conservatives, warning of a Labour–SNP deal.

In the end, Miliband had felt pressured to rule out a coalition before the formal election campaign had begun. Many of those around him now concede he should have done so even sooner. He had failed to be as explicit earlier in the month when addressing Scottish Labour's pre-election gathering in Edinburgh. One insider said: 'Ed and Douglas and Jim were all in different rooms, barely talking to each other.'

So when the anti-SNP line was at last articulated, the anticipated slap in the face for 'not listening to Scotland' was subsequently delivered by the attendees at Labour's Scottish focus groups. But it wasn't as vicious as had been imagined, partly because the announcement had been made south of the border, and partly because voters had by then seen it coming. It's also possible, though, that they were less bothered about it because they had little intention of returning to the Labour fold.

Once Miliband made the anti-SNP announcement, one of Labour's spin doctors triumphantly but hubristically declared 'we are not going to talk about this for the next eight weeks'. They assumed the ticking time bomb had been defused. But there were secondary devices.

As Charlie Falconer had predicted, the ground swiftly moved on to other options – especially as Nicola Sturgeon said she wasn't asking for a coalition anyway. But she did offer to help Labour keep David Cameron from going back through the door of Downing Street, so speculation about what type of deal could be struck continued to mount.

More damaging for Labour in Scotland was the finding in their focus groups that the argument that you need to vote Labour to get a Labour government wasn't being believed. The SNP had said they would help 'lock' the Tories out of office, and, as the Nationalists were the one party that hadn't co-operated with the Conservatives on the referendum, this was seen as credible. Frankly, Lord Falconer believed it too.

Following the election, Labour is now nearly 100 seats behind the Conservatives – and has 55 seats fewer than the SNP in Scotland. So the party is still likely to face questions over whom – and on what terms – they would work with to form a government in future. Taking a hard line with the SNP could mean closing off options they would prefer to keep open, so the dilemmas Ed Miliband faced still exist for his successor.

The Battle for Downing Street

26 March

- Ed Miliband chooses to let David Cameron take questions first in the opening television encounter of the election.
- Despite that defensive decision, he goes on the attack and attempts to appear 'tough'.
- He highlights how he stood up to Rupert Murdoch – but he is told the 'price of going to war with the media is too high'.
- The new Labour leader may have to choose their enemies more carefully.

IT SMACKED OF defensiveness, not decisiveness. A coin was tossed to determine whether David Cameron or Ed Miliband would take questions first from Jeremy Paxman in the inaugural 'non-debate' of the election campaign. Ed Miliband had won that toss of the coin, but had chosen to go second.

The broadcasters still had the scars on their backs from vicious negotiations with the parties, but had finally come up with a formula which the Prime Minister in particular could accommodate. He – and his strategists – felt the regular debates had 'sucked the life' out the last election campaign, which is another way of saying they had inflated Nick Clegg's profile, and possibly cost the Conservatives an overall majority. Now, as David Cameron's personal ratings far outstripped Ed Miliband's, why put them at risk by allowing viewers to see the Labour leader on an equal footing with the Prime Minister?

So, this time, he grudgingly agreed he would take part in only one actual debate. It would involve seven parties soon after the formal campaign got under way. The broadcasters' original proposal of a 'head-to-head' clash between the only two candidates who could make it to Number 10 had been reduced to having them in the same studio on the same night, appearing consecutively not concurrently.

The format would involve a 'grilling' from Jeremy Paxman followed by questions from an audience, moderated by Sky's Kay Burley, and would still be adorned with the dramatic title *The Battle For Number 10*, even though no hand-to-hand combat between the candidates would take place.

Miliband's decision to let Cameron take the initial flak allowed him to respond to anything which the Prime Minister had said, but had the disadvantage that he would still be jousting with Paxman on Channel 4 and Sky when BBC and ITN were showing 'highlights' packages on their main news bulletins at 10.00pm. This would certainly mean that the impact any disastrous encounter with 'rottweiler' Paxman would be lessened that night – but, equally, any triumph would be diluted.

Still, great store was put on 'unmediated access' – Ed Miliband's strategists would rather viewers saw for themselves how he could perform rather than see an edited version.

But this wasn't exactly unmediated access. There was a mediator who had a reputation for asking searching, even insolent, questions. Paxman likes not just to shock, but disarm, his prey.

Very early in my career I worked with him on the 1997 BBC *Election Programme* and conducted in-depth research into each possible guest, providing him with some of his apparently *ad-hoc* one-liners – for example, when he asked the former Conservative Party Chairman Cecil Parkinson: 'You are chairman of a fertiliser firm. Just how deep is the mess you're in tonight?'

He now tried a similar approach with Ed Miliband. It was just the opinion of a 'bloke on the tube', of course – but that man felt that if Ed Miliband went into a room with Vladimir Putin and the door was locked, then two minutes later Putin would emerge smiling while puny Ed Miliband would be 'all over the floor in pieces'.

Ed Miliband initially responded with humour – wondering aloud if the man on the tube had, in fact, been David Cameron. There had been a rather lively internal debate amongst his close advisers about how Ed Miliband should conduct himself. One of his longest standing supporters and key strategists had been pushing for him to be presented as 'tough' and 'strong'. Another equally senior adviser felt this might seem inauthentic. If voters were asked in those awful *vox pops* in the street what qualities come to mind when you think of Ed Miliband, he argued, people might say 'principled'. You would hope they would say 'decent'. They would not say 'tough' – he might have wanted to 'weaponise' the NHS as an election issue, but he was no Arnold Schwarzenegger.

But there was a bit of Ed Miliband, close friends say, that liked the suggestion of toughness – that looked in the mirror and saw a strong champion of the poor and dispossessed staring back at him. In the end, Paxman himself resolved the issue since his line of questioning revolved round the idea that Miliband was a 'north London geek', too weak to be Prime Minister.

Ed Miliband had no choice but to resist that narrative. So when it was put to him directly that 'the point is, people just don't think you are tough enough', he answered with the most memorable line of the night, the rather transatlantic, 'Am I tough enough? Hell Yes, I'm tough enough.' And the Labour Party swiftly showed its entrepreneurial side when t-shirts emblazoned with the phrase 'Hell Yes, I'm Voting Labour' were produced and marketed.

Miliband had prepared well for the encounter. The ex-*Times* journalist Tom Baldwin – who became his chief adviser on communications and strategy – had alternated with Tony Blair's former chief spokesman Alastair Campbell to play the role of Paxman in rehearsals. But the 'Hell, Yes' line was Miliband's alone and appeared to be spontaneous. Perhaps the phrase, or something like it, had been lodged in his sub-conscious from his time at Harvard, on sabbatical from Gordon Brown's team in 2002, or possibly from further back. He had accompanied his academic father Ralph to Boston as a 12-year-old and credits this period for his love of baseball.

Team Miliband were impressed with his performance and genuinely shocked when the instant polls suggested David Cameron had had a better night. They were spitting blood, too, that Paxman had appeared to patronise what at that stage was still a potential prime minister by asking at the end of their bout, 'Are you all right, Ed?' when the microphones were still open. But he had acquitted himself well and had responded with a 'Yeah – are you?'

But on closer examination, what had been a fired-up performance masked some underlying weaknesses. When giving examples of his toughness, for example, was he also exposing flaws in his own judgment?

Ed Miliband told the TV audience he had been brought into a room with David Cameron and Nick Clegg and they had just been on the phone to Barack Obama about the bombing of Syria – following the apparent use of chemical weapons by the Assad regime in 2013. His opposition to a 'rush' to air strikes had been controversial inside his Shadow Cabinet – not least with Jim Murphy, who was later to become the leader of the Scottish party – but he and the Shadow Foreign Secretary, Douglas Alexander had resolved to oppose the government and had defeated David Cameron with the help of Conservative rebels. So he could have presented this as a victory against a prime minister who was impetuous and hawkish – and who, after all, was his principal opponent at the election. Instead, he said he had 'stood up against the leader of the free world'. If there were doubts that he was statesman-like enough to strut the world stage, he was telling his sceptical audience he was out of kilter with the US and had tweaked the American President's nose. And this President was not George Bush. He wasn't a Republican. He was a Democrat, and one whose personal ratings in this country tended to be positive. Miliband expanded on his theme in his encounter with Paxman:

> People have to decide – do they want my ideas, do they want my principles when I stood up not just to President Obama, but Rupert Murdoch, the energy companies, the banks, fighting for ordinary people, which is what I believe in and what I came into politics for?

And in this long sentence he tended to crystallise what he was against, not what he was for. Perhaps that need to demonstrate 'toughness' had got the better of him, but his ideas were also about increasing productivity, fostering high-value jobs, building better housing, all of which were argued less convincingly. Even if he defined himself by what he was against, had he chosen the right enemies? And if the right enemies, the wrong battles?

Following the phone hacking scandal which led to the closure of the *News of the World*, and the imprisonment of David Cameron's former Director of Communications, Andy Coulson, Rupert Murdoch had become something of a pantomime villain. So to have a pop at him wasn't at all unpopular. But the long battle to bring about a new system of press regulation was seen as one of the biggest strategic errors of Miliband's leadership by the man who was in charge of dealing with the press.

Bob Roberts was Labour's director of communications, but much to the chagrin of some in the party, was the almost constant companion of Ed Miliband throughout the election. A former political editor of the *Daily Mirror*, he rarely dropped the ball – usually dispensing wise advice and soaking up much of the pressure from a sceptical and increasingly hostile media. But on the handling of the thorny issue of press regulation, he felt his party leader had scored an own goal.

> The vehemence with which some of our people wanted to attack the Murdoch empire – not that they would have done us any favours – made the media more generally suspect that Labour was somehow out to get them. And that wasn't just execs – that was subs, and general reporters.
>
> We knew we couldn't win them over but we could have won a fair hearing. We needed to maintain the respect of other media outlets, if not Murdoch's. In the end some our attacks had been too aggressive and they retaliated. We got 1992-type coverage.

That was a reference to the often personal attacks the then Labour leader Neil Kinnock was forced to endure when it looked like he, too, might have either led his party to victory, or at least deprived the Conservatives of an overall majority. It was typified by *The Sun* front page on Election

Day featuring Kinnock's head inside a light bulb alongside the legend 'would the last person to leave Britain please turn out the lights?'

So while Ed Miliband was boasting of standing up to the vested interests of the Murdoch empire, his own press chief believed: 'The morality of it was unanswerable but the political effort and expenditure of going to war with the media was too high.'

From Builder to Soldier: Britain Succeeds When Working People Succeed

27 March

- Ed Miliband unveils the main theme of the campaign.
- The Labour battle bus isn't all that it seems.
- The new leader will have to find language that encapsulates a broader electoral appeal.

'THIS IS THE PLACE where all of the United Kingdom came together and showed the world what we can do.' It wasn't exactly a subtle message from Ed Miliband. He was getting his retaliation in first by firing the starting gun on Labour's election campaign just days before David Cameron would go to the Palace and formally begin the race for Downing Street. The venue was London's Olympic Park and clearly Miliband was hoping to associate himself with the success, patriotism and optimism of 2012. He had packed a large number of journalists, activists, and most of the Shadow Cabinet into a very small space 300ft above ground, in the pod of the Orbit – Sir Anish Kapoor's sculpture-*cum*-observation tower. The structure's contorted metal construction – which gave it the appearance of a dysfunctional helter-skelter – would probably have made a better metaphor for a general election which was going to bring all sorts of unexpected twists and turns. The UK, however, didn't exactly come together on this occasion when extremely disgruntled visitors found they had been barred from the attraction until the Labour team had left the building.

I was there with BBC producer Dan Grant, whose cruel and unusual punishment for being resourceful and creative would be to spend six weeks 'on the road' with me following the Labour campaign from target seat to target seat across the UK. We had primarily wanted to give some new broadcasting equipment a dry run – and take a peek at Labour's 'battle bus' which was being paraded for the first time, and on which we assumed we would be travelling. But it soon transpired that there were to be two buses. These were similar, but not the same.

Ed Miliband would be ensconced in one vehicle with his entourage and it would be used only to travel short distances between train stations and speech venues. The other coach would convey the broadcast media and the Press Association across the country. It had one advantage over the Labour leader's coach – its facilities included a WC. But its lack of Labour politicians meant we would use the bus only fleetingly, usually when Ed Miliband deigned to pop on board for a chat. Instead, we would often anticipate which trains Miliband and his aides would be using, and then book tickets on the same service.

There was, however, a story to cover today, too – it was one of the mini-announcements with which we would become familiar. In this case a five per cent profit cap on big NHS contracts won by private sector companies. This small, but new announcement would be used to attract press interest, and then the Labour leader would re-announce existing but more significant policy, such as plans to fund 20,000 more nurses and 8,000 more doctors in the NHS in England. A similar template would be applied to other policy areas.

But what was far more valuable on the cusp of the campaign proper was to hear Ed Miliband's announcement of the theme for Labour's forthcoming political contest. It, too, by now was familiar but was about to become far more prominent.

> This election is not simply a choice between two different parties and two different leaders. But two different visions of our country. That Tory vision that says Britain succeeds when only a few at the top do well... Or a Labour vision based on the idea that Britain only succeeds when working people succeed. That's why this election matters so much.

It formed just one paragraph in Ed Miliband's speech but distilled his approach to the election. He wanted voters to think about who was on their side. In the jargon of his aides, he had been a 'builder' earlier in his leadership – reaching out for new support to construct a majority. But now with an economic recovery which didn't appear to be spreading the benefits fairly, he was to be transformed in to a 'soldier' who would battle on behalf of those who were losing out. This was a recognition that the Conservatives had a solid lead on the economy which would be difficult to challenge head-on so now here was an attempt to change the terms of the debate. Political arguments should no longer simply be about who could best deliver growth, but about who should reap the rewards.

The message had taken the best part of a year to refine – especially the key phrase 'Britain only succeeds when working people succeed'. Labour insiders had been worried that there had been a lack of clarity about what the party stood for – not just in the minds of the target voters it needed to convince, but even amongst its core support. And no wonder. There had been huge frustration at the party leader's previous willingness to chop and change.

Initially, he had championed the 'squeezed middle' – his pollsters had liked the phrase as it had suggested broad appeal, and not simply a focus on the least well-off. It had even played well with *Telegraph* readers. But it had been squeezed out following a frankly embarrassing interview with John Humphrys on the BBC's *Today* programme in November 2010 when Miliband appeared to have trouble defining exactly whom he had in mind. Then there had been the 'Promise of Britain' – which was supposed to be about the next generation doing better than the last. Labour's pollsters said that once the idea had been explained to voters, it had proved powerful – but, unfortunately, they found the phrase itself meaningless. In June 2011, in what was unofficially referred to as a re-launch of Miliband's leadership, he gave his 'responsibility' speech – stressing the need for responsibility both at the top and bottom of society. In turn this theme was subsumed in a wider message of 'rebuilding Britain' – a slogan that would be replaced at the 2012 conference by a new 'One Nation' narrative. This, in turn, was slowly smothered by the emerging 'cost of living crisis'. This is when, at last, those around Ed Miliband felt the party had really broken through but Labour's own polling suggested that around the turn of the year – January 2015 – the falling oil price was having a positive impact on family budgets, so the 'crisis' had become less resonant with key sections of the electorate.

There had, however, been an earlier recognition that a phrase which encapsulated a political attack would be inadequate as a general election slogan in any case, so work had already been undertaken to find new words that would sum up Labour values.

A transatlantic current flowed in to Labour's thinking. Former Obama aide David Axelrod was appointed as a campaign strategist just over a year before the election. For all of his talk of standing up to the Leader of the Free World, Miliband was quite keen to engage one of the President's former staffers. Axelrod had helped mastermind Barack Obama's victory, first to be the Democrat nominee for the White House, then to be elected the 44th US President in 2008. He had gone on to advise him for more than two years in office and had returned for the successful 2012 re-election campaign.

Labour had wanted a 'big name' for their own campaign, following the Conservatives' successful signing the previous year of Jim Messina, Obama's former campaign manager. With his pedigree, 'the Ax' didn't come cheap. Some insiders have suggested he was paid more than £300,000. And he didn't come to Britain often. One insider told me:

He earned more in a month than I got in a year. He was a senior member
of the team. I saw him in the office no more than twice.

Instead he dispensed his advice in weekly telephone calls. But he was
ideologically compatible with Labour.

He had initially propelled Obama towards the White House on the
promise of change, but also of bringing the country together – a not
dissimilar approach to Labour's abandoned 'One Nation' theme. But in
2012 he had changed tack – majoring instead on tackling economic
unfairness, or what some sections of the conservative press in the US
dubbed 'class warfare.' He had been influenced by a book co-authored by
the Labour, and Democrat, pollster Stan Greenberg and straight-talking
strategist James Carville.

Both men had been key figures in the 'war room' which had overseen
Bill Clinton's presidential campaign more than 20 years previously and
which will always be associated with the well-known political catchphrase 'It's the economy, stupid.' Their new work was entitled *It's the
Middle Class, Stupid!* and it chronicled the falling living standards and
insecurity from which a broad swathe of the American workforce had
suffered even before the financial crash struck. It highlighted growing
income inequality – while the majority worked longer hours for fewer
rewards. And it exhorted Obama to take up the cudgels on their behalf.

In 2012 it had been clear who Obama had been for – and what he was
against. In other words, he had successfully gone from being a 'builder'
to a 'soldier.' In a rare meeting with Miliband in London in May 2014,
Axelrod had been critical of what some in the Labour Party had described
as the series of 'retail offers' or 'small scale bribes' in the absence of an
effective overarching story. According to Patrick Wintour's account of the
meeting in the *Guardian* (3 June 2015), he had characterised the party's
approach as 'vote Labour, win a microwave'.

So with Axelrod's input, Labour's strategists spent the spring and
summer months in heated debate over what slogan might encapsulate the
party's appeal. The American 'middle class' were substituted for British
'working people'. One attempt at a new phrase – 'Putting Working People
First' – had the benefit of clarity, but was felt to be too divisive. In a speech
to the Blairite Policy Network think tank in July 2014 Miliband tried out
various phrases – he talks about 'people succeeding' and 'Britain succeeding.' He also highlighted what he saw as the 'broken link between work
and reward' – which could have been lifted from Greenberg and Carville's
call to action. What he said in the speech about 'reforming markets' was
tested in a focus group in the marginal Harlow seat in Essex – but voters
simply assumed he was going to interfere with their street stalls.

Axelrod assisted with language and definition. Finally, the phrase 'Britain Succeeds when Working People Succeed' was agreed. Obama's former aide liked the fact it mentioned people, and the idea of 'success' implied that Labour would grow the economy. But above all he approved of the link between an individual's self-interest and the country's well-being. This elevated Labour above mere traders in free microwave ovens, in his view.

Miliband used the phrase in anger in his 'zero-zero' speech in November that year – when he was fighting back after the failed coup against his leadership. In a reference to attempts to undermine him he said: 'I am willing to put up with whatever is thrown at me, in order to fight for you.' Then he went on to denounce both the insecurity of zero hours contracts and corporations which pay 'zero' tax. He saw real substance behind the phrase which is why he subsequently insisted it wasn't just a slogan. But it certainly had been designed with that purpose in mind. As one insider said, it could go on a banner in the way that 'a cost of living crisis' could not. Though it would have to be a rather big banner. Or, in truth, a metaphorical one.

And now it would become a key theme of the campaign, and would almost always be juxtaposed with an attack on the Conservatives for standing up for those at the top. Miliband would subsequently use it in his brief opening address at the only TV debate of the campaign in which he and David Cameron would appear together – and it would be prominent on the cover of Labour's manifesto.

But not everyone had been chuffed with it. One adviser said it gave the impression of a 'big offer' to voters but in fact concealed a 'small, scratchy offer' which didn't speak adequately to the concerns of those in the middle. And the emphasis on 'working people' would also focus attention on Labour's policies towards those who employed many of them – British businesses.

Funny Business

30 March

- Labour's campaign comes close to disaster early on by blurring the line between business backing for a specific policy on Europe – and an endorsement of the party itself.
- Senior party figures fear Ed Miliband's rhetoric on business could cost votes.
- Jeremy Corbyn is far less able to use a pro-EU stance as a substitute for wider engagement with business.

ED MILIBAND SPENT the first official day of the election campaign trying to eliminate a negative. No trip to marginal seats. No rallies. No knocking on voters' doors. No significant new policy announcements. Instead, as David Cameron travelled to Buckingham Palace to tell the Queen what she already knew, now that we have fixed-term parliaments – there would be an election on 7 May – the Labour leader made almost as short a journey from the City of Westminster to the City of London to look into the whites of the eyes of prominent business leaders.

* * *

In 2011 in his party conference speech in the less affluent city of Liverpool, he had delivered his attack on predatory capitalism – though he had some difficulty in naming specific predators when pressed to do so the following morning on the BBC's *Today* programme.

His speech was seen as the most decisive break with 'New Labour' – amplified when a mention of Tony Blair was greeted by some in the auditorium with jeers.

Since then his opponents had developed the narrative that not only was he far less pro-business than his two immediate predecessors, but that he was not comfortable with the process of wealth creation. And this view extended beyond his natural political enemies.

Largely under the radar, the Shadow Chancellor, Ed Balls and the Shadow Business Secretary Chuka Umunna had been trying to repair what they judged to be a rather damaged relationship with those at the top of finance and industry. But, according to some of those close to both men, they believed not only that they lacked their leader's full backing but that Ed Miliband was being urged to move them from their portfolios when safe to do so – and almost certainly would have considered this had he become prime minister. They say he had been too reluctant to meet with business leaders himself, and – in the words of one of them – when he did engage, he had simply left them with the impression that 'he wanted to hit them with a big stick'.

Ed Miliband's approach had been highlighted by his decision not to attend the annual meeting of the British Chambers of Commerce at the Queen Elizabeth Conference Centre, about 500 steps away from the leader of the Opposition's office at Westminster in February.

It had been explained at the time by the Labour press team as a 'diary clash' but subsequently leading figures admitted it was no such thing. He hadn't wanted to attend.

The dilemma, though, for the Shadow Chancellor's team was this. Business needed to hear reassurance directly from Ed Miliband. That's the message they had received from many unpublicised business dinners, and from one-to-one meetings with senior executives.

But was it better in the end for Ed Balls to attend the BCC bash and dress his speech up in pro-business tones, or was it better to have the symbolism of the party leader there – even though his rhetoric would have stressed the responsibilities, or frankly, burdens he was going to place on business leaders? As Ed Miliband wouldn't attend, then Ed Balls had no choice but to substitute himself – but he didn't fight too hard against his leader's absence.

While there may have been only a narrow gap between the preferred policies of the two Eds, an ally of the Shadow Chancellor identified a crucial difference in approach:

> You could justify each and every single policy. The problem was the rhetoric. We would describe the sort of things we were trying to do – for example, getting the big banks to lend to smaller enterprises – as 'sensible reforms.' Ed Milibands's office would present it as 'a day of reckoning for the bankers'.

Ed Balls himself has indicated he was uncomfortable with some of the language used by his namesake. In other words, Ed Miliband had done little to dispel the anti-business image the Conservatives had created for him.

* * *

The Labour leader chose to launch his party's business manifesto in the Square Mile at the plush headquarters of Bloomberg – business broadcaster to the so-called predatory capitalists, amongst others. The auguries, however, weren't entirely favourable.

The document itself was in the form of a little red book and, as he introduced his leader, perhaps the most pro-business member of the Shadow Cabinet, Chuka Umunna, unapologetically announced, to silence: 'We are the Labour Party – the clue is in the title.' The 22 pages included a repeat of Labour's pledge to cut and freeze business rates for small and medium sized enterprises. Though as the eligibility for the rate cut would be based on the floor size of a business, many local branches of Boots – run by a Monaco-based Italian who had re-domiciled his HQ from Nottingham to Switzerland – would benefit every bit as much as a corner shop.

But there was much to come in Labour's actual manifesto that some businesses wouldn't like. An increase in corporation tax. A repeat of the bank bonus tax. A root and branch reform of HMRC to focus not just on tax evasion, but to scrutinise 'tax efficiency' – or legal loopholes that allowed enterprises to minimise their tax bill.

So, expecting negative headlines for much of this agenda, Labour's strategists were privately rather proud of discovering a way to accentuate the positive. Their unique selling point to business was that they wouldn't burden them with the uncertainty of an EU referendum. But this policy wasn't universally popular in the Shadow Cabinet and wasn't quite as straightforward as it sounded.

* * *

Ed Miliband had come under intense pressure from some in his Shadow Cabinet to back an EU referendum as it became clear that in some parts of the country, UKIP was picking up support – not just from Conservatives and disillusioned non-voters, but from some former Labour supporters too. Miliband hadn't quite stood firm on opposing a referendum but swayed only ever so slightly in the breeze of internal criticism. He and the Shadow Foreign Secretary, Douglas Alexander, decided they would use the language of David Cameron and Nigel Farage and talk about an in/out referendum. But there would be a high barrier to overcome before granting a vote.

The British people would only be consulted if there were to be a further transfer of power from Britain to Brussels. Previously, Labour would have held a plebiscite only on the specific transfer of sovereignty but now – on the surface at least – the whole issue of EU membership would be on the ballot.

One adviser to a pro-referendum Shadow Cabinet member said this was seen by some around the Opposition's top table as a shoddy compromise. He opined that time and again when Ed Miliband had the chance to make the political weather, he ran instead for shelter from the elements.

Labour, he argued, should have been bold and committed to an early referendum as the best way 'to end uncertainty for business' – and to catch opponents on the hop. The idea of a mid-term referendum – as put forward by David Cameron – was potentially disastrous as voters might deliver a verdict on an unpopular government. But several months out from the election he conceded:

> We are stuck with the current policy because for Ed to change now he would look not just weak but an arse. And that's even worse than the policy.

Labour's pollsters took a different view. They found that even voters who disagreed with Ed Miliband on Europe admired the fact that he was giving a clear answer and discernible leadership by opposing Cameron and Farage on an early referendum. They felt it was an opportunity to show he was strong. In fact they were finding that the public liked him to show fortitude on issues which weren't their top priority. So what they heard on the EU was the apparent strength, and not the policy. But strength had its weaknesses, too. Had he, for example, strongly argued the case for higher immigration or higher spending, voters would have focused on the message – because they cared about these issues more – and not the conviction with which he said it. So he had to be careful when and how he appeared unwavering, but on the EU he seemed to have hit a sweet spot.

As the internal sniping began to abate as polling day approached, Ed Miliband became more and more comfortable with his opposition to a referendum. He spent an increasing amount of time highlighting just how unlikely it would be for a Labour government to hold one, as a further transfer of powers to Brussels just wasn't on the horizon.

He more confidently recast Europe as a hard dividing line with David Cameron. He stressed that while he too wanted to see reforms in Brussels, these would best be brought about by alliance-building rather than by banging on the exit door.

* * *

So this journey had now brought him to the city where party strategists had decided that the most pro-business policy of all would be an emphasis on Britain's continued EU membership – and resistance to a referendum on an 'arbitrary' timescale. But not all went to plan.

A lack of the kind of consensus-building that Labour wanted to see in Brussels very nearly undermined the central point of Ed Miliband's appeal to business. As the audience and the cameras were finally admitted to the speech venue, I ran in to my old BBC colleague Lucy Thomas who was now working for a pro-business campaign group. She whispered that at least one member of the invited audience wasn't very happy.

The head of UK operations for the German engineering giant Siemens, Juergen Maier, had featured in a full page Labour ad in the *Financial Times* that morning, denouncing the uncertainty that a referendum would bring. But this hadn't been a new quote. Rather it had been lifted from an interview with another newspaper well before the election campaign got underway. Had he even been consulted on its use beforehand? I was determined to find out.

Not usually rubbing shoulders with blue chip bosses, I asked Lucy how I would identify him. He certainly stood out from the crowd. 'Oh he is in a flowery shirt and looks just like Paul Mason' (the *Channel 4 News* economics editor) she replied. Indeed, the resemblance was uncanny. I kept an eye on my prey – ready to pounce for an exclusive interview as soon as the event was over.

Time and again in the run up to the campaign I had attended seminar after seminar where it was stressed that this – infinitely more than in 2010 – would be a social media election. Now this threat to traditional ways of conducting journalism became all too real. To his credit, the BBC's Business Editor, Kamal Ahmed had rung the press offices of all the companies featured in Labour's FT ad alongside the Siemens boss. And while some businesses had been perfectly content to be included, Siemens had said the party had 'over stepped the mark' in using the quotes in a political context. And he had tweeted this response. This, in turn, had alerted my competition to Juergen Maier's worth. I saw rival broadcasters – who had probably quickly googled images of the Siemens' boss – hover near his seat. Had there been a window in this basement venue, the idea of a civilised one-to-one interview would have just gone out of it. So the moment Ed Miliband brought proceedings to a close, I moved in.

A startled Mr Maier moved in the opposite direction, into the clutches of Channel 4's long-standing Political Editor, Gary Gibbon, who is more streetwise than his polite public-school demeanour suggests. I was quickly joined by our camera and began firing questions at the Siemens CEO. Labour had a lucky escape. He wasn't quite as outraged as his press office had believed. His comments became mildly damaging and not devastating. He said he had been consulted by Labour about the use of his quotes in advance. And he stood by his criticism that an EU referendum would mean uncertainty for business. However he hadn't fully appreciated the overtly party political nature of Labour's advert and he told me he felt 'uncomfortable' with the way in which his opinions had been exploited. Other broadcasters then pursued him out of the venue to get their own words with Mr Maier. This soon included my colleague Lucy Manning, when it was discovered that the microphone I had been handed to record his comments hadn't worked.

The business launch was close to descending in to farce... on both sides. Quick as a flash, the previously invisible Bob Roberts appeared rather like the shopkeeper character from the children's TV show *Mr Benn*. In a damage limitation exercise, he wanted to assure me that Labour has indeed checked the quotes with Mr Maier before publication. But in effect the Labour operation had been rumbled.

Given the lack of high profile business backers, they had settled in the wheeze of republishing pro-EU quotes which happened to coincide with their own position, but looked at first glance like an endorsement on the day they unveiled their business manifesto. This option isn't available to Labour's new leader in future as first, there is now going to be a referendum in any case – and second, he opposes the EU/US trade deal that's currently being negotiated which won't exactly endear him to some large domestic and transnational businesses.

The shallowness of Labour's support amongst business leaders was about to become more apparent – but there was a split at the top between those who worried about this, and those who welcomed it.

Zero Sum Game

1 April

- Ed Miliband's rocky relationship with business continues when he announces new employment rights, and there are worries amongst Shadow Cabinet members that he is too relaxed about business support for the Conservatives.
- The Labour leader genuinely believes his employment policies would be popular beyond his party's core supporters – and has to be restrained from going even further.
- But Jeremy Corbyn is likely to latch on to Labour's poll findings, suggesting some voters believe the party was too soft, not too hard, on big business.

APRIL FOOL'S DAY was one of the most earnest of the campaign. Yes, there were internet spoofs – Ed Miliband 'photoshopped' to portray him as blond. The joke was that party strategists had been mulling over how to imbue him with the 'Bojo' (Boris Johnson) effect – an ability to reach voters who don't usually back his party – and could only come up with giving him a disheveled mop of hair. Then there were the 'leaked details' of a 'meeting' between him and Nigel Farage to discuss deals in a hung parliament. But it was no laughing matter that the start of the new month also signalled the beginning of the most divisive phase of the campaign. It had little to do with either fringes, or fringe parties – it was much more fundamental than that.

Much has been written about 'the end of history' and how class politics had been consigned to the era of the Cold War. But on this day in 2015, the old parties of Capital and Labour met on the election battlefield. And while there were now clearer divisions between the political parties, this was also a day when Ed Miliband's leadership became more clearly defined, too.

* * *

The Conservatives' wealthy co-chairman Andrew Feldman had coordinated a letter signed by 100 business leaders, many of whom were associated with companies that were household names – from Primark to Iceland to Costa Coffee – calling for the continuation of the current government's economic policies. It was splashed, traditionally enough, on the front page of the *Telegraph*. Labour expected something of this nature early in the campaign so the business manifesto had, in part, been an attempt to pre-empt this. But it coincided exactly with the day Ed Miliband had chosen to announce a tightening of labour laws. The Confederation of British Industry denounced Labour's plans, the Trade Union Congress warmly applauded them.

At an event to launch the new policy I ran into Rachel Kinnock, Ed Miliband's charming and highly competent *aide de camp* who could get him out of most scrapes – including in this case, a late change of venue. We were in a 19th century factory near Huddersfield which now manufactured hi-tech defence equipment and had a small but highly skilled workforce. The planned visit to a supermarket headquarters in Leeds had been called off when it had been discovered that the leader of the opposition would have to wear a hair net, or alternative head covering, when touring the premises. This potential image hadn't passed the prime ministerial test so the venue had been moved at short notice west along the M62. But I was reminded of the era when Rachel's father Neil, a staunch supporter of Ed Miliband's leadership, had been portrayed simultaneously as anti-business and as just not prime ministerial enough to occupy Number 10.

The current Labour leader believed he could escape the same fate because he felt after the financial crisis, people were now more sceptical towards big business – and with living standards lower than at the time of the last election, voters were more open to ideas on how the economy could be run differently.

* * *

I had been told the previous day that – just 48 hours after Parliament had been dissolved – Ed Miliband was about to change one of his own policies. Some members of his Shadow Cabinet told me they got more notice than I did, but not too much more.

Following a review led by Norman Pickavance – the former personnel director of Morrison's supermarkets – in 2014 Labour had pledged to reform zero hours contracts. The party announced that, if in government, it would give workers on these terms – which give employers maximum flexibility and employees no guarantee of regular working hours – the right to request a regular employment contract after six months, and the legal right to one after a year. But Ed Miliband was now going to propose to give workers the right to a regular contract not after 12 months, but after just 12 weeks. It was fully anticipated that it would be denounced by some employers and many of those around him appeared unperturbed at the prospect.

* * *

So what had motivated the change? There is one apparently glaringly obvious answer. To get himself out of a fix after the row over union influence in the selection of a candidate for the Falkirk seat in 2013, Ed Miliband had instigated a review of Labour's links with the party's industrial wing. This had culminated in reducing the amount of guaranteed funding from the trade unions. Members would no longer be 'affiliated' to Labour *en bloc* but would have to make a personal and positive decision to pay a fee, and it had been assumed that many simply wouldn't get around to doing so. At the time, even the very personification of New Labour, Peter Mandelson, confided to me that he believed Ed Miliband had acted rashly and should have made any reform of Labour's funding conditional on a wider review of how all the main political parties were financed. He believed cross-party agreement to take 'the big money' out of politics, including limiting the influence of wealthy Conservative donors, had been close in 2007 – but had been scuppered by Gordon Brown, who had wanted to play to the union gallery before making his move from Number 11 to Number 10 Downing Street.

The apparently unintended consequence of the Miliband reforms was, however, to make Labour more and not less dependent on the union leaders. As affiliation fees from the members were set to fall, the party became more in need of large discretionary donations from general secretaries and executive committees at the top of the unions' hierarchy.

And back in 2013 – just ahead of the TUC annual congress – Labour's spin machine had gone into overdrive suggesting that Ed Miliband's speech to trade unionists would include a commitment to clamp down on zero hours contracts. The accompanying behind the scenes briefings floated the idea of permanent contracts after 12 or 24 weeks of being on 'zero hours'. So many union leaders – including those in charge at Unite and the GMB – were, to say the least, bitterly disappointed when Ed Miliband didn't set out such a specific timescale in his actual speech, then subsequently said there would have to be a 12-month wait for regular contracts. They had been pressing hard for Labour to take a tougher stand on flexible working in its manifesto. So, on the surface there was a transactional relationship. A cheque in the post for £1 million from Unite just as the campaign was about to begin, a change in employment policy a matter of days later.

But that is far from the whole story. As one Shadow Cabinet member told me:

> It wouldn't be so bad if he was just caving into pressure. There is little doubt that this was a change that Ed himself wanted to make too.

In fact there had been fears that too little that was new was being kept back for the election campaign. So, far from last minute pressure being exerted from the unions, the party leader's office had agreed to toughen the policy – with no resistance from the Shadow Chancellor – but the announcement was to be made only when the formal campaign got under way.

Indeed I discovered the Labour leader had contemplated going even further. There had been a certain rationale to revisiting the Pickavance proposals. It was possible that employers would turf out those on a zero hours contract after 11 months work before having to offer them a regular contract of employment. Reducing the period to 12 weeks would make it more difficult for employers to recruit replacements, and therefore make it trickier for them to avoid their responsibilities. Then there were the numbers. The Office of National Statistics estimated that 697,000 people were on 'zero hours' in their main job in 2014, up by more than 100,000 from the previous year. This was characterised by Ed Miliband as an 'epidemic' of insecurity in the workplace, though this represented just 2.3 per cent of the workforce. But even if there hadn't been a proliferation of these contracts, Ed Miliband had been contemplating toughening Labour's stance. At one level, he wanted to motivate Labour's core vote to well, actually vote. But his most senior and long-standing strategists believed that a message on improving working conditions and living standards would stretch beyond this electoral redoubt. In short, it would symbolise that Labour in government would run the economy differently – pushing up productivity through better skills and higher wages.

Those close to him say there was an emotional element to Ed Miliband's approach too. He discussed employment issues often beneath the media radar at 'People's Question Time' events in marginal seats. And time and again – rather like George Orwell shocked by the extent of the working-class poverty he witnessed as he took *The Road to Wigan Pier* in the 1930s – he was moved by listening to people's personal experiences. It wasn't so much the two per cent or so of employees on zero hours complaining about their working conditions which had made the impression. It was the mums and dads of young workers relating how insecurity in employment was leading to insecurity in their personal lives and creating tensions in their families. So he felt he was being ahead of the curve in recognising that a stronger stance on zero hours contracts would be potentially popular.

In fact, he had considered announcing a complete ban on zero hours contracts all together. Employment lawyers had been consulted to assess how difficult this might be. In the end, the argument that some flexibility for those who chose it – thought to be perhaps around in one in ten of those on zero hours contracts – prevailed. But so too did politics. While it was striking that unlike his New Labour predecessors, Ed Miliband was content to take it on the chin from business by interfering in the employment market, the symbolism of ending zero hours contracts entirely was seen by enough of those around him as a step too far. One highly influential aide told me: 'We would be massacred if we were seen to end the flexible labour market.' And while Ed Miliband's press team declared it serendipitous that the Conservatives had hailed support from the boardroom on the same day as Labour stood up for those on the shop floor, not all Shadow Cabinet members were as sanguine. With the polls apparently deadlocked, one of them remarked: 'This will motivate our 34 per cent. But God' they added, 'it will motivate *their* 34 per cent too.'

* * *

Those close to the Shadow Chancellor, Ed Balls, were not talking about serendipity. Other words starting with 'S' came to mind when they got wind of the letter from business leaders which would endorse Conservative economic policy. As it was being circulated prior to publication, they rang round their contacts. They were pleased that they managed to limit the number of FTSE 100 chief executives who signed the missive to half a dozen. But they knew this was merely an exercise in damage limitation. Others around the Shadow Cabinet table insist that Ed Miliband's office had been warned that businesses hadn't felt the party leader was taking their concerns seriously enough. But when this had been raised at a meeting, an unnamed member of the leader's staff had suggested that the captains of industry should 'f*** off.'

Jon Cruddas recounts that when Jim Murphy was in the Shadow Cabinet, he would ask much the same question every few weeks following lengthy policy discussions – 'what are we doing to create as well as spend the wealth?' This usually received brief mutters of approval until – as Cruddas puts it – 'we all said "yes, now let's talk about NHS week…"'

But did Ed Miliband's attitude to business cost his party seats and votes?

The deputy leader Harriet Harman, who toured the country in a pink minibus and talked to thousands of female voters in particular, told me that the policies on big business and the banks were rarely denounced. Instead, there were fears that Labour wouldn't be tough enough on people at the other end of the scale – those claiming benefits. And some polling evidence backs this up. In a survey of nearly 5,000 voters, commissioned by the TUC and carried out in the week after the election by Labour's own pollsters Stan Greenberg and James Morris, 42 per cent of respondents said the party was too soft on big business, compared with 22 per cent who thought they were too tough.

Morris himself doesn't believe the party's attitude to business shifted many votes in one direction or another because compared with issues such as the deficit, public spending, welfare and immigration, any government's attitude to business was – electorally at least – far less important. 'People didn't care if companies paid a bit more or a bit less corporation tax. Or if they did, it was unimportant to how they cast their vote.'

But Harriet Harman's travelling companion on the pink bus, the Shadow Women and Equalities Minister, Gloria De Piero believes that apparently anti-business rhetoric narrowed Labour's appeal amongst aspirational voters who weren't CEOs of big corporations but owners of small companies:

> Sam runs a bakery in my constituency, the Country Kitchen, employing three people in Sutton-in-Ashfield. She comes from a family who had worked in Nottinghamshire's mining industry and she had always voted Labour. But she told me she was voting Conservative for the first time because she felt she couldn't do anything else – she had no enthusiasm for Cameron and Osborne but felt we were a risk to her business.

For some advisers, the eventual result of the election demonstrated that Labour hadn't been forgiven for presiding over the financial crisis. In the polling, the party might have been interpreted as 'too soft' on banks because they hadn't been tough enough with them in power.

The more significant finding in the TUC poll suggested there was a massive deficit when it came to which party could be trusted with the economy – with Labour 39 points behind the Conservatives. Some say suggestions that Labour simply didn't understand business may have accounted for some of this gap. Bob Roberts certainly felt, from a communications perspective:

> The perception we were anti-business had been allowed to thrive and was deeply damaging. We never really emerged from the predators versus producers soundbite – a phrase we had never even intended as a soundbite.

So, with the exception of the victor, Jeremy Corbyn, those who were vying to replace Ed Miliband all advocated 'resetting' Labour's relations with business. They didn't believe standing up for employees and employers should be a zero sum game.

They each said they suppressed their own concerns at Ed Miliband's approach in the run up to the election out of 'loyalty'. But not long after his departure as opposition leader, Yvette Cooper denounced Miliband's division of businesses between 'predators' and 'producers' as 'unhelpful'. She pledged to set up an advisory council which would include business leaders who might never themselves vote Labour. Within days of the election defeat, Andy Burnham said he would value entrepreneurs every bit as much as nurses – and Liz Kendall talked about giving more support for new business to grow.

Those close to Ed Miliband believe that this bunching together of pro-business voices was partly responsible for creating a large swathe of abandoned territory on the left which Jeremy Corbyn's supporters were then able to occupy without a fight.

Miliband's former adviser, the Labour peer Stewart Wood believed the mainstream leadership contenders had jumped to conclusions too quickly:

> The soft left was in retreat and a vast expanse of land was created – some of the people who voted for Ed's approach on these issues voted for Jeremy Corbyn in this election.

Now, while conventional wisdom says Labour's new leader will need a new relationship with business, the polling suggests – and some close to Ed Miliband believe – the next leader could still, if desired, find a polite way of telling captains of industry to 'f*** off'. But that attitude to business would need to be decoupled from a perceived lack of economic competence, and other credible measures would need to be taken to address the lack of trust in Labour's ability to manage the economy.

We're All Labour Here

2 *April*

- Ed Miliband appears unable to motivate some of Labour's core voters as he prepares for his televised clash with David Cameron.
- The analysis that Labour lost the election because it was too left-wing appears simplistic.
- He is 'egged' on his way to a public meeting – but not in a way that suggests he's made enough impact to upset anyone.

IT DIDN'T LOOK LIKE much of a demonstration. I arrived on a clear, crisp morning at Bury Town Hall – venue for another of Ed Miliband's 'People's Question Time' events – and soon spotted two very neatly dressed women in their 40s or 50s (I was too polite to establish which) flanking the entrance, handing out leaflets to council workers and audience members alike. It transpired they were canvassing to elect a slate of left-wing candidates to the national executive of the big public sector union; UNISON. If their presence didn't make Ed Miliband feel uncomfortable, it should have.

Mary Eadie told me she felt her union leadership had been too kind to the Labour leadership 'and it's time to hold them to account'. Dave Prentis, the union's general secretary, wouldn't speak out against austerity for fear of embarrassing Miliband, she opined. The women weren't on the far left. Members of the Trade Unionist and Socialist Coalition who revered the late RMT leader Bob Crow would show up outside similar events to protest against austerity and Labour's apparent acceptance of it. But today's leafletters were solid Labour. Mary's colleague Bernie Gallagher was standing in the UNISON election herself – but it was the general election which worried her. In a matter-of-fact tone, with a hint of resignation but not bitterness she said:

> He's not been radical enough, has Ed. We thought when he stood against his brother he was going to be more radical, more passionate but it hasn't turned out that way.

And this had been proving a problem on the doorsteps. As a party activist, she was experiencing exactly what Labour's own internal polling was suggesting – having felt the political necessity to stress deficit reduction to a wider electorate, it was becoming difficult to motivate some traditional supporters to go out and vote. Her union would subsequently back Jeremy Corbyn's successful leadership bid.

In his analysis of why Labour lost, the former Shadow Cabinet member in charge of policy, Jon Cruddas, told the left-leaning Institute for Public Policy Research think tank that there had been a substantial loss of traditional working class support – those from so-called social classes D and E – between the time of Tony Blair's leadership in 1997 and Ed Miliband's in 2015. I asked the women what they thought their party leadership could do to tackle this problem of motivation, with little more than a month to go to polling day. Bernie said:

> The zero hours will make a difference – the unions were right to push him but he should go further and ban them altogether. He also needs to say something about housing. But the main thing is to come off the cuts.

Mary took up the theme: 'He has to stop saying he will cut public spending and public services.' With much of the tabloid press – with the exception of the *Mirror* – attacking Miliband from the right, it was worth remembering that there was always a left flank too – something which would become very obvious in the seven-party television debate that would take place that evening in Salford.

In north-west England, those who felt Ed Miliband hadn't fired them up with enthusiasm would have a choice between staying at home and rushing a Conservative government. But in Scotland and Wales other choices, as they say, were available.

The official Labour line was that the best preparation for that evening's clash was 'meet the people' events such as the one about to unfold in Bury. The Manchester MP Lucy Powell – Miliband's former deputy chief of staff – had been appointed as vice chair of the election campaign in November 2014 following the coup-that-never-was and she had encouraged her leader to front these 'People's Question Time' events twice-weekly from December to build up his confidence and public performance skills. But these had usually taken place well away from the media spotlight. However, now getting into and out of these events was more tightly controlled – as was the guest list. Haunted by the Gillian Duffy incident – when the opinionated Labour supporter had broken through Gordon Brown's protective cordon at the last election in nearby Rochdale to interrogate him on immigration policy, only to be denounced as a 'bigoted woman' when he was safely back in his car but with his radio microphone still on – the Labour machine were especially keen not to make their current leader the victim of the unguarded moment. So much so that even the 'arrival shots' – much valued by the media for the opening pictures of a TV package – at events were rarely offered and largely avoided. Even if that meant Ed Miliband getting to an engagement extremely early, or finding the least public way of accessing a venue.

Matthew Laza – the party's broadcasting guru who had previously worked for the full gamut of BBC programmes from *The One Show* to the *Politics Show* – was a bespectacled ball of nervous energy outside the venue as this time, pictures of Ed's arrival hadn't actually been banned outright. 'If I screw this up, I'll have to answer to Rachel Kinnock!' he exclaimed, in a tone that mixed mirth with fear. There had been sceptical voices internally, he said:

> But I had to tell them this is an election, it's a democracy, and people are actually allowed to photograph our leader on the street.

The problem, though, was less with Rachel Kinnock and more with those running the Labour campaign back at the party's London HQ. They had decreed that Miliband must look 'prime ministerial' at all times – preferably behind a podium. With his TV background, Laza knew this was unsustainable but had to broker a path between the extreme nervousness of the HQ team whenever Miliband was at risk of spontaneously meeting the public, and a travelling press pack who were looking for images that would work on television or in press photos.

Laza had been recruited after the unflattering pictures of Miliband's struggle with a bacon sandwich in May of the previous year, in the run up to the European elections. His adviser, the Labour peer Stewart Wood, had had to remove the offending snack but not before the snappers had made a meal of it and photographed Miliband's contorted face. The rest of Labour's press team had ink in their veins, and he was the only one with a background in popular television, not print journalism. But with such a fear of a negative image of the party leader being spread far and wide, he was struggling against some others in his own party to get the opportunity to create more positive portrayals of his boss. As it turned out, he had nothing to worry about this time.

Ed Miliband strode off his campaign vehicle and wasn't punched by members of the public. But he was 'egged'. No, not like John Prescott in 2005, who hit out as a protestor threw a hard boiled oval object at him. Instead four-year-old Jennifer Torbet-Bagnall blocked Ed Miliband's path and handed over a nest of mini-egg encrusted Easter cakes.

The pictures were TV gold. Ed Miliband beamed naturally but there was an awkward moment when he was calculating whether to take the gift, hand it to her nearby parents, or to the local candidate – the more telegenic James Frith – who was accompanying him.

A 'natural' like Tony Blair or Bill Clinton would have instantly bent down, accepted the child's offering and smiled. So the caution from mission-control that was making Laza's life so difficult hadn't entirely been the result of paranoia. This was one leader who was never going to be truly relaxed in front of the cameras.

Back at base, the man brought in the previous year to deliver a 'smooth, professional' campaign – Spencer Livermore – was unapologetic for his, and his team's, approach. He took the view that 'there is no such thing as too much control freakery'. While restricted access to a party leader might prove frustrating for broadcasters, nonetheless Ed Miliband had never looked as ready for Number 10 as he did in the controlled environment of a modern day campaign. This view would, however, be tested to near destruction subsequently. But for today a successful balance had been struck between spontaneity and shut-down.

* * *

So much for ingress. Egress proved more controversial. My colleague Callum May – a technically superb radio producer but also a fine journalist – spotted that the luminous green exit sign had been shrouded in the kind of black felt you might see on a magician's table and, abracadabra, had temporarily disappeared. As if by magic – and I didn't see who was responsible – the sign was unveiled again within minutes of Miliband's departure.

Following Ed's leadership victory over his brother David at the 2010 Labour conference, the elder brother was pursued by a press pack through the venue, with the legendary 'Gobby' at its head. 'Gobby' was an appropriate nickname for the loquacious trader of information that was BBC producer Paul Lambert. He could often be heard lobbing a witty 'shout' at passing politicians. He left to become UKIP's head of communications – then swiftly departed following Nigel Farage's failure to win a seat in parliament. Unlike his leader, there was to be no resurrection of his political career, but back then he was at the top of his game. A frustrated David Miliband said he was simply trying to leave the building: 'I am looking for the way out.' Quick as a flash Gobby – in an accent that would make the late Sid James sound refined – roared 'Are you on your way out?' as the elder Miliband made his way to the door.

So it was perhaps to stop something similar happening that the exit sign had been unofficially suspended. Had Ed Miliband flopped in the debate, a sharp snapper would have had a very recent image symbolising his downfall. But Callum checked whether the avoidance of a PR disaster could potentially lead to a real disaster. A spokeswoman for the Association of Chief Fire Officers told him 'Covering an exit door is a serious matter. It puts people at risk if fire breaks out.' Callum tweeted a picture of the concealed exit and members of Ed Miliband's staff could be heard discussing how many views it had had. But with all media eyes on that evening's ITV-hosted debate, the story failed to ignite wider interest. The Labour leader had at least one lucky escape today.

The event inside Bury Town Hall itself was no less subject to control. Labour's spin doctors insisted that the question time participants had been chosen by the local party. Through their canvass returns, they had apparently identified 'swing voters' who needed perhaps that extra push from a prominent politician such as Ed to get them to the polling booth. But when I followed Miliband inside the faded art deco surroundings of the venue, I was pleasantly accosted by a regular and benevolent BBC viewer who confessed 'we are all Labour here' with a knowing smile.

Ed Miliband was certainly bombarded with a range of questions on very diverse topics – from tackling anti-social behaviour to the terms and conditions of the teaching profession. He was mildly berated by Jennifer's dad – who said she wanted to be a doctor when she grew up – for not promising a bigger cut in tuition fees in England. And a Labour councillor wanted him to cut rather than freeze VAT. But the tone and substance of the vast majority of the questions were neither difficult nor hostile. He was asked – for example – just how soon he would get rid of the 'bedroom tax' – a key plank of his policy. In order to maximise the number of questions but minimise the dissatisfied number of follow ups, he tended to group the audience's contributions in threes and answer on a swathe of subjects all at once. So – soft questions, no interruptions, and adequate thinking time – that didn't look or sound like the preparation for the only television debate to include both him and the Prime Minister. And indeed it wasn't.

Alastair Campbell had just tweeted that he had been playing the moderator of that night's TV debate in what had been secret (but widely assumed) preparations. Ed Miliband's advisers had warned him not to take questions on the debate from what one member of the Bury audience had dubbed 'the toxic media'. But he was rather more relaxed about it than they were.

So amidst the throng of Labour questioners, I asked him if he thought Alastair Campbell had made a convincing Julie Etchingham, ITV's anchorwoman for the seven-party stand-off, and if he could share with us more details of his debate preparation. He said Alastair Campbell should stick to his day job but he did admit his key tactic would be to talk 'directly to the British people' – the unsaid logic was that he was going to attempt to rise above the fray and appear prime ministerial. There would be put downs of opponents but the main focus of those would be David Cameron and not the leaders of the more minor parties. It was thought more important to frame the debate as a choice of who viewers would prefer to see in Number 10, and to neutralise the Conservatives' emphasis on his personality rather than policy.

Although he said he regarded the debate as no more intimidating than his appearance at Bury Town Hall, Ed Miliband had been eschewing a heavier schedule of campaign visits in favour of practicing to take on the Prime Minister. He had been holed up at the Radisson hotel in Manchester honing his direct address to camera – and rehearsing some of the key messages he would deliver that night with his brainy inner circle of Stewart Wood, Torsten Bell, and Greg Beales – the former Gordon Brown adviser who had become one of his earliest supporters for the Labour leadership.

Beales had begun 'prepping' for the possibility of debates since the previous December and had anticipated David Cameron's reluctance to take part so had carried out rehearsals with and without the Conservative leader's participation. When 'Cameron' was in the room he was usually played by Alastair Campbell.

Stewart Wood admitted that Campbell hadn't always found it easy to stay within his role. His most spectacular breach, however, had occurred not at this election but in 2010 when he had been 'prepping' Gordon Brown. He had been playing the then opposition leader when someone tweaked the mock David Cameron's tail over his support for the Iraq war. Alastair Campbell apparently responded by saying 'I am just going to step out of role for a moment' and launched a foul mouthed defence of his own role in the run up to war. In this campaign, he often emphasised – whatever role he was playing – that more needed to be done to defend the record of the last Labour government. In debate preparations, Wood himself tended to play Nick Clegg, though the Shadow Chief Secretary to the Treasury, Chris Leslie occasionally came off the subs bench.

But perhaps the most significant addition to the team came from Scotland. So concerned was Ed Miliband with the prospect of taking on Nicola Sturgeon that a mere backroom adviser couldn't be trusted with playing the SNP leader.

So he transported the party's most senior figure in the Scottish parliament – Labour's then deputy leader, and now leader, in Scotland Kezia Dugdale – 200 miles to sharpen his anti-SNP lines. As Jim Murphy didn't have a seat in the Scottish parliament, it was Dugdale who had been taking on Nicola Sturgeon at First Minister's Questions at Holyrood, and could best analyse – and mimic – her opponent's strengths and weaknesses.

Another Scot, Ayesha Hazarika – a talented former stand-up comedian who worked for Harriet Harman – played the leader of the Green Party in England and Wales, Natalie Bennett. I was told by one of the inner circle that if the real leader of the Green Party had been as sharp and effective as Hazarika in her role-play, Ed Miliband would have struggled in the real debate. She also 'stood in' as Plaid Cymru's Leanne Wood – though she attempted neither Bennett's New South Wales accent nor Wood's old South Wales tones. If you ever had to describe an intellectual, Miliband's policy guru Torsten Bell would look like one, so it seemed like miscasting to turn him into Nigel Farage. But like the old TV show *Stars in Their Eyes* – where members of the public played their favourite pop stars – the lack of a physical resemblance was eclipsed by the strength of the performance.

Until now, the names and roles of most of the cast list that helped the Labour leader prepare to take on his opponents have remained secret. But other preparatory work for the debates became embarrassingly public very swiftly indeed.

Happy Warrior

2 *April*

- Ed Miliband's debate preparations are exposed when he leaves confidential notes behind in a TV dressing room.
- He fails to follow his own advice in dealing with Nicola Sturgeon, and also fails to land a killer blow on David Cameron.
- Labour's new leader will need to work out how to oppose both the Conservatives and the SNP yet appear principled and consistent.

THERE WAS NO NEED to speculate on Ed Miliband's tactics for the debate or – as is inevitable in political journalism – simply trust the word of good sources. Rather helpfully, Ed Miliband left behind his prep notes in the dressing room of the ITV Salford venue and these, perhaps unremarkably, found their way in to *The Sun on Sunday*'s possession for subsequent publication.

So, just as he had revealed to me in Bury, Miliband's main tactic would be to talk directly to the British people rather than spend too much time parrying his opponents. And his advisers' faith that the public's doubts about him as a potential prime minister would be dispelled the more they saw of him were spelled out in almost cringeworthy detail. His notes reminded him to 'relish the chance to show who I am' and talk to the camera to 'use the people at home'.

He was to be a 'Happy Warrior' – the title of a Wordsworth poem written after Nelson's death – a generous, compassionate man at arms. It was a phrase not unknown in political, especially American political, circles. Barack Obama had described his Vice President Joe Biden as 'a happy warrior' and Franklin D. Roosevelt had used the phrase nearly a century before. In Britain, though, it invited tabloid ridicule.

Those close to him say that the notes reveal a lot more than the papers realised. The messages he wrote to himself didn't contain lists of policies he had to recount, and not much was directly about attacking his opponents. Instead they largely focused on his own self-confidence and how to exude that confidence more widely. His inner circle had been impressed with how much better he was coming across in interviews and in public since debate preparation first got underway in the dying days of 2014. Some regretted not starting the process even earlier. He had to distil ideas and complex arguments and he had his beliefs – and how he explained them – tested to near destruction but it was felt he had emerged stronger from the process.

In the event, Ed Miliband was forced to abandon some of the advice he had been cramming in to his brain before tonight's debate began – to remain 'calm and never agitated'.

He pretty much stuck to this approach when dealing with David Cameron, and some critics say he was almost too Zen-like in the face of jibes from Nigel Farage – by not challenging robustly the UKIP leader's claims that foreign HIV sufferers were coming to Britain specifically to benefit from NHS treatment. He was however less relaxed and a bit more agitated when dealing with the personification of Britain's changing polit-ical landscape.

* * *

While 50 years ago two parties took almost every vote between them, and while just five years ago viewers of the television debates might well have thought the era of three-party politics was permanent, now the Labour leader wasn't just facing Conservative and Lib Dem opponents. There were six other politicians on stage with him. And three of them were women.

The SNP's Nicola Sturgeon had dressed boldly in red – perhaps to underline her determination to supplant Labour as the main party in Scotland. And she derided the 'old boys network' in SW1.

It appeared that Natalie Bennett from the Greens, and Leanne Wood from Plaid Cymru as well as Sturgeon had consulted each other over launching an early concerted attack on the austerity advocated by the main parties at Westminster – including Labour. Ed Miliband had fully expected to be mocked for a policy of austerity-lite so he tacked to the left by stressing an end to what he called 'the bedroom tax' – and advocating an extension of the tax on bankers' bonuses.

But he was dragged further and further in to what some on the night dubbed 'the Ed and Nicola' show. Ed Miliband felt he had to counter-attack – suggesting that the Scottish government which Nicola Sturgeon now led, had also made cuts. In the end each party leader had got their message across, so while this may have been a defining moment in putting the fragmented nature of our politics on display on prime time television, it didn't really feel like a defining moment in the election. Only two of the participants could have become – or remained – prime minister, and it appeared that David Cameron had been to an extent insulated from attack as Ed Miliband battled the SNP leader.

Dividing lines were blurred between the two men by the very nature of a seven-way debate. And that outcome suited the incumbent. He had argued for a wider field and avoided the risk of a head-to-head clash with Miliband during the course of the campaign. This had been Ed Miliband's only chance to tackle the Prime Minister directly in debate and he found plenty of obstacles had been placed in his path.

A vast 'spin room' was located in an old sound stage near the debate venue which had the rather unshowbizzy name of the Pie Factory. The verbal equivalent of the custard variety was very much in evidence as the politicians and party strategists lobbed around derogatory comments about their opponents' performances.

Within minutes of the closing titles rolling, the Conservative spokes-people, led by none other than the chancellor George Osborne, were quick to talk up Nicola Sturgeon rather than point to David Cameron's rather low-key performance. The stronger Sturgeon appeared, the more Conservative strategists could portray the 'threat' of her dominating a 'weak' minority government led by Ed Miliband. However the instant-reaction polls showed a mixed picture.

So who 'won' the debate? The near-instant ICM poll suggested Ed Miliband and David Cameron had been neck and neck – at the top – on 25 per cent each with Nicola Sturgeon finishing behind Nigel Farage, though YouGov handed the honours to the SNP leader. ComRes more or less reported a dead heat amongst the leading politicians – Cameron 21 per cent, Miliband 21 per cent, Farage 21 per cent, and Sturgeon 20 per cent. So no clear victor.

Ed Miliband had indeed been a warrior tonight – but as he had indeed been a warrior appeared to have few reasons to be singing along to that infuriatingly ubiquitous Pharrell Williams song. But everything felt more harmonious when pollster James Morris delivered his assessment several days later as part of his weekly briefings to Miliband's inner circle. Both the party and the party leader's ratings had risen in the wake of the debate – and this would happen after every set-piece TV event, apart from the last one when no polling was done. This suggests David Cameron had been right to avoid more than one head-to-head clash, and to get that out of the way more than a month before polling day.

Perhaps journalists and even some politicians, however, are a little too obsessed with the topline of the polls and who 'won' a debate. Because lurking in the undergrowth of detail there was much better news for the Conservatives and a big warning for Labour. For all the heat and occa-sional light generated by the seven-party slanging match, the man already in Number 10, according to ComRes, was ahead on having the best ideas for Britain's future (27 per cent). And 40 per cent of viewers' polled believed David Cameron was the 'most capable of leading the country'.

Chips off the Old Block

3 April

- Ed Miliband exposes his family to the cameras on a bank holiday trip to Blackpool.
- The press pack get treated to fish and chips but there's not much food for thought.

GOOD FRIDAY. A bank holiday in Britain so no prizes for guessing the weather. The sky seemed appropriate for a day that marked Christ's crucifixion. Pitch-black angry clouds burst open to soak all and sundry in Salford as the press prepared to take a not so magical tour to the seaside in the Labour battle bus. Five years ago when I covered the last general election, news desks were grateful if I filed some lines of copy on my Blackberry. Such is the speed of technological advance I was now expected to broadcast live when I was literally on the road. The BBC News Channel had lots of airtime to fill on this long weekend so as I sat, and swerved, around on the bus I chatted into a camera about what we were being given for breakfast. Under the eagle eyes of Miliband's press team I then had to get in to the less comfortable terrain of talking about their leader's performance at last night's debate.

When I was finished, someone in the TV gallery – where the director, and often a programme's editor, sits – back at the BBC's New Broadcasting House in London shouted in to my ear: 'Brilliant.' I was momentarily feeling chuffed with my performance and the quality of my analysis until she added swiftly 'the picture didn't break up once'. So a technical triumph, if nothing else.

On arrival in what was once England's premier resort – and the location for a few holidays early in my life – the rain redoubled its efforts. Ed Miliband was coming to Blackpool not just because one of its constituencies was a Labour target, but because he was about to demonstrate he was a regular guy. After meeting bedraggled activists at the Imperial Hotel – once home to gossip and intrigue when Labour wasn't too snooty to hold its conferences here – he took a tram to Harry Ramsden's fish and chip shop.

Most cameras were kept outside the eatery while he, wife Justine, and sons Daniel and Samuel were fed inside. But they were filmed through the windows. Labour's battle bus drew up outside and we hopped on swiftly followed by the Labour leader, who brought us the gift of a traditional fish supper. I think there is an electoral law against 'treating' but the vinegary aroma of the food was too much to resist.

I asked Ed Miliband how his sons coped with the attention. 'Well they do cope with it but they are still too small for it really to register. I think they may hate it as teenagers and find it embarrassing'. And he joked: 'They would probably want an iPad in return for appearing with their dad on telly.'

He had largely managed to protect his children from the glare of publicity but the scrutiny he himself faced as Labour leader was intense. My own scrutiny at this point, however, was brought to a halt as the bus started up and began making its way to Morecambe while the BBC News Channel wanted me to stay in Blackpool – so I had to ditch the chips and hare off the vehicle, leaving my bag to be retrieved later, or I would have found myself in the wrong town.

I made my way to a waiting camera back at the windswept entrance to the Imperial Hotel, and the gallery spoke to me:

'Are you with Ed Miliband?'

'No, he's on a bus to Morecambe.'

'Is anyone with Miliband?'

'My colleague Peter Hunt is on the bus.'

'Ok we will speak to him then.' And with that I was dismissed.

A Bit of Politics

4 April

- Stars of the '80s and '90s endorse Ed Miliband at a Labour rally.
- The Labour leader urges activists to have more conversations with voters.
- The next leader will have to distinguish better between activity and support.

IT WAS LIKE A trip to my past. A colourful poster on the wall of the Pyramid Arts Centre in Warrington announced it was soon to welcome Basil Brush to the venue. Despite Labour's ban on fox-hunting, though, he wasn't on the bill for the late-afternoon Labour event. I had been a regular viewer of his cheeky vulpine antics as a child, but as a student I had preferred *Saturday Live* – a showcase for alternative comedians, hosted by a fast-talking guy in a spangly suit who injected 'a bit of politics' in to his motor-mouth monologues. Since then Ben Elton had written books and screenplays and starred in his own TV shows – then had started hanging out with Andrew Lloyd Webber, Queen, and very possibly real members of the royal family. But now at a rally here in Warrington the comedian announced 'I am back. Well, actually I have never really been away.' No witty one-liners, though, just an appeal for the better-off to put something back into society. There was humour from his cross-dressing co-star Eddie Izzard, who said 'I have to wear this lipstick because it's the Labour Party colours.' Soap star Sally Lindsay took to the stage, too, before the main act – Ed Miliband himself.

His was an impassioned performance in front of nearly 1,000 people who had packed in to this rather grand Victorian theatre. But perhaps because of some of the cast list, this really had the feeling of an opposition rally, not a gathering of a government in waiting. He gave the first outing to what would be the peroration for almost all his subsequent speeches – in the tightest election for a generation, he urged his audience to put off 'weddings, and DIY' until after polling day. But in order to meet his then target of four million conversations, he implored his activists to 'do him a favour':

> I want each of you to knock on 500 doors in our key seats. Some of you are doing that already. And I want you to do something else. I want you each to bring with you a friend to do the same. That could make the difference in this general election.

But however many doors were knocked upon, neither of the two seats he mentioned in his speech – Warrington South and nearby Weaver Vale – were regained on election night from the Conservatives. So his conversations were not having the desired effect, but at this stage in the campaign he still seemed to be confusing activity with support – stressing the need for further doorstep chats, rather than assessing their value.

There is also a rather obvious but valuable lesson for Jeremy Corbyn here – packing out venues and delivering well-received speeches or just knocking doors at election time aren't enough in themselves to shift sufficient votes.

When Miliband left the theatre this bank holiday weekend, around 20 Conservative activists wearing Alex Salmond masks were there to greet him. Yesterday's storm clouds appeared to have blown in from Blackpool.

A Taxing Issue

8 April

- The abolition of non-dom status appears to open up a gulf between Ed Balls and Ed Miliband.
- One of the biggest days of the campaign nearly falls flat.
- The Conservative counter-attack causes confusion in the ranks.
- The policy is denounced privately by some senior Labour politicians.

'AN EXPERIMENT RUN BY CHILDREN'. That was a senior Labour politician's private denunciation of Ed Miliband's tenure as Labour leader – and the left of centre policies developed by his advisers. Other Blairites, such as Alan Milburn, have now made similarly withering verdicts public.

So the International Digital Laboratory of Warwick University was perhaps an appropriate place for Ed Miliband to launch one of the flagship policies of his political experiment. The foundation stone of the sleek building had been laid by Gordon Brown in 2007 and the former Prime Minister had returned here just ahead of the election campaign in 2010, appealing to voters to 'take a second look' at him, just in case they had initially come to the conclusion he had been useless in Number 10. Now his former adviser was in the same venue about to unveil an eye-catching proposal. He was going to announce the abolition of 'non-dom' status which 115,000 of the super-rich used to limit their tax liabilities on overseas earnings.

The non-dom rule was as old as income tax itself, dating from 1799 and the era of Pitt the Younger. Back then Colonists who weren't regarded as domiciled in the UK were exempt from taxation on income and assets held aboard unless they tried to repatriate profits. Successive governments had been wary of abolishing the rule outright in case wealthy investors who still had to pay tax on UK earnings fled the coop. But Gordon Brown had introduced a non-dom charge and George Osborne had increased it. So not too much of a dividing line there, and Ed Miliband wanted a bigger one at this election – a strategy usually favoured by his old boss.

I had got wind of what he was proposing to do only the previous day. Labour were worried to the point of paranoia that details of BBC planning diaries were being leaked to the Conservatives, and they tried to keep the pin in this grenade for as long as possible. But one of their press officers had been rather loose-lipped. That said, advance notice hadn't really helped Labour's opponents as they had to calculate how to respond – if they said it would be a disaster, were they siding with the super-rich? So they were reduced to criticising the 'small print' of the announcement.

They latched on to Labour's proposal that temporary workers would still have an exemption from paying tax on their worldwide income in the UK. The suggestion was that Labour's policy on non-dom status was a con. So the briefing from the Labour press team was robust – yes, sure, there were some footnotes to the policy, but make no mistake this was the *de facto* death of non-doms, they argued.

The morning papers had carried news of Labour's policy change pretty positively, so when I sauntered past security straight in to Ed Miliband's rehearsal of the announcement I was greeted warmly, and not with suspicion. With a wave of the hand, he dismissed the argument that the small print undermined the principle that long-standing UK residents should pay tax on the same basis and waxed lyrical that most capitalist economies had a much stricter system than Britain. He then feigned horror and said 'oh my announcement doesn't affect you does it? Do any of the BBC's top reporters have non-dom status?' I responded by saying my circumstances were so straitened that – unlike him – I wouldn't even be eligible for his mansions tax.

The good humour would evaporate when it became clear that the BBC had been sitting on an unexploded bomb. It was detonated by the Conservatives, who had unearthed it, and highlighted the most dangerous parts. The full force of the blast then came when the Corporation broadcast the unedited version of an interview the Shadow Chancellor Ed Balls had given to his regional radio station, Radio Leeds, back in January. He had said complete abolition of the non-dom status would lead to people leaving the country and probably cost money – in stark contrast to his leader's announcement that it would raise 'hundreds of billions of pounds'.

Ed Miliband had been so proud of the policy he had declared that it must be kept back for the election campaign, to gain maximum impact. There had been a panic just a couple of weeks before when insiders convinced themselves that George Osborne might try to spike their guns in the budget. There were suggestions that the policy would have to be rushed out. But the Shadow Treasury team prevailed upon them to hold their nerve. 'Frankly,' one of Ed Balls' advisers, Alex Belardinelli, admitted: 'there was a realisation that there wasn't going to be much that was very new in the manifesto. This was one of the best policies and we couldn't throw it away.'

He had felt that Ed Balls' January interview could have done just that on the day of the policy launch. When he watched my report on the *One*

O'Clock News – which featured extensive sections of the Balls interview – he felt disaster was looming. So he worked hard to square the circle and convince journalists there was no major inconsistency between the two Eds. The aftermath of the political explosion turned out to be conventional, when it could have gone nuclear. The interview had been given at a time when Ed Balls was under instructions from Ed Miliband not to reveal that the party was considering abolishing non-dom status. That must not leak out before the campaign was under way – so Balls dutifully obliged on that score by refusing to admit it was on the agenda. But because this was several months before the announcement would be made, not all the details had been worked out.

There wasn't a bitter battle over it but Balls was very clear there had to be exemptions for business people coming into the country for genuinely temporary stays of three or four years – and similarly for people studying here – otherwise the prospect of having to rearrange their tax affairs may dissuade them from coming at all. So in his calls to journalists, Alex Belardinelli maintained that as Balls' caveats had all been conceded by Miliband, he was in full support of the policy – indeed he would have been, too, back in January with those exemptions.

What had caused the problem was that in an attempt to counter Conservative accusations that the policy was somehow half-hearted or a 'con', Labour's press operation had been failing to point out or give sufficient emphasis to the footnotes – the exemptions – which Belardinelli had argued were 'a fundamental part of the policy.' In trying to eliminate one negative, another had been created. But by the end of the day Labour considered themselves to be in a good place. Despite the ropiness of the launch, the policy had made an impact and had put the Conservatives on the back foot. Indeed, senior Conservatives admitted privately that they had been 'panicked' by Labour's initiative and how well it was playing.

Not everyone in the Labour Party was quite so satisfied. A senior politician with a business background who was at the policy launch denounced it off the record as 'gesture politics of the worst kind' which would raise very little cash. In fact he sounded that day rather a lot like Ed Balls had done back in January. Nonetheless the policy seemed generally popular within the party – and the Conservatives' fears spurred them into launching a spectacular diversion the following day.

Education, Education... Fratricide

9 *April*

- The launch of Labour's Education Manifesto is blown off course by an apparently over the top Conservative attack.
- Labour's strategists are pleased with their counter-attack but their own message on education is obliterated as the party is forced on to the defensive.
- Senior Labour figures are astonished so little of the campaign was devoted to 'helping people get on' – and the next Labour leader is advised to say more about social mobility.

SHOCK AND AWE. Those were the tactics developed by the Defence Secretary. Michael Fallon is a very experienced and highly astute politician – he can be affable and charming but he also likes to stay close to the centre of power. So what he was defending today – apart from his own job – was an apparently very narrow Conservative poll lead and he used every political weapon at his disposal to do so. Writing in the pages of *The Times*, he confirmed that a Conservative government would back a four-boat replacement of the nuclear deterrent. But then he swiftly took aim at the Labour leader in what could hardly be described as a 'clinical' or 'surgical' attack. He raised the prospect of Labour forming 'a backstairs deal' with the SNP that could threaten the renewal of the nuclear deterrent. But he didn't stop there. He then chose to remind voters of how Ed Miliband came to lead the Labour Party and conflated a political battle and a possible family feud with the safety and security of the nation, saying:

> Ed Miliband stabbed his own brother in the back to become Labour leader. Now he is willing to stab the United Kingdom in the back to become prime minister... We saw in that leadership election just what he would do to get into power. We saw what he did to his own brother.

Even Conservative commentators such as Tim Montgomerie, the founder of the influential but unofficial Conservative Home website, thought the attack was OTT. However, Isabel Hardman, writing on *The Spectator*'s site, recalled the mayor of London Boris Johnson's description of a political tactic deployed by the Conservatives' strategist Lynton Crosby, described here as 'an Australian friend':

> Let us suppose you are losing an argument. Your best bet in these circum-
> stances is to perform a manoeuvre that the great campaigner describes as

'throwing a dead cat on the table, mate'. That is because there is one thing that is absolutely certain about throwing a dead cat on the dining room table – and I don't mean that people will be outraged, alarmed, disgusted. That is true, but irrelevant. The key point, says my Australian friend, is that everyone will shout 'Jeez, mate, there's a dead cat on the table', in other words they will be talking about the dead cat, the thing you want them to talk about, and they will not be talking about the issue that has been causing you so much grief.

So, the previous day's non-dom policy and the former feline were about to suffer the same fate – to be dead and buried. And as for setting today's agenda – well that was going to be as difficult for Ed Miliband as giving the cat CPR.

* * *

Ed Miliband was set to launch Labour's education manifesto at the hi-tech London offices of Microsoft, at the other end of Victoria Street from Parliament Square. The event was being hosted by a former presenter of *Tomorrow's World*, Maggie Philbin. To coin a phrase, she had been the future once but this had also been intended as a showcase for two of the party's rising stars Tristram Hunt, Mandelson confidant turned TV historian turned Shadow Education Secretary, and Chuka Umunna, the Shadow Business Secretary. But these apparently attractive faces of the Opposition front bench were consigned to a supporting role.

As soon as I had cleared the pleasant but persistent security to gain access to the venue, Bob Roberts performed his now familiar magic trick of appearing from nowhere to have a quiet word. 'If you were to ask about Trident, I am sure we would be happy to provide an answer.' With this Labour had all but given up on getting education stories into anything but the specialist press. The best form of defence from a potentially damaging accusation, it had been calculated, was counterattack. Some in Miliband's inner circle felt, however, that this would only enable the Conservative line to gain a wider audience, but that view hadn't prevailed.

Ed Miliband was robust in his response. On the substance, Labour was committed to Trident renewal. Ed Balls' 'value for money' test – could you have continuous at-sea deterrence with one fewer submarine? – was junked. As Balls had only ever introduced it as a sop to Miliband, he wasn't too bothered. The Conservative policy was matched. This probably did little to win back former Labour supporters in Scotland who liked the SNP's no-nukes stance. But Ed Miliband felt he couldn't afford to let his own character be assassinated in this political battle.

He took aim not just at Michael Fallon, but the Prime Minister too. He said in a tone which conveyed regret more than anger:

> Michael Fallon's a decent man but today he's demeaned himself and demeaned his office. Decent Conservatives across our country will say – come on, we're better than this. David Cameron should be ashamed. Why does a campaign descend into the gutter? Because a campaign is failing. They are desperate. Lynton Crosby is behind the scenes, pulling the strings, sending out minions. David Cameron should get a grip.

Many of those around Ed Miliband felt a moment of danger had passed and took comfort that the Conservatives had had to change their line of attack – some misinterpreting that their main opponents had lost strategic direction and that the scattergun nature of this latest assault would backfire. Labour had challenged the accusation that they couldn't be trusted on defence or would 'barter away' the deterrent. But not everyone in Ed Miliband's camp was so sure that they had witnessed a 'failing' in the Conservative campaign.

One senior adviser told me he had felt that Labour, by this stage, already would have taken a pounding on the questions of economic competence and leadership. Yet this just hadn't happened. While Labour trailed on both issues, the Conservatives hadn't – if the polls were to be believed – romped ahead either. The Conservative tactic of simply comparing Cameron with Miliband hadn't caused the latter's lower ratings to collapse further. But he discerned that Conservative strategists were finding new and more creative ways to raise the leadership question. They had successfully reminded the uncommitted voter about the first 'fact' they knew about Ed Miliband – that he had somehow betrayed his own brother by running for leader. Another adviser privately described Fallon's intervention as the 'cleverest dog whistle of the campaign. They got what people were whispering about him – what he did to his brother – back up the agenda.'

And though the SNP weapon had not yet been fully deployed by the Conservatives, they had successfully floated the idea that as prime minister in a minority administration, Ed Miliband would either be unwilling or too weak to stop a leftwards drift in order to appease the SNP. The adviser said:

> In the end, which I didn't predict, we were f***ed on the SNP – but in a way, that was just another means for the Conservatives to raise the leadership issue.

One Nation, No Vision?

9 April

LET'S SUPPOSE THE dead cat hadn't been thrown on the table. Then the party's education policy would have been launched as one of a series of 'mini manifestos', which at the time many senior Labour figures felt had helped them to set the political agenda.

The idea was to remind – or in some cases inform – a less than fully engaged electorate of Labour's policies in key areas, but with a smidgen of novelty in order to interest the press. Unless there was incoming fire from the Conservatives that was likely to score a direct hit, Labour pretty much stuck to their pre-agreed plan. So much so that some strategists smugly believed that everything *was* going to plan.

The 'new' education policy to be launched today was to offer pupils 'one to one' careers advice. But there were murmurings that the overall education policy wasn't radical enough. Following Labour's 2010 defeat, the Blairite former cabinet minister Alan Milburn accepted the role as chair of the Social Mobility and Child Poverty Commission, and produced report after report which had highlighted how difficult it still was for intelligent, well-educated people from working class backgrounds to get on. And in 2014, his Commission had attracted controversy when it pointed out how many of the top jobs in society were occupied by fewer than ten per cent of the population which attended independent schools – including 71 per cent of judges, and more than half of the most senior civil servants.

Baroness Hilary Armstrong – a former Labour chief whip – told me she was astonished that her party leadership hadn't exploited this impressive body of work for its own ends, siding and sympathising with those from ordinary backgrounds struggling to achieve, as well as those who had to live on low pay. And she wasn't the only one.

In a post-election speech to the Centre for Social Justice – seen as a centre-right think tank because of its early links with the Work and Pensions Secretary Iain Duncan Smith – Milburn not only declared that Ed Miliband, in his view, had been the wrong leader and should have been ditched the previous year when there was a failed attempt to encourage Alan Johnson to oust him, he also attacked his party's policy focus during the campaign. After his speech, he told me:

I was bamboozled at the lack of education policy in the campaign. Tristram (Hunt) kind of got social mobility. Ed didn't... no, Ed doesn't... He was obsessed with the two per cent at the top that he wanted to tax and the eight per cent at the bottom on zero hours contracts.

There had been unhappiness, too, over what became the most memorable and distinctive of Labour's education policies – a cut in tuition fees in England from the £9,000 annual maximum to £6,000, and which would have featured prominently if Michael Fallon hadn't attempted his character assassination. Unlike over non-doms, the differences between the two Eds on this policy had genuinely been profound and long-lasting.

Like a tip of an iceberg, occasionally parts of the dispute came in to public view but much of the tension remained submerged. Strategically, Ed Balls knew his best chance of becoming Chancellor was to bolster the other Ed and hope that Labour could get enough votes to form a government. So he had no interest in advertising the full-scale nature of the difficulties. Some of the Shadow Chancellor's closest allies felt in January 2015, Labour simply couldn't win under Ed Miliband's leadership but that it was too late to ditch him, and Balls himself tried to make the policy add up during the early part of the year, before its unveiling in February – ahead of the formal election campaign. He knew that it had to appear that Labour could account for every penny it intended to spend. But as one member of Labour's treasury team put it: 'The question was if we had £3 billion to spend, could we have spent it on something better?' Some others around the Shadow Chancellor subsequently reflected on whether they had been 'too loyal'.

The biggest frustration for the Shadow Chancellor was, however, that he had had to find credible funding for a very large scale retail offer and burrow away on the detail for a couple of months – then, having delivered his leader's wishes, the policy would barely feature during the election campaign itself.

* * *

Some senior Labour figures saw the eventual 'Hurry! Hurry! 30 per cent off tuition fees!' policy as a worrying example of what voters might see as stand-alone offers which did little to reinforce a wider view of what society would look like under a Labour government. Jon Cruddas, as head of the party's policy review, had been fighting a rearguard action to prevent so much of the party's policy offer being transformed into what he had termed 'small scale bribes.'

One of Ed Miliband's closest aides felt that an opportunity to convey a wider vision of society in 2012/13 when the party had been re-branded

'One Nation Labour' had been subsequently squandered. That terminology had allowed the party to move on from being New Labour – Ed Miliband's avowed approach as the 'change candidate' when he successfully swiped the leadership from his front-running brother – without regressing to 'old' pre-Blair Labour either. The language conveyed a degree of political cross-dressing, entering territory first carved out by Disraeli with his denunciation of 'two nations' a century and a half ago. Slowly but surely this wider narrative had been reduced to what this adviser called 'antagonistic retail offers.' He went on:

> We have a crisis in education – and that is not solved by, for example, forcing companies to freeze prices or getting banks to sell off branches they don't want.

A frustrated Peter Mandelson – who had remained relatively tight lipped about his concerns – had gone public over the tuition fee row. In February – just three months before polling day – he expressed his worries about the future financing of universities, argued for Labour to put off any decision on fees until after the election, and said: 'Participation levels in higher education have risen from every level of British society, including the most disadvantaged. Higher fee levels have not undermined this.'

Ed Balls, too, had argued for a post-election delay. But despite widespread, high-level concerns, it wasn't entirely obvious that a tuition fee cut would undermine education funding or had to come packaged as part of a wider vision for education or for the nation. Or indeed that somehow the public were resistant to 'retail offers' and preferred loftier ideas. While working class students hadn't appeared to have been dissuaded from going to university because of high fees, Labour's polling suggested their parents and even grandparents did have concerns about the debts being foisted on the younger generation.

There had been a powerful case made by a middle-aged man at a focus group who had three children, all of whom he believed were capable of going to university. He thought of the total amount that three children would owe in tuition fees and regarded this as 'family debt.' That debt would be higher than the value of his home. It was this type of voter that Labour's policy was targeting rather than aspiring students.

A major survey of nearly 5,000 respondents carried out from the moment polls closed on 7 May by Labour's own pollsters for the TUC suggested that more than three quarters – 77 per cent – of voters wanted 'concrete plans for sensible change' compared to 15 per cent who opted for 'a big vision' for radical change – and a tuition fee cut, while not visionary, was a 'concrete plan' for change.

In fact some people Labour were targeting didn't even recognise 'One

Nation' as an attempt to describe a bigger vision in any case. At a focus group, one voter assumed it was the name of a boy band – like 'One Direction.' Pollster James Morris defended the decision to move away from this narrative. He told me:

> 'One Nation' didn't mean anything to voters. It didn't connect with any of the issues they cared about – immigration, the deficit, having a better standard of living. For some it conjured images of traditional Labour levelling down, for others it was just vapid. It replaced a focus on 'responsibility' that did make sense to people, but Ed hadn't been comfortable with making this his ongoing theme. The commentariat loved it, but it made no sense to those we needed to convince.

He added that the term has far more resonance for the Conservatives, who have now taken it up – it challenges the perception that they are too narrow in outlook, too privileged in their make-up. But for the Opposition: 'there was just no tension here with the Labour brand.'

In the end the tuition fee policy was not a game-changer. This was not because it was a 'retail offer' according to some close to Miliband. The bigger problem was that Labour was perhaps not in the right place to be trusted to make the wider argument about cutting 'family debt' when they had racked up the nation's overdraft and hadn't apparently come to terms with it. And the other 'retail offers' suffered a similar fate. Capping energy prices, for example, was a popular policy. But if too many voters believed Labour fundamentally couldn't be trusted with the economy, then they also believed the party would never be in a position to deliver the nice things they were promising.

Unions and the Union

10 April

- In his first visit to Scotland during the campaign, Ed Miliband narrowly avoids focussing attention on his rows with the unions.
- But there have been high-level arguments and serious divisions over how to handle the SNP.
- Jeremy Corbyn will have potentially fewer problems with trade union leaders but is likely to face many of the same dilemmas in defending the union.

IT WAS TO have been a flying visit to Scotland. We had left the night before, and drove a bit less than an hour north-west from Edinburgh airport to what looked like a magnificent castle which looked out across rolling plains. Sadly the building – parts of which dated back to the 14th century – was largely used as a wedding venue and we were billeted in a building which was architecturally more barrack room than baronial in nature. On arrival, we were greeted by the familiar faces of our ITN and Sky News counterparts.

So here we all were, overlooking the Forth Valley, because it was one of the nearest hotels to Grangemouth, where Ed Miliband would pop in briefly to see the staff at a supermarket's distribution centre.

Yes, that was the same Grangemouth where management had recently very nearly closed Scotland's last remaining refinery and the Unite convenor there, Stevie Deans, had resigned amid much publicity. And yes, that union official was the same Stevie Deans who had been chair of the Labour Party in the neighbouring constituency of Falkirk in 2013 – and had been accused of trying to fix the parliamentary selection there for Karie Murphy, a close friend of Unite's general secretary Len McCluskey. Both Deans and Murphy had been suspended from the Labour Party, though later cleared of wrongdoing, following a protracted, bitter investigation and subsequent wrangle which had led to the resignation of the high profile campaigner, and now the party's deputy leader, Tom Watson from the Shadow Cabinet – and from a key role in the general election campaign. Watson employed Karie Murphy in his office and once shared a flat with Len McCluskey (though he points out he also shared a flat with the altogether more Blairite Gloria De Piero). And yes, that was the same Falkirk where the retiring MP had been none other than Eric Joyce, who had been expelled from the Labour Party following a violent brawl in the House of Commons.

So even before we had been shown to our rooms, it came as no surprise to be told the Grangemouth trip was off, and the Labour leader would be confining himself to the Scottish capital. We were now in the wrong place but at least by the skin of his teeth Ed Miliband had not come to what would have been the wrong place for him. Both Falkirk and Grangemouth were lost to the SNP on polling day but he had narrowly avoided inviting his opponents to re-examine his relations with his trade union funders.

At the top of the Labour Party there was huge frustration that he hadn't got on the front foot having been seen to have been the choice of the unions for leader. Some of his closest advisers and allies had urged him to reform the relationship with the unions within a broader context of restoring trust in politics well before the Falkirk fiasco. He had been urged to make that the centre point of the 2011 Labour conference speech, where his attack on 'predatory' capitalists had instead captured the headlines. But as one of those advisers put it: 'He lacked the courage to seize the moment.'

Worry Points

10 April

- The Two Eds – Miliband and Balls – attack the SNP's economic plans.
- Scottish Labour leader Jim Murphy denounces Nicola Sturgeon's 'Full Fiscal Austerity'.
- Voters like Labour's message, but continue to distrust the messenger.
- The scale of the challenge for Labour's new leader is larger than previously imagined.

LABOUR'S BIG GUNS were ready to fire at the SNP. The hastily-arranged alternative event for this morning turned out to be rather more spectacular than the previously planned glad-handing in Grangemouth. Instead, Ed Miliband now would be at the Doubletree hotel, close to Edinburgh's city centre. The reason for choosing the venue was obvious once we arrived. The press conference was to take place on the top floor of the hotel's conference centre. This afforded a panoramic view across the city skyline, dominated by the austere majesty of Edinburgh Castle perched on one of the Scottish capital's extinct volcanoes.

This view was intended to form the backdrop to Ed Miliband's speech. The image could well have conveyed strength and a sense of history. And with the union flag flying over the medieval landmark in a city which had decisively rejected independence, this might just serve as a reminder that Labour had helped deliver victory – rather than suffered defeat – in the previous year's referendum.

There was, however, a snag.

Uncharacteristically for showery April, today had turned out to be a scorcher. The temperatures were balmy but worse still, the skies were clear blue. So the TV crews were, in the end, faced with a choice. As Ed Miliband stood against the floor-to ceiling-windows of the conference centre with the Castle – and sunny Edinburgh – behind him, the bright background played havoc with the cameras. To compensate either the backdrop would have to be 'burned out' – losing the imagery and sense of place – or the Labour leader would have to look as though he was skulking in the shadows. In the end, the choice was to see the key speaker distinctly but to all intents and purposes, when watched on television, he could have been in an anonymous office block just about anywhere in the western world.

The late change of venue – and indeed story – created some other problems, too. I had got up in the wee small hours to file a piece for Radio 4 on Labour's new line for the day, but discussions over whether or how to cover it for the BBC1 *One O'Clock News* were continuing frantically even after Ed Miliband had arrived. So the small but committed cadre of advisers and activists that had been brought in to form an audience tried to 'shoosh' the TV crews, apparently missing the fact that – rather like the tree falling in the forest – if Miliband's remarks weren't broadcast then they might as well never have happened. The event was purely a media confection and was not a public meeting.

* * *

The subject matter was Full Fiscal Autonomy – yes, you can see why the *One O'Clock News* might not have been immediately sold on covering it, as it might take the entire half-hour bulletin to explain it – and Ed Miliband's small band of supporters were treated to a surprise. This was to be no solo speech. He was to be flanked by the party's Scottish leader Jim Murphy and the Shadow Chancellor, Ed Balls. Just a month later two of the trio had lost their seats in parliament, and the other had resigned the party leadership. But today they were stars in the party's firmament, and although they had never been the best of friends they had come together to take on a common enemy – the SNP.

In his valedictory speech in London a month after Labour's catastrophic defeat, Jim Murphy said that the campaign had united the former Blairites and Brownites in common cause and he cautioned against further division under a new leader:

> In the last two months of the election campaign I spoke more to Ed Balls than I did in the previous two decades and I realised how wrong I had been before. I had no closer support from any colleague during that election campaign than Ed Balls. At times I thought if he'd spent more time in his own constituency than in my campaign in Scotland, perhaps he'd have won his seat. But how wrong to wait until so late in the day to work together properly.

And the attack on the prospect of austerity under the SNP – a party that was apparently campaigning to end it – had clearly come too late in the day too. But today's event was about pinning back the nationalist advance, not an attempt to achieve the impossible, and gain victory. Labour had been handed a weapon by the well-respected, independent think tank the Institute for Fiscal Studies.

Following the March budget, the Institute had upped its estimate of the costs of Full Fiscal Autonomy from £6.6 billion to £7.6 billion, largely due to deteriorating oil revenues. It explained why:

> (Under FFA) all taxes and the vast majority of spending would be devolved to Scotland – with the Scottish Government making transfers to the UK government to cover things like defence, foreign affairs, and Scotland's share of the UK's debt interest payments... The Scottish Government would have to borrow if its spending were greater than its revenues. It would also have to bear the risk of volatile North Sea and other tax revenues... In cash terms this is equivalent to a gap of £7.6 billion. Unless oil and gas revenues were to rebound, onshore revenues were to grow more quickly than in the rest of the UK, or government spending in Scotland were cut, a similar sized gap would remain in the years ahead.

Labour had acquired this addition to their armoury – which allowed them to say the anti-austerity SNP's own policies might lead to further austerity – just after the budget the previous month. Ed Miliband had warned of the risk of 'ending redistribution within the UK' in a speech in what had once been the solidly – but by then decidedly shaky – Labour town of Clydebank before the election campaign had got under way. But then they were aiming at a moving target, because the SNP hadn't put a timescale on their ambition to introduce fiscal autonomy – which, in any case, would need the approval of Westminster.

What triggered the Labour attack now had been the debate on BBC Scotland two days previously, where the SNP leader Nicola Sturgeon had said she would accept full fiscal autonomy as soon as the other parties agreed to grant it, and hadn't demurred from the suggestion that this could be as soon as next year. Murphy had been trying to manoeuvre her in to saying this, or something like it, for some time. He swiftly assessed this to be 'a stupid strategic error' when she did so – as Nicola Sturgeon was in effect admitting that she would be willing to see austerity in return for greater autonomy. In other words apparently the powers vested in a nation mattered more than the welfare of its inhabitants. The well-being of working class communities would be sacrificed on the altar of an ideological attachment to greater independence. Murphy's political attack on her was described by some Scottish papers as a Full Fiscal Assault – and he admitted it had put a much-needed spring in Labour's languid step.

So that's partly why the UK leader and Shadow Chancellor were weighing in too. But the other reason was that Labour's focus groups in Scotland had been trying to find chinks in the SNP's rather heavy armour. These were what insiders termed 'worry points'. And amongst some former Labour supporters who had backed a 'Yes' vote in the referendum and were now intending to vote SNP, there was just a bit of disquiet about what might lie ahead in a Nationalist dominated Scotland. So the idea that Nicola Sturgeon might – or might have to – impose austerity on Scotland rather than save the nation from it was one such 'worry point'. For Labour, the SNP policy of Full Fiscal Autonomy was to be rebranded Full Fiscal Austerity.

But worries don't always determine actions. People concerned about their jobs don't always leave them or immediately look for alternative employment – they hope for the best. So while Labour had picked up a useful weapon, it didn't contain a silver bullet. The then Shadow Scottish Secretary, Margaret Curran, said the attack had a limited impact on the doorsteps. 'People just weren't buying'. The message might have been powerful, but the messenger wasn't trusted.

Following Labour's high-powered triple-headed Full Fiscal Assault, Nicola Sturgeon had been quick to offer up her response on the streets of Glasgow – a city whose voters had backed independence – amid enthusiastic supporters waving saltires. She defended the policy – more fiscal freedom could help the Scottish economy expand so a high level of cuts wasn't necessarily the consequence. But mostly she took the view that the best form of defence was attack, and her denunciation of 'fears and smears' by the pro-Union Labour Party struck a chord with at least some of those who had been dismayed at the apparently negative nature of the 'No' campaign in the referendum. This was a campaign which the Nationalists had dubbed 'Project Fear', following reports – officially denied – in the pro-independence *Sunday Herald* that this terminology was being used internally by the Better Together hierarchy to describe their tactics.

Senior SNP strategists tell me that their own focus groups picked up that those voters felt Labour were just re-running the referendum campaign and hadn't learned from it. But Labour's own quantitative and especially its qualitative research – its focus groups – subsequently suggested the problem was much, much more serious. And this is likely to mean it will be monumentally tough for the new Scottish Labour leader Kezia Dugdale to take on the SNP in the short term.

In an internal memo, it was revealed that voters felt Labour's attack on Full Fiscal Autonomy and the 'black hole' in the Scottish finances that would ensue was credible, but it didn't worry them. Project Fear had lost its terror. The memo said:

> People find the black hole plausible but not particularly scary – people believed that the SNP would have to borrow or raise taxes to make up the difference. They didn't think they would have to make £7.6 billion-worth of cuts. Borrowing and raising taxes was seen as necessary and worth it if it meant more power for Scotland.

Or as one voter in a focus group put it: 'a divorce always ends up costing you.'

Now, that one phrase was particularly toxic for Labour. In the campaign for the first elections to the Scottish Parliament in 1999 – which I had covered for the then politically-neutral *Sunday Herald* – I reported on how Labour, which had been initially trailing the SNP in the polls, had distilled a powerful message from their focus groups: 'Divorce Is An Expensive Business'. This may sound all too stereotypical, but this is what Labour's research said at the time: By and large women voters hadn't liked the idea of separation and break-up while men hadn't been keen on the cost – so they put their, and their nation's, well-being ahead of a risky future striking out on their own. Now some of the same demographic were saying in 2015 that while they didn't like the cost of greater autonomy, it was to be expected and probably a price worth paying.

That wasn't the full extent of the grim news. Under attack by the Conservatives for not reining in spending, it might be assumed that the one part of the UK where voters were more relaxed about Labour's own fiscal record was in Scotland where support was greater for higher public expenditure. But a Labour internal poll, conducted at the beginning of 2015, suggested that while 62 per cent of voters across the UK thought Labour would borrow more than Britain could afford, in Scotland the number was also high – at 55 per cent. In fact there was slightly more concern about this than there was about Labour putting 'the needs of Westminster ahead of needs in Scotland' – at 53 per cent. And in post-election polling, that concern over whether Labour could be trusted with its hands on the purse strings had risen, not fallen, in Scotland to nearly two-thirds of voters. In other words, the SNP were more trusted to borrow responsibly than Labour. One insider conceded: 'Full Fiscal Autonomy was a cul-de-sac we ran in to and spent a lot of time running around in it.'

* * *

When the failure to turn concerns over fiscal autonomy in to votes for Labour became apparent, there was a dramatic change of course.

The focus on winning over 'soft' SNP supporters – those who wanted a Labour government at Westminster, or who had voted Labour in 2010 but were now tending towards Nicola Sturgeon's party – shifted towards much narrower, but potentially more fertile, ground. Those who had voted 'No' in the referendum and who hadn't been traditionally Labour but might switch in the hope of pinning back the onward march of the Nationalists were to be recruited to the party's focus groups. It was believed their attitudes might determine whether Labour could still hold on to a small number of seats. Wider ambitions to win back significant sections of Labour's former support in central Scotland were abandoned.

Even in the overwhelmingly pro-union city of extinct volcanoes in which Ed Miliband was speaking there were rumblings that should have worried him. True, the one seat where the new emphasis on these 'switchers' worked was in Edinburgh South, but that was the sole success in Labour's desperate salvage operation.

The constituency which contained the Castle – and which had been intended to form the backdrop to today's event – was about to change hands.

A Flock of Starlings

10 April

- The more sophisticated SNP campaign exceeds expectations.
- Labour support in once safe-seats drifts towards the Nationalists, even in areas where voters had rejected independence.
- The next Labour leader will have to address political and organisational failings in Scotland.

'THE LABOUR COLLAPSE WAS BIBLICAL'. That was the verdict of a former assistant general secretary of the Labour Party in Scotland. Just minutes away from where Ed Miliband had been attacking Full Fiscal Autonomy, Tommy Sheppard had been politically attacking his former Labour comrades, as he battled to seize the Edinburgh East seat for the SNP.

He had taken redundancy from his position as a Labour Party apparatchik in 1997 and was astounded to be denied a place on a panel of his party's candidates to contest the first elections to the Scottish parliament in 1999. Hailing from Northern Ireland, for him there had neither been a Damascene conversion to Scottish nationalism nor a spiteful defection to the SNP following what he had regarded as a shoddy stitch-up by his internal opponents to prevent him from becoming an MSP. He had instead sunk his redundancy money into a comedy club venture and soon had venues in Edinburgh, Glasgow and Newcastle. He remained interested in politics but not active in any party.

Around 2005 he identified a 'tipping point'. Disillusioned with the Blair government, he felt that the social democratic society he would like to see was more likely to be achieved in an independent Scotland. But still he didn't sign up to the SNP. He took an active part in the 'Yes' campaign in the 2014 referendum, impressed by a rekindling of enthusiasm and political activism in his adoptive homeland – 'a feeling we can plough our own furrow, achieve things for ourselves.'

He finally joined the SNP only in September 2014, five days after the referendum. Just eight months later, he was the party's MP for Edinburgh East, seizing a constituency which takes in large parts of the city's historic centre, as well as housing estates to the east and north, from Labour's Sheila Gilmore – and achieving a smidgen less than 50 per cent of the total votes cast.

The scale of victory surprised him. He said whole streets in the former

Labour stronghold of Craigmillar were backing the SNP – and he couldn't quite believe his party's own data at this stage in the campaign, which later turned out to be true:

> I liken it to a flock of starlings, changing direction – suddenly but firmly. And it doesn't look like they will be changing direction again any time soon.

Labour's Jim Murphy has said: 'Put simply we weren't good enough in terms of our policy, our personnel or our organisation.'

The battle of Edinburgh East tends to underline that. Policy was perhaps the least of Labour's difficulties. Labour's focus groups had found that voters had wanted to see 'a distinctive Scottish party'... though one attendee had joked 'come round my house on a Saturday night and you'll see a distinctive Scottish party all right!' Plenty of policy prescriptions followed – including perhaps a bespoke one for that focus group member – a lifting of the ban on selling alcohol at football matches. There were ten election pledges – rather than the six which Ed Miliband launched – designed to motivate Labour's potential supporters in Scotland. The bigger problem – according to one of the most senior figures in the Scottish party – was that:

'We had plenty of policies but I felt I didn't have an argument.'

And campaigning just across the Forth, in what was then Gordon Brown's seat of Kirkcaldy and Cowdenbeath, the former Scottish First Minister Henry McLeish didn't get the impression that the campaign would be won on policy – not even the best 'retail offers' would shift voters:

> We could have offered people a lottery win every week and not made a difference. There was no policy discussion on the doorstep. The minimum wage, anything we wanted to mention, their eyes glazed over – what we were facing was a mood. They were questioning what Labour was for, not our individual policies.

The SNP had distilled their message into three words, tested and refined in their focus groups: 'Stronger For Scotland.' While Tony Blair had three words – or rather the same word thrice – to describe Labour's appeal as leader of the Opposition in the '90s –'education, education, education' – the party had far more trouble defining itself now. SNP campaigners in Edinburgh East, and elsewhere, reported that the 'Stronger for Scotland' message managed to appeal to those who hadn't backed independence but trusted those who had to stand up for the nation's interests at Westminster. Labour's own focus groups tended to suggest that, post-referendum, key voters felt the party was keener to keep the UK together than to put their interests first. In the words of one focus group participant: 'You won

the referendum. Get over it.' In other words, I've done what you wanted
– and voted no – now it's time I did something for me.

When it came to personnel, though, Jim Murphy was onto something.
He was leading the Scottish party because – frankly – no one at Holyrood
was seen to have as much of a profile or personality to take on the challenge of turning Labour's dire prospects around in time for 2016, never
mind the looming Westminster election.

A 'talent-trawl' under the party's then deputy leader Anas Sarwar to
find candidates for the 2015 general election and the Scottish elections the
following year only got under way after Labour had suffered the severe
setback of 2011 when the SNP won an overall majority in Holyrood. As
Labour's position deteriorated in the polls, well-placed sources have
suggested some of the party's MPs were reluctant to give up their seats to
more energetic campaigners because a defeat would bring a severance
payment. Jim Murphy's parting shot as Scottish Labour leader was to
re-open selections for Holyrood, and to have in some seats 'primaries'
where not just members of the party, but members of the public, could
have a say over who should be Labour's candidate. But the seeds of disillusionment and near-destruction were sown many years before. Tommy
Sheppard may inevitably have drifted towards the SNP, but it does seem
odd that an experienced and articulate Labour organiser, and former
councillor turned entrepreneur was thought to have no place as an MSP.

But it's worth dwelling on the organisational failures that Murphy
identified. Some in the SNP feel that their superior tactics in the ground
war pushed them up from winning, say, 40 seats to the near-clean sweep
of 56. The SNP didn't conduct their entire campaign like Edinburgh East
but it does demonstrate how they exceeded expectations in an historically
Labour-held seat, and raises questions over whether Labour's conversations were being conducted with the right voters.

13,000 Conversations

10 April

- SNP's campaigners concentrate on winning new support rather than getting committed voters to the polls.
- Labour's technique of 'getting the vote out' has been overtaken by events.
- The new Labour leadership will have to find ways of gaining a better understanding of their electorate.

THE SNP IN Edinburgh East fought a predominantly ground campaign. There were high-profile visits, and three campaign shops where anyone could just drop by, but largely this was a street-by-street fight.

And the SNP felt they had the better weaponry. Partly as a result of Labour's historical dominance of central Scotland, their canvassing operation had been geared towards 'getting the vote out.' So the focus of the effort was on identifying where Labour voters lived, checking if they were still Labour, then cajoling them to go to the polling station and giving the elderly amongst them a lift. The operation wasn't planned with a dramatic shift in voter allegiance in mind. Indeed there wasn't much wrong with a system that delivered 41 MPs and more than 40 per cent of the vote at the last general election. The only flaw was that it wasn't fit for purpose when voters *en masse* changed direction.

At the previous Westminster election, the SNP got a little under 20 per cent of the vote and six seats. So just 'turning out the vote' would never have been an option for them. Their whole approach to canvassing was different. Their canvass cards measured the degree of likelihood that someone would vote SNP and allowed the bulk of the work to go in to persuading people who were on the brink rather than simply ensuring the die-hard bravehearts got to the polling station.

So when SNP activists went on the doorsteps they put voters in one of eight categories, building on an already sophisticated database. Category one would be those who said they had voted SNP at the last three elections, and the electoral roll would be checked to ensure that they had indeed voted. In the second category were those who identified with the SNP, but hadn't necessarily voted in the three previous elections. Category three were SNP supporters but with no record that they had previously voted. The gradations continued all the way to category eight, which contained those who were against voting SNP. Because the party was already doing well in the polls, it was able to concentrate its efforts on those in the middle categories... those who were undecided or wouldn't say how they would vote, or on whom the SNP had no data at all – and in the end, the activists were also able to have conversations of persuasion with those who had previously opposed the party.

The assumption was that those who had previously voted SNP would do so again, so they got less attention. The state of the art database had filters which would take out regular supporters, or those who were eligible to vote in EU but not general elections, and leave those who required the most effort to bring them round. Tommy Sheppard said politics was about priorities:

> There was debate within the party because some of our supporters would say 'we haven't seen you', so for some we also needed to make sure they got motivational material, the leaflets, and so on – but they didn't get canvassing effort. You can't talk to everyone, it's a tactical decision.

Canvassers were instructed not to get into arguments on the doorstep but conversations with the candidate were arranged and some people were won over in this way.

In the end, the ambitious target of talking to 20,000 voters in the constituency wasn't met – but the success rate amongst those who were approached was high. 13,000 were contacted and the party had data on a further 15,000. Combining this information, the organisers assumed 14,000 voters would back the SNP. In fact, 23,000 did – nearly 50 per cent of those who voted, and not the 40 per cent the organisers had originally hoped for in what had been a Labour seat. 'In the end,' Sheppard admits, 'we thought it would be close – but the national swing was unstoppable.'

Labour campaigners say the SNP also had an advantage as they were better at 'pavement politics' – taking up and reflecting local issues in their campaigns. But Sheppard insists his focus was very much on the big picture: 'Our campaign was about the people of Scotland taking control – not about how often the bins were collected.'

As a former Labour official, the message that his old party had let its traditional supporters down played well in working class areas. But he also felt that the SNP was seen as a more acceptable vehicle for social democratic policies than Labour amongst some voters in the more affluent parts of the city.

The SNP in Edinburgh also managed to put the squeeze on the Green vote. Although the Scottish Greens also favoured independence, left-wing voters who were disillusioned with Labour and who voted 'No' in the referendum were likely to find them more acceptable than the Nationalists.

The SNP benefitted from such defections as this reduced the Labour vote. But there was considerable 'churn' in the Green vote as the SNP campaigners attempted, with some success, to persuade long-standing Greens to vote tactically for them to keep Labour out. The SNP already had reliable information on voters' party preferences and whom they would back if, in theory, their first choice wasn't available – so they could target those Green voters who had said they might opt for the SNP in the absence of a candidate of their own. Sheppard said: 'For years Labour made the strategic assumption that their voters had nowhere else to go. Well, in Scotland they have.'

Three months on from the election, on 12 August – the day she was elected as Labour's new leader in Scotland – Kezia Dugdale appeared to back this up this analysis:

> Having spent the summer thinking this over, I think there are two reasons that led to so many people losing faith in us. Firstly, a large part of the population have simply switched off from us. It's not so much that they don't like what they hear – they've stopped listening to us altogether. And secondly, those who are willing to give us a hearing tell us they don't know what we stand for anymore.

She has promised to give her party a new determination and to be clearer about whose side it is on. But some of Labour's most senior figures in Scotland are warning colleagues that the crumbling of traditional loyalties could become more dramatic across the UK. Certainly there is no social-democratic competitor to Labour in England (if the Lib Dems were ever that, their five years in coalition with the Conservatives has left them on life support). But the party was far less successful there than the Conservatives at bringing potential defectors to UKIP back in from the cold. And if people break with their traditional voting habits once, they are likely to do so again.

Voters seem more willing to look for alternative options. Although UKIP and the Greens ended up with just one seat apiece at Westminster, between them they garnered five million votes – so their level of support can, at the very least, greatly influence the outcome even in constituencies they don't win and in an electoral system that doesn't do them any favours. Andy Burnham has suggested that Labour may not yet have reached a nadir, and a senior Shadow Cabinet colleague of his said to me: 'My message to the party is don't believe it can't get worse. It can.'

In Good Health?

11 April

- Labour fail to match the Conservatives' spending pledges on the NHS.
- Shadow Cabinet tensions come to the surface.
- The next leader will have to calculate if the fiscal straitjacket can be loosened without losing votes.

'A GUN WILL be fired towards the end of the second half of this performance.' That was the warning sign on the stairway of the venue Labour chose for the launch of its 'mini-manifesto' on health. Now, back in November 2014 the BBC's then Political Editor, Nick Robinson reported 'a phrase the Labour leader uses in private is that he wants to "weaponise" the NHS' – but surely this was ridiculous!

Perhaps the firearm had something to do with one of the works staged by the resident amateur operatic society in the Victorian-era Guiseley Theatre near Leeds which today played host to Ed Miliband, the Shadow Health Secretary, Andy Burnham and the Shadow Care Minister, Liz Kendall. In other words, the then leader of the Labour Party, and two MPs who wanted to succeed him, all took to the stage – and it made for an occasionally nail-biting performance. Liz Kendall – whose former partner is a comedian – was the warm-up act but both Burnham and Miliband strode the stage simultaneously. There may not have been guns involved, but they were at times at daggers drawn. Andy Burnham, said, 'When I am health secretary' then glanced to Ed Miliband and added 'hopefully...' But confirmation came there none. Miliband hadn't just defeated his own brother for the party leadership, but also Ed Balls, Diane Abbott – and Andy Burnham. He knew that his Shadow Health Secretary still coveted the top job and although he had confirmed that Ed Balls would be chancellor if he won, Miliband gave Burnham no similar assurances about his future. Burnham subsequently complained about a lack of consultation even over the health aspects of Labour's manifesto and a watering down of the commitment to a more comprehensive health and social care service.

But it had been the Conservatives who had been quicker on the draw on the NHS today. Without bothering to set out how the money would be raised, the chancellor George Osborne and the health secretary Jeremy Hunt had said they would meet the £8 billion which Simon Stevens, the chief executive of the NHS in England, calculated would be necessary – over and above efficiency savings – by 2020.

Although Labour had a clear lead in the polls on the NHS, the Conservative ploy did wound them on the day when they wanted the media to focus on their own plans. Suddenly, the Labour pledge of £2.5 million looked puny. But they came back with a confident response. They had already decided the key message they wanted from the launch of the actual manifesto at the start of the following week was one of fiscal responsibility. It was just possible that the Conservative commitment – in an attempt to 'de-weaponise' the NHS – might backfire. So they decided against trying to match the £8 billion. Instead, Miliband delivered a memorable line: 'You can't fund the NHS with an IOU.' He then attacked the Tories for irresponsibility and a lack of credibility – spraying around unfunded commitments like there was no tomorrow. Publicly at least, he seemed to relish the role reversal.

Ed Miliband wasn't so confident when I spoke to him after the event, on Labour's battle bus *en route* to Leeds station. I reported on that night's PM programme on Radio 4 that senior sources had begun describing Labour's £2.5 billion as a 'down-payment.' Those sources could not be more senior than the leader of the opposition. He said that Labour would always give the NHS what was necessary. But he had a problem. Everything in the manifesto had to be costed so Labour could not be accused of plans to 'max out the nation's credit card' again. So as resources became available, of course the NHS would be a priority. But it would lack credibility to scrabble around to match the Conservatives' 'off-the-cuff' announcement.

This inability to 'match-fund' the Conservatives nationally was causing problems in local campaigns too. Senior Party officials say that from an organisational point of view, the failure to establish fiscal credibility before the formal campaign got under way had proved costly. That's because with more trust in their ability to run the economy, the Conservatives could – to an extent – roll out the pork barrel. Conservative candidates had very targeted messages about what local improvements would be funded on their re-election. As Labour had more heavy-lifting to do to regain trust with the nation's purse strings, their local candidates were more constrained in what they could say a Labour government would deliver for their area. While there may have been too many national 'retail offers' – such as the energy price freeze – for some in the party, others say there were too few at grassroots level.

But the message on financial stability and responsibility was about to be put in the political equivalent of neon lighting.

Hold the Front Page

13 April

- Labour launches its manifesto – with an eye-catching front page.
- Putting a commitment to fiscal responsibility in a prominent position had been a controversial late decision.
- Ed Miliband tries to correct the damage inflicted by not mentioning the deficit in the same city the year before.
- Jeremy Corbyn will still have to re-establish trust on the economy.

AN UNCONVENTIONAL venue was chosen for what turned out to be an unconventional manifesto. The document's launch was held on home turf for Labour – Manchester, a city wholly devoid of Conservative councillors and indeed MPs. But perhaps in an attempt to add popular appeal to a dry 20,000 word document which had a lengthy phrase – *Britain Only Succeeds When Working People Succeed. This is a Plan to Reward Hard Work, Share Prosperity, and Build a Better Britain* – in place of a proper title, the event was held at the old Granada studios where for many years *Coronation Street* had been filmed. Now another phrase unlikely to roll off the tongue of the average Rovers Return regular is 'budget responsibility lock'. Yet that is what appeared on the very front page. Because whether at the Rovers or the Dog and Duck there was still enough muttering that Labour couldn't be trusted to run the economy. To keep the hostelry analogy going, some voters felt they would do to public money what a drunk would do later with the alcohol he had consumed in the pub.

So the policy was audacious – an attempt to correct Ed Miliband's failure in the same city the previous year to mention the deficit in his conference speech. According to insiders, this had been disastrous – with the Conservatives pulling ahead soon after in Labour's private polling.

So now the new budgetary lock would commit a future Labour government to reducing the deficit on current spending each year until it had been eliminated, bringing down debt as a percentage of national income 'as soon as possible' – that is by the end of the parliament – and getting all future manifesto commitments audited by the independent body set up by George Osborne, the Office for Budget Responsibility.

This was a raid deep within Conservative territory. Indeed it was the clearest sighting of prudence since she had been banished when Gordon Brown moved from Number 11 Downing Street to Number 10 and the economy crashed. Ed Miliband declared that Labour was now the party not just of change but of responsibility. His position had resulted from a series of meetings with the other Ed – the Shadow Chancellor Ed Balls – culminating in a speech Ed Miliband had made on the economy in December 2014. Aides had been pressing for him to be more robust on deficit reduction since his memory had failed him in that notes-free speech to activists two months previously. At a social gathering soon afterwards I had asked him if he should have made the December speech sooner. He grinned as he said it, but I had touched a raw nerve. His response had been brief and to the point: 'Oh, f*** off.'

He now delivered his lecture on fiscal responsibility with much more confidence, even impressing a *Daily Mail* correspondent. But what was the paean of praise to Prudence doing on the very first page of the manifesto? My colleague Allegra Stratton, of BBC's *Newsnight*, had tweeted her scoop that it had been a late addition. For a leader who boasted of the millions of conversations his members were having with the voting public, he had precious few chats with some senior party figures about the most important page in the manifesto.

Just a few calls established that it had been an older version of the document – with a commitment to fiscal responsibility, but not on page one – that had been seen by the party's Clause V committee the previous Thursday when it had formally approved the contents. This committee is often described as 'the parliament of the Labour party' – bringing together members of the Shadow Cabinet, the national executive committee, and trade unionists – and its purpose is to be consulted on, and to approve, the manifesto. The party's deputy chairman Jon Trickett is on the record – in *The Guardian* (4 June 2015) – as saying he wasn't consulted and the prominence given to deficit reduction was damaging:

> It changed the whole character of the manifesto. The document itself was about transforming Britain while also having a deficit reduction strategy. In the end, the document was subordinated to a statement about a programme of austerity.

Jon Cruddas told me he understood the need to get a headline – 'they needed a story for the day' – but was concerned that:

> It looked like we were playing fast and loose with the internal democracy of the party. We had reset the policy agenda around the National Policy Forum (on which activists and trade unionists were represented) and arguably we united the party around a tough economic story but the danger was we were driving a coach and horses through that process.

A lid had been successfully kept on the row during the campaign itself and those close to Miliband say there was nothing sinister in rearranging the contents. It was presentational not political.

The manifesto was supposed to embody the twin themes of reassurance and inspiration. But polling in the week before the document was to launch had suggested that voters still doubted that Labour was serious about bringing the deficit down and would not repeat the mistakes of the past. Senior aides were concerned that the party was still getting blamed for the financial crash happening on their watch. In particular Ed Miliband's policy chief Torsten Bell and his campaign director Spencer Livermore believed something more symbolic needed to be done. Douglas Alexander was said to be keen, given the lack of new policies, to use the manifesto launch to try to slay the deficit dragon.

So it had been decided to give far more weight to the message of fiscal responsibility before the Clause V committee even met. What was agreed after the event was what to call the approach to deficit reduction to make it sound new. Torsten Bell worked on a phrase that is now so unmemorable many of the Labour politicians I have spoken to recently couldn't recall it. But just like the government had a 'triple lock' to protect pensions, it was felt that there needed to be a name for the newly prominent policy – so 'budget responsibility lock' was forged. The document wasn't finalised until the early hours of Friday morning – a long weekend away from the televised manifesto launch. 'If you ever need a good rate for a late printing job, there someone I can recommend', a Shadow Cabinet adviser joked.

Labour's treasury team had outlined every component which made up the budget 'lock' over the past 18 months but were supportive of the rebranding. Ed Balls was also instrumental in the prominence given to fiscal responsibility. He had been asked to give a round of media interviews on the morning of the manifesto launch. He was determined that Ed Miliband wouldn't leave him to deliver the monochrome message of belt-tightening so the leader could then concentrate on the colourful sunlit uplands at the launch itself. Balls was insistent that the entire event, and the document itself, should be subordinated to the need to re-establish economic credibility. So placing the repackaged policy on the front page, Balls believed, would make it difficult for his leader to backslide.

Ed Balls undertook many of the media interviews just before the manifesto launch. And Ed Miliband's press team were pleased that the manifesto now told a story in itself and wasn't just a pull-together of existing positions. But some of those close to the two Eds – Miliband as well as Balls – felt that once fiscal responsibility had been highlighted, the party leader almost lost interest. 'In his mind a box had been ticked', one of them confided 'and he felt he could move on to things he was really interested in.' 'This was front and centre of the manifesto launch,' said another observed, 'but it should have been front and centre of the general election campaign.'

Spencer Livermore's view was that:

We really did something counter-intuitive that day and some Conservatives will admit we put them on the back foot. But it didn't overcome the fact that we hadn't done enough over the previous five years.

Missing a Trick?

13 April

- There's another late addition to the manifesto – aimed squarely at the SNP.
- But Labour downplays its significance, to its potential cost.
- It's unlikely this policy will survive a Jeremy Corbyn leadership.

ANOTHER LINE HAD been inserted late into the manifesto with the minimum of consultation. With the benefit of hindsight, some say Ed Miliband should have made more of it. The SNP were advocating 'coming off austerity' with modest increases in departmental budgets. The manifesto now made clear that Labour wouldn't work with any party that didn't sign up to its approach to deficit reduction.

After the lines that 'Labour will cut the deficit every year' and 'we will get national debt falling and a surplus on the current budget as soon as possible' comes the killer sentence: 'This manifesto sets out we will not compromise on that commitment.' Both Labour's treasury team and Ed Miliband's press team said the line had been inserted with the SNP in mind. But its importance wasn't emphasised. This seemed logical at the time, in case a renewed commitment to fiscal responsibility would be overshadowed by more speculation about coalition. The general election co-ordinator Spencer Livermore – who had been through the 2010 campaign with Gordon Brown – felt that any more talk of the SNP would be at the expense of Labour to making its own case to the public.

Yet in this one line Labour had some armour to protect themselves from a Conservative assault in England. That attack in essence was that the SNP would move a weak Labour Party to the left as a price of sustaining them in power. The SNP couldn't abandon an anti-austerity message at Westminster without potentially damaging their prospects at the Scottish elections in 2016. So had Ed Miliband gone on the front foot, and said that it was because Labour was so committed to balancing the books that an SNP deal was unviable, he might have stood a chance of blunting the sustained attacks from Conservative strategists. As his successor Jeremy Corbyn doesn't believe in an arbitary timescale for eliminating the deficit then this option won't be available to him but Ed Miliband never used it to his full advantage.

Instead he appeared to be behind the curve, incrementally hardening the anti-SNP rhetoric in response to the continuing speculation about what he would or wouldn't do in a hung parliament. But it would all have seemed more complicated then – because if Labour were to say too loudly in Scotland that their attachment to spending cuts made it impossible to work with the SNP they knew they could wave goodbye to many of those voters who had previously backed them but who had voted 'Yes' in the referendum. They needed to make a strategic decision to write Scotland off if they were to utilise fully their 'deficit reduction deal-breaker' for protection in England. Instead of doing so stridently, they tip-toed towards this position.

Indeed, an earlier decision to 'call' Scotland could potentially have given Labour organisational as well as political advantages – for example, by diverting the resources used unsuccessfully to defend Douglas Alexander's or Jim Murphy's seats across the border to Carlisle, a marginal constituency Labour failed to gain. But those conversations their activists were having didn't suggest at that stage that there would be a simultaneous loss of some seats in England and a near-total meltdown in Scotland which would end the careers of two of its 'stars'.

And one of the most senior figures at the heart of the party's organisation told me that while it would have been the right strategic call to abandon Scotland earlier, it would have been politically impossible to do so. First, because 40 angry MPs would have made a huge fuss and the ensuing headlines would have been ghastly. But second, with elections to the Holyrood parliament in 2016, Labour still needed to maintain a base – MSPs and prospective MSPs would have assumed their chances were being written off in that process, too. Douglas Alexander did sanction a shifting of resources within Scotland but organisers say that many English target seats were already spending to capacity so it would have been of limited value to transfer more effort to them in any case.

But Labour was blindsided to the possibility of giving more assistance to some vulnerable seats south of the border as a net loss of seats in England wasn't expected. No polling whatsoever had been done in the seats Labour were battling to defend, and lost on the night. The Conservatives by contrast were publicly defending 40 – in reality 50 – seats with as much vigour as the constituencies they were targeting to win.

'The mind-set,' a senior organiser told me:

> Was that Labour had suffered its second worst defeat since the war in 2010 and while there were special circumstances in Scotland, it just couldn't get any worse in England so the only way was up.

But it could – and it wasn't.

Invitation Only

14 April

- The Labour campaign almost goes off the rails.
- Ed Miliband narrowly avoids causing offence to black and ethnic minority voters.
- Attempts to control and restrict the media are stepped up.
- The new leader may have to rethink the balance between transparency and control.

LABOUR NARROWLY avoided making the headlines for the wrong reasons on the day the Conservatives launched their manifesto. 'I hope he hurries up – I need to go to the toilet' said a tall man in a dirty boiler suit. He was one of around 80 'extras' at the Brush Traction factory on the outskirts of Loughborough who had been corralled outside to await the arrival of the Labour leader. The Leicestershire factory refurbishes and repaints old railway engines for reuse on the freight network – and such a transformation was there for all to see with a 'before' and 'after' display in the factory yard. A makeshift stage had been built, astutely enough, in front of the shiny rolling stock from where Ed Miliband would speak, and not beside an old decaying British Rail diesel nearby – though no doubt Conservatives would have drawn an analogy that far from being New Labour, Miliband was simply putting a contemporary gloss on old statist ideas. 'We have been here 20 minutes. I didn't come to work to see him!' said an older man in an equally dirty boiler suit. His name was Don and I encouraged him to ask a question to compensate for his long wait. 'I have nothing to ask him – I don't think anything of him', was his curt response.

It looked like all this not-so-eager anticipation would be over when a helicopter was spotted making a descent and landing in an adjacent field. Was this hubris after what was seen as a successful manifesto launch? The snappers darted to the wire fence around the factory, got their zoom lenses attached in – well, a flash – but soon confirmed it wasn't Ed Miliband at all. The night before I had chatted to a senior media executive who had been mulling over whether broadcasters had done enough to introduce voters to the idea that the Labour leader could become the next prime minister. Had they simply bought the line from most newspapers that he wasn't up to the job and it couldn't happen? Would voters wake up on 8 May and say 'how the hell did that come about?' And I wondered if the police and security services had suddenly embarked on a similar thought process.

The Labour bus containing Ed Miliband arrived at Brush Traction flanked by two sturdy armoured vehicles whose occupants, never mind the cars, looked like they could withstand a nuclear blast. And there was already security on the ground well before the Labour's entourage arrived.

Soon the restless audience had a chance to hear from Ed Miliband and ask questions. The media had infiltrated the sea of boiler suits, mostly to get a response to the policies in the Conservative manifesto, and he and his press team were satisfied with his answers. Perhaps too satisfied.

We decamped to make the journey to Leicester, a city where more than half the population is from an ethnic minority background. Where better then for the national launch of the party's black and ethnic minority manifesto? *Sky News* had agreed to provide pool camera coverage even though the event might get less media than it deserved, clashing, as it did, with the main manifesto launch by the party's prime opponents. Then *en route* I got a call. The pool camera had been well – pulled.

Party strategists in London had apparently taken the view that the first event had worked so well, then why risk anything else going wrong? The closer they appeared to power, the tighter the control they wanted to exert. There was to be no media access – except for the black and ethnic minority press. So I resolved that my key task was to get in. The suspicion was there might be someone at the event – organised by the resourceful and sometimes controversial Leicester East MP Keith Vaz – that Ed Miliband didn't want to be seen with. Or that he was likely to face hostile questioning.

When we arrived, we couldn't fail to notice that a massive billboard had been erected beside the venue, declaring that Leicester welcomed Ed Miliband. His face was beaming benevolently from it like a dictator of a Central Asian republic. But we, on the other hand, were not welcome. Two Labour press officers and two security personnel guarded the locked entrance and barred our way. I was under instructions if they did not relent to 'Crick' Miliband. We had beat him to the community centre venue, so when he alighted from his vehicle I would then become a pale imitation of the determined, but always affable and engaging, Channel 4 political correspondent Michael Crick, stick a microphone under the opposition leader's nose and ask why they were launching their policies for ethnic minorities in secret.

I decided to start the process early and we began filming our refusal to be admitted. We sought to get answers for our barring on tape from the usually highly-capable Labour Press officer Anna Wright, whose slight frame concealed a steely and tribal determination. The health and education manifesto launches hadn't just been restricted to the specialist press so was Labour now ghettoising ethnic minorities, I ventured? I kept getting a stock answer – 'It's an ethnic minority event'.

I had a calculation to make and I am still not sure I made the right one. Instead of publicising Labour's attempts to control the campaign and restrict scrutiny, I did all I could to gain entry and in the process possibly helped save them from themselves. Partly it was because I was intrigued by what might be going on inside that they didn't want us to see. So I made a further attempt to gain access by calling a couple of contacts in London who would put more pressure on Miliband's press chief Bob Roberts to relent. I didn't know this at the time, but Roberts too could see a media disaster looming, and I was told had already been on to the senior strategists in London who had been refusing steadfastly to open the doors.

Uppermost in their minds had been the need for Ed Miliband to appear prime ministerial, as his personal ratings still lagged behind the actual PM. They were worried that he would be photographed in a garland. And because of the now infamous images of his struggle with a bacon sandwich, they were concerned that he would have to try to consume 'weird' food – their word, not mine – so as not to offend his hosts, but would not cope well with this in front of the cameras.

As it transpired Ed Miliband – travelling with Roberts – was far more relaxed about the event than his very senior aides in London. Attempts had been made throughout the campaign to ensure the 'on the road' team and those in the London HQ were signing from the same song sheet. Spencer Livermore, as campaign director, had instituted a daily call around 7.30am usually involving Livermore himself, Douglas Alexander and Tom Baldwin at head office and Bob Roberts, Rachel Kinnock, Stewart Wood, and often Miliband himself from some more distant part of the kingdom. Sometimes the cast list expanded, sometimes it contracted. There would be another conference call around lunchtime each day, too. Despite this, tensions were not unknown.

Roberts very rarely overruled the campaign team at the party's HQ. He has a reasonable manner and could usually use his powers of persuasion to effect change. This time he simply had to ignore their instructions. He knew Labour's exclusion of the press from an ethnic event – when David Cameron was given the appearance of welcoming all comers to the unveiling of his manifesto in Swindon – would make a stark, and unflattering, contrast. So Roberts called me and told me a pool camera would be allowed in. I then negotiated access for me, and an ITN journalist as well as Sky.

The event was far more impressive than the launch of the previous mini-manifestos. It was a full Keith Vaz production – very much what you would expect from someone about as shy and retiring as an extrovert on speed. He had organised a gospel choir, drummers from the Indian sub-continent and a stellar list of black and ethnic minority politicians through the years from Paul Boateng to Chuka Umunna. Vaz's 17-year-old daughter took to the stage to declare when she came of age – though 'as a teenager I have mind of my own' – she would be voting Labour. He asked if I was going to do a piece to camera – I told him, to his chagrin, that cameras had very nearly been banned. I was subsequently given a lovely gift of sweet meats.

The event should have been a credit to the Labour Party but nearly resulted in very negative publicity. At one stage in denying entry, the press office had cited a breach of 'fire regulations' if too many journalists were to go in. Presumably that concern hadn't extended to covering up fire exit signs in Bury. And it turned out there was plenty of room inside, with no exits blocked.

Labour had lost a by-election in Leicester to the Lib Dems following the Iraq war and would not want once again to drain what was usually a sturdy reservoir of support for the party. But very senior officials in London at the centre of the election campaign had come within a hair's breadth of being seen to treat voters from ethnic minority backgrounds with less respect and importance than teachers, or those who worked in the NHS – because far from being turned away, the media had been heavily encouraged to cover both the education and health manifestos.

To be transparent with our audience we probably should be honest about the extent of restricted access on a general election campaign – though this had been by far the most serious yet ludicrous example.

The irony was the decision was subsequently taken to redo Ed Miliband's response to the Conservative manifesto – thus negating his clip against the much-loved backdrop of the train factory. The focus was moving further towards the Conservatives' uncosted commitments in the wake of a snap analysis by the Institute for Fiscal Studies. So I got a call from a sheepish Bob Roberts. He apologised for the initial decision and asked if we would like a new clip of Miliband for the teatime bulletins? I said we would be happy to accommodate it outside the ethnic minority event, so long as he took a full range of questions.

Just as we were awaiting his return, a pensioner in a rather fast motorised scooter came by: 'Who's here? Miliband? Oh, I got a thing or two say to him. I am going to vote UKIP this time,' she snarled. We fully expected him to drive back into a scene reminiscent of his old boss and Gillian

Duffy, but then I got another call. Yes, he wanted to do a new interview but he was 20 minutes away and wouldn't be coming back here. So on a day of narrow escapes, the possibility of an encounter with a real and highly sceptical voter had been avoided.

Campaign Stop

16 April

- Ed Miliband gets mobbed on a brief visit to a marginal seat.
- Jeremy Corbyn is in the crowd.
- The Labour leader's decision to take part in a debate with Nicola Sturgeon – but without David Cameron – splits opinion in his team.

THE PURPOSE OF the visit was primarily to deliver a message to the media. We had been told Ed Miliband would make a 'campaign stop' in Crouch End – a trendy, and more recently, also an affluent north London suburb – but it transpired he wasn't actually *en route* to anywhere else. He would speak on a little platform outside the Art Deco Hornsey Town Hall. Its intricate and impressive interior would do a grand ocean liner proud but its exterior unfortunately resembled a municipal crematorium. So the Labour bus was parked directly outside to provide a branded and less morbid backdrop to the party leader's remarks.

Around 100 local activists had gathered with posters on a weekday morning. I used to live in the area so I knew some of them, and others recognised me. None that I spoke to expected Labour to get an overall majority – but they were correctly confident of winning the Hornsey & Wood Green seat back from the wealthy Lib Dem minister Lynn Featherstone. She had overturned a massive Labour majority in 2005 in the wake of the Iraq war, which had so offended the small 'l' liberals of north London. But confidence was not exuding from the Miliband entourage on arrival. 'Right,' one of them told me 'we have to get him in and out of here as quickly as possible'.

Tonight was to be the so-called 'challengers' debate' on television. The BBC was to broadcast a clash which would exclude the governing parties. Of the five party leaders who would take part, only Nigel Farage would be positioning himself to Ed Miliband's right. Miliband's director of strategy, Greg Beales, was strongly in favour of participation – but many of his colleagues were so sceptical he was told, perhaps not entirely in jest, he would have to resign if it turned out he had made the wrong call. Some advisers had scratched their heads in puzzlement over why Miliband had agreed to the debate as they anticipated that he would face a concerted attack from the Greens, SNP and Plaid Cymru and be portrayed – in Cameron and Clegg's absence – as a proxy for Westminster austerity.

Beales, in contrast, felt that Miliband should once again take the opportunity to gain unmediated access to people's living rooms – but also to
make an issue of Cameron's absence. And the advice was that while the
Prime Minister wouldn't be a participant, Miliband should act as though
David Cameron was right there. This would then force parties to his left to
focus on Cameron's record and not simply to attack Labour. So his press
team were determined to deliver a blow to David Cameron before the
debate even began. But they also realised the importance of nothing going
wrong in advance of the evening event that would put him on the back foot.

Just in case opponents, or even just random members of the public,
heard that the Labour leader was in Crouch End, his remarks would be
brief. He would take no questions from his own activists, or from a brace
of left-wing London MPs – the future leadership candidate Jeremy Corbyn
had joined Diane Abbott in the crowd (she assured me, with a grin, that
she wouldn't heckle) – and especially not from reporters. So his speech,
at barely more than three minutes duration, lasted little longer than a
soundbite. He was cheered when he said that David Cameron was refusing to turn up for the job interview to be prime minister. He stressed the
importance of the election, then surrounded by his security detail, he
headed off to a crowded cafe less than a two-minute walk away.

Nervous press officers shouted to each other 'Where's Michael Crick?
Where is Crick?' They feared the legendary political journalist would
'doorstep' him and ask an inconvenient question. So today, unlike in
Leicester, I didn't have to impersonate him or adopt his MO – he was here
in person to do it all himself. There was near panic as much of the
100-strong crowd decided to follow the Labour leader to the cafe and the
persistent Channel 4 reporter could not be seen. One of Ed Miliband's
armed close protection officers told me that this was one of the most
challenging days of the campaign because the briefest of walkabouts was
on the edge of chaos – protestors would have been easier to target, isolate
or frankly manhandle but he was having to clear a path through well-wishers who were simply disappointed not to hear more from their man. And
there were TV cameras to record every moment.

Ed Miliband regained his cool inside Riley's ice cream cafe and
Michael Crick and myself positioned ourselves outside amidst the
well-wishers and bemused local residents. A row of uniformed police
formed along the pavement. Inside the local media had been granted interviews while the national media were denied access. On emerging, one of
them briefly announced his verdict on the interview: 'The usual bullshit,'
he huffed as he made his way out. Then apparently random members of
the public were plucked from the crowd to meet briefly Ed Miliband. I

asked one of them – who said his name was John – if he had just turned up on the off-chance of meeting the Labour leader. No, he said – he had been emailed the day before and told he had to register his interest before being given details of the venue. And so too had Elaine, a party member who had wanted to raise concerns about the policy on disabilities.

The press office insisted the event was not as controlled as it appeared. Certainly they didn't want it to become any less controlled. So two offers were proffered. Michael Crick would get a clip with Ed Miliband inside the cafe if he didn't 'doorstep' the Labour leader on the way out. He wanted to ask about the tax affairs of David Axelrod, Miliband's American adviser. So this offer was subsequently withdrawn. I would be given a 20-minute off-camera interview with Ed Miliband – once he was safely ensconced in Labour's battle bus – along with a colleague each from Sky, ITN, and PA. There was a further reporting restriction – that the whole interview was 'background' and no remarks could be attributed directly to Ed Miliband. He was accosted briefly *en route* by a protestor campaigning for better rights for prisoners but apart from that, was unscathed.

If Miliband hadn't been confident about that night's debate, he gave no hint of it aboard his campaign bus. He asked my advice, and laughed when I said 'don't do it'. He admitted he had had the same counsel from other quarters but in the end 'the opportunity for unmediated access to voters is too important to pass up'. Tapping the oak brown veneer on the table of his executive coach, he added 'touch wood, it's worked so far.'

He had been pleased with his performance with Paxman, and in the seven-party debate, and said: 'Look I know it sounds like managing expectations, but we felt we had won the first debate,' in fact, not quite a debate but the separate Paxman interviews with him and the Prime Minister, 'and that's not what the first, instant polls showed, but they came round.' He anticipated that the BBC's David Dimbleby would intervene more between the participants than ITV's Julie Etchingham had done and he may well have to attack, rather than ignore, Nigel Farage, but his main mission would be to 'talk directly to the British people'. He and the ubiquitous Bob Roberts derided the Conservative criticism that Cameron's reluctance to debate was a 'process issue' of no relevance outside the Westminster bubble. They got 'cut through' with voters, they said – it had been mentioned spontaneously on the doorsteps – and it went to the core of the Prime Minister's character.

So it was of little surprise when the debate came that Miliband highlighted Cameron's absence and renewed the offer of a head-to-head clash. But the actual head-to-head clash with the SNP's Nicola Sturgeon didn't go quite so well.

Not a Big Enough Difference

16 April

- Ed Miliband performs well in debate, and appears more prime ministerial than ever.
- But Nicola Sturgeon lands a blow that appears to seal Labour's fate in Scotland.
- Jeremy Corbyn will find it challenging to win back both defectors to the Conservatives in England, and to the SNP in Scotland.

THIS WAS THE high water mark of the Labour campaign. A risky venture for Ed Miliband, the instant poll from Survation declared him the winner – and actually more prime ministerial than the absent incumbent. The bookies had made him the favourite to get to Number 10 for the first time. And several days after the debate, the pollster James Morris gave his weekly presentation to Labour's campaign team. The party's own bespoke research showed that Ed Miliband had been seen to perform well. As with the previous debate, his ratings had been given a fillip. Labour was ahead in the marginal seats. But this time something else had happened – for the first time in the campaign the party was polling well enough plausibly to become the largest party in a hung parliament. The mood was optimistic. It appeared that it really was all to play for.

The debate had apparently gone to plan. While at the margins, Nigel Farage had turned on the audience and accused them of bias, Ed Miliband was parrying accusations from the parties on the left that he was 'austerity-lite.' Meanwhile, as prepped by his team, he had stared down the barrel of the camera and delivered a message to David Cameron: 'If you think this election is about leadership, then debate me one-on-one. Debate me. And let the people decide.' And he refused to be dragged to the left, offering further reassurance that he would bring the deficit down year-on-year.

His attack lines on Nicola Sturgeon had been well-rehearsed. The only guarantee of getting rid of a Conservative-led government was to vote Labour – backing the SNP would be 'a gamble.' He also threw in a denunciation of Full Fiscal Autonomy. And he not only repeated the 'no coalition' line – he highlighted the differences he had with the SNP, including on Trident.

It had been a confident performance. But Nicola Sturgeon's responses inflicted more damage than he immediately realised. First, she said she could make Labour 'bolder' – for example on funding the NHS. She asserted that Miliband was 'too weak' to shut the Conservatives out of power without her help. This played entirely in to David Cameron's narrative to voters in English marginal seats that the nationalist tail would wag the Labour dog.

But what most delighted SNP strategists was her response to Miliband's well-practised attack against the anti-austerity parties. He said:

> I have fought the Conservatives all my life... Let's not pretend there isn't a difference between me and David Cameron. There is a huge difference between me and David Cameron.

Her apparently spontaneous reply was: 'I don't say there is no difference between Ed Miliband and David Cameron. I say there isn't a big enough difference between Ed Miliband and David Cameron.'

In fact this line – or one similar to it – had been tested in SNP focus groups, when voters were asked if they thought there was 'enough of a difference' between the two leaders. And it was at least one key on the ring that was unlocking support for the SNP amongst those who had voted 'No' in the referendum.

The SNP's claim to be 'stronger for Scotland' was already playing well. But as one senior strategist admitted, this wasn't a fundamentally different message than the party had put forward at previous Westminster elections, only to win half a dozen seats. The changes to the political landscape now made this a potentially more fertile seed to sow. The main difference was the fact of a coalition government, not the theory. So SNP claims that they could hold the balance of power after the next election – with the polls pointing to another hung parliament – no longer looked fanciful. The argument then moved on to who would be best to stand up for Scotland's interests: Labour MPs – more of the same, and who might not be able to defeat Cameron anyway – or the SNP, which hadn't campaigned alongside the Conservatives at the referendum? And the phrase 'not enough of a difference' seemed to reflect the views of 'No' voters who might under different circumstances have voted Labour.

It will be hard for the SNP to claim that Miliband's successor Jeremy Corbyn doesn't have big differences with the Conservatives – after all, he has large enough differences with senior MPs in his own party. But the change of leadership might never have happened if those around Ed Miliband had deflected this silver bullet and held on to more Scottish seats. They were aware of the dangers. One of Miliband's closest advisers said he had seen this problem coming the previous summer when Alistair Darling, as leader of the 'No' campaign, felt compelled to reject SNP allegations that the Conservatives would be in a position to privatise NHS services in Scotland – while of course Labour was warning of similar dangers in England. While Alistair Darling may have been right about the devolved health service, this adviser felt he was not appearing 'different enough' from the Tories. But being able to see a tsunami coming and being able to turn back the tide are two different skills. The latter is more useful, but less achievable.

So although the UK-wide instant poll suggested Nicola Sturgeon came second to Ed Miliband in the debate, her advisers were content that her support had a Heineken quality, and was starting to reach parts of the body politic other parties couldn't reach. Subsequent focus groups suggested she had hit the spot.

Put to the Test

17 April

- Labour launches its 'youth manifesto' – to mature students.
- Ed Miliband proposes a ban on paid internships.

WAS IT BIG head or big balls? That was the topic of conversation amongst some sections of the media *en route* to the launch of Labour's youth manifesto at the unusually named Bishop Grosseteste University in the cathedral city of Lincoln. While it is almost certainly the former – from the French, *'tete'* – just in case it's the latter, local people tend to refer to the higher education institution as 'Bishop Grost.' A former teacher training college, it became a university as recently as 2012 and has a high number of mature students. So this might not have been the obvious place to launch a 'youth manifesto' that could have a little less relevance to them, given their average age. But the venue had been moved from Birmingham to this highly marginal seat where the Conservatives had a majority of little more than a thousand votes and precious few members, as Labour had become increasingly confident of snatching it back. They were to be disappointed come polling day.

The new announcement to help provoke interest in the manifesto – which contained otherwise familiar policies on student finance – was a ban on any internships lasting for longer than four weeks. It was another controversial reform of employment law – following the stated intention of getting rid of around 90 per cent of zero hours contracts. Interns would have to be paid at least the minimum wage after a month. This would be another front in Labour's battle against exploitation. It was also a demand of the party's biggest single source of income – the Unite union, which pays its own interns the 'living wage', higher than the minimum. In the week of the announcement Labour received £700,000 in donations from the unions. But it was the Blairite Liam Byrne, the Shadow Higher Education minister, who had championed the policy – and had been expropriated from him.

An article had appeared in *The Independent* in December 2014 suggesting he was about to announce that a future Labour government would ban them. In fact privately he had gone further and drafted amendments to the government's small business legislation to ensure interns would be paid. But he was told by Miliband's office to pull the amendments and instead announce a 'consultation' on internships.

They had bigger plans – paid internships would form one of their 'retail offers' at the election. It would create a dividing line with the Conservatives – who were expected to defend unpaid internships which Labour would then claim were making some professions, the media included, the preserve of people with well-off middle class parents. So Labour could claim to be on the side of social mobility while energising their core vote with a bit of class politics. While the policy was unashamedly controversial and designed to hit the headlines, in the wake of the previous night's debate it received less publicity than anticipated.

Instead much of the focus – to the Conservatives' delight – remained on whether Ed Miliband would need a deal with the SNP in the event of a hung parliament. Variations on this theme would continue to dominate the next week's campaigning.

Immigration and Exploitation

18 April

- Ed Miliband gives a keynote speech on immigration amid internal arguments over how tough he should be – and some confusion over the policy.
- There are fears that floating voters hear only that he opposes the 'exploitation' of migrants, not limiting immigration.
- His distinct but complex argument is difficult to convey.
- The challenge for the new party leader is to have a distinctive Labour approach to immigration, but one which doesn't play down their own voters' concerns.

NOT FOR THE FIRST time Ed Miliband was to issue an apology of sorts. When he battled for the Labour leadership in 2010, he acknowledged that 'we need to be willing to talk about the issue of immigration'. Then in Kent, in the local elections four years ago, Ed Miliband had identified falling living standards and immigration as the two main reasons that Labour had lost trust with working class voters in the South of England. Maurice Glasman – *eminence grise* of campaign group London Citizens, and the leading light behind the socially conservative Blue Labour movement whom Ed Miliband had ennobled – had been rather more outspoken, suggesting the previous Labour government had lied about the scale of immigration. This, he argued, had created a massive 'rupture of trust' with the electorate.

In response Ed Miliband had said, 'I don't think we lied but we got it wrong in a number of respects. We underestimated the number of people coming from Poland. And the pressure on people's wages.' The Conservatives had denounced this is a 'partial apology'. Some in his own ranks – including his parliamentary aide and former minister John Denham, who represented the highly marginal southern English seat of Southampton Itchen – had been urging him to go further. So in December 2012, I was summoned to a college above a supermarket in Tooting in south London to conduct a BBC interview just before Ed Miliband delivered a speech to a multicultural audience.

For him, sorry still indeed seemed to be the hardest word. He couldn't quite bring himself to utter the 'S' word but he did concede that immigration 'had been too high' under the last government, particularly low-skilled immigration. He said again that 'we got it wrong' and 'lessons had been learnt'. And this time he came armed with a new policy to enable – but also to insist that – migrants working in the public sector achieve a higher standard of English.

So that drab December day in south London was now a sunny Saturday afternoon on the Wirral, nearly two and a half years later, but not much else had changed. At a public meeting aimed at wresting the marginal Wirral West seat from the Conservative employment minister Esther McVey, Ed Miliband began his speech with almost exactly the same words he had used in Tooting: 'Let me be clear. Labour got it wrong in the past. We have listened. We have learned and we have changed.'

Labour officials had been stung by accusations that the campaign had not only been tightly controlled, but was now actually looking like it. So 10,000 voters on Merseyside had received notification of today's Q&A with Ed Miliband at Pensby High School. Not only was it standing room only, an overflow room had to be hastily set up.

When the questions came, however, very few were on immigration. He was criticised by an accountant for not winning over the confidence of business. He was quizzed over votes for 16-year-olds. He was urged to go further in pushing out private sector providers from the health service.

So Ed Miliband was perhaps fortunate that immigration – which according to some polls had for a time been voters' number one concern – had now been replaced by the far more fertile territory of the NHS. But it hadn't gone away.

Opposite the school, the occupants of a comfortable semi-detached home, adorned with a union flag that would make those flown atop most public buildings look puny, told me they hadn't been invited to the meeting and were very concerned about immigration. But few inside the venue seemed as bothered.

So the first question on the topic came from me. I asked Ed Miliband why Labour had not rebuilt trust on immigration, despite recognising it as a problem at least three years ago, and why he couldn't be straight with people that there was very little he could do to control unskilled immigration from inside the EU. His answer was almost as long as his preceding speech. And that was in part Labour's problem. He didn't want to play a numbers game with David Cameron – who in any case had significantly failed to get net migration down to the tens of thousands as he had promised at the last election. He wanted to address the issue in a distinctly Labour way. But that meant giving me – and therefore voters – a long and complex answer.

His solution to low skilled EU migration was encapsulated in the phrase 'immigration policy doesn't stop at the border'. But there were many complex steps voters had to follow to discover just how immigration would be controlled. He was promising a crackdown on bad employers who paid migrants less than the minimum wage. Forcing wages up was designed to appeal to traditional Labour voters and trade unionists who had seen their, or their members', salaries undercut by low paid migrants. But they could also be reassured that the migrants themselves would be saved from further exploitation. And by pushing pay up, employers would have less incentive to 'import' unskilled eastern European labour. That in turn would cut immigration. But it was perhaps a too subtle message for a party that hadn't won back public trust.

As every policy had to be costed, this message was to be accompanied by 100 more Home Office staff who would seek out rogue employers, paid for through increased visa fees. This number seemed modest compared with the 5,000 officers currently deployed on enforcing immigration law.

So one of Ed Miliband's aides briefed that the new 100-strong unit would grow over time, as fines from rogue employers would fund its expansion. Within hours another senior aide flatly contradicted this. Fines would go to HMRC not to the Home Office unit. So this had all the hallmarks of a tactic for the election not a strategy for government.

Then there was the small matter of how the story was playing in the press. There had been robust briefing that Ed Miliband's remarks on immigration would be 'measured' and 'prime ministerial'. 'We won't be pandering to UKIP' I was told. When most of the media reflected that and also reported the first half of Miliband's message – the action to stop migrants being exploited, rather than the subsequent expected fall in immigration – one of his closest aides did a pretty good but unintentional impression of the fictional spin doctor Malcolm Tucker from *The Thick Of It*: 'F***, f*** – this is not playing well for us. It now sounds like he is too soft on f***ing immigration.'

Having to keep the liberals of Crouch End and the workers of Gravesend happy was proving quite a challenge.

A senior Shadow Cabinet member was dismayed by the performance. He told me:

> Sure, there was a pledge on immigration. But Miliband never wants to do the heavy lifting. He won't talk numbers and time and again his whole attitude to the issue is to tick the box and walk away. Yes, he will talk about exploitation but people won't hear him on immigration. They just hear 'exploitation'. Some of the tougher messages just have to come from the party leader.

And indeed there were tougher Labour messages than had been mentioned on the Wirral.

The previous November the Shadow Work and Pensions Secretary Rachel Reeves wrote 'exclusively' for *Mail Online* that Labour would make EU migrants wait two years before they could claim jobless benefits. The policy had been signed off by the party leader and part of Miliband's own press team convinced Reeves that an article on the *Mail* website would hit a good target audience but also it would then get picked up by the broadcasters. When the toughest message yet from Labour – a policy that might well breach EU law – barely rated a mention, I was told Reeves was furious.

Some in Miliband's office were far from furious as they had wanted to use this approach to 'test the water' on the tough message before Ed Miliband himself had to articulate it. But with very little reaction – negative or otherwise – some of those close to both Ed Miliband and Ed Balls felt the party leader now had a golden opportunity to lead from the front, and make some former Labour voters who had been quietly drifting off to UKIP sit up and take notice. The policy would also challenge the 'something for nothing' image the party was trying to shake off. And he would get his retaliation in first, as it was widely expected that David Cameron would announce his own restrictions.

When Ed Miliband unveiled Labour's election pledge on immigration the following month in Great Yarmouth – a seat the party had held until 2010 but failed to win back at the general election – he did speak about the two-year benefit wait. But to the disappointment of some senior Shadow Cabinet members and their advisers it wasn't the central message. The line in the speech – 'We will make it a criminal offence to undercut pay or conditions by exploiting migrant workers' – attracted the most attention, especially when it was admitted by his aides that undercutting pay in itself wouldn't actually lead to prosecutions.

So the policy that attempted to tackle twin toxic issues for Labour – benefits and immigration – got second billing. It also hadn't helped that a leaked document for canvassers was reported as advising those on the doorstep to respond to inquiries on the issue, but then to move the conversation on to topics more favourable to Labour. Ed Miliband denied that he hadn't wanted to talk about immigration – and indeed he talked about it a lot. But his internal critics believed that the message could have been stronger and not enough was said about the entire issue during the course of the election campaign itself. So while activists undoubtedly had conversations with voters about EU migrants, the feeling at some senior levels in Labour was that these conversations were unlikely to prove productive if the party sounded more worried about the welfare of the migrant rather than those whose wages had been undercut.

Professor Tim Bale studied Miliband's time in opposition in *Five Year Mission* and suggests that the emphasis on exploitation might have been an answer to the wrong question:

These sort of solutions made a degree of sense, even if they reflected the wholly predictable tendency of social democratic parties to come up with an economic answer to what is to no small extent a cultural question and therefore a much harder one to answer.

But even during the campaign there were serious splits over exactly what – and how much – to say about immigration. Some of Ed Miliband's advisers were urging him to return to the theme again after his Wirral speech. This is a box that couldn't just be ticked. The voters weren't allowing it. His own private pollsters – Stan Greenberg and James Morris – were telling him the issue was still resonant and potential Labour voters hadn't had adequate reassurance that he 'got it.' One adviser close to the pollsters said:

> The way we talked about immigration wouldn't win over dyed-in-the-wool right-wing UKIP voters. But those drifting away from Labour did find our arguments compelling. The problem was they weren't hearing our message enough, it just wasn't front and centre enough.

And James Morris pointed out that after the pre-election launch of the party's immigration pledge, while concern amongst voters about Labour's approach remained high, it had begun to diminish. If the policy had become a more central part of Labour's campaign, it's possible this effect may have continued. But, equally, Morris believes it may in any case have been too late by then:

> When Ed ran for leader, he emphasised the need for change on immigration. But very quickly that change became marginal and technical, rather than a deep repositioning of the party. By the time of the election campaign, it was hard to get voters to believe that Labour had really changed – particularly as UKIP had emerged and were filling the working class, populist space we should have occupied.

Unlike on welfare, the Conservatives were judged to be vulnerable. As well as arguing against exploitation of migrants, Ed Miliband could potentially have done more to exploit Conservative weaknesses. David Cameron had broken his promise on net migration. Some of his former voters were looking to UKIP. So some strategists believed Labour had the potential to occupy counter-intuitive territory – rather as Cameron himself had done by stressing in opposition how much the health service had meant to his family. He had put himself in election posters saying he would cut the deficit, not the NHS.

Others close to the then leader disagreed. They said they were at the limits of the 'authenticity issue.' Ed Miliband, the son of an immigrant and from a small 'l' liberal, north London background could not reinvent himself as Nigel Farage, or claim to be from some of the working class communities where immigration and identity were proving to be potent concerns. He had to argue a case he felt comfortable with – one which suited his character and his party. That's why the distinctly Labour solution of linking immigration with exploitation – and in tackling one, you tackle the other – was settled upon. To rip this up just before polling day could have looked desperate, and a tougher message from his mouth might in any case still not be believed. And as one adviser put it:

> Not just Ed, but the whole Shadow Cabinet looked youngish, special advisory, middle class so there was an issue as to how well they could carry the message. Don't forget Tony Blair had John Prescott. He could say to traditional supporters why Tony should be trusted. Perhaps we should have used an older figure like Alan Johnson who could speak more authentically to working class communities. In the end perhaps we shouldn't have been surprised we did better in multicultural London and in metropolitan areas.

An independent post-election analysis being conducted by the former policy chief Jon Cruddas suggests that in some areas outside the capital, UKIP hit Labour much harder than the Conservatives. Cruddas believes that there was a 'double digit loss of seats for Labour' because of a drift to Farage's party – though it's difficult to know if a different policy on immigration, or a different emphasis placed on the same policy, would have carried any more credibility without a change of party leader.

Whatever the internal arguments over the prominence and presentation of the immigration policy, Bob Roberts commends the legacy the former leader has bequeathed his successor:

> He neutralised that attitude Gordon Brown and others had towards Gillian Duffy and similar traditional voters – he said it was not wrong or racist to discuss immigration. Now, we may not have made the issue into a positive. But if I told you when he was elected in 2010 we would restrict benefits to EU migrants, you would have laughed at me. Ed successfully and sympathetically moved the party on, and that will help the next leader.

It's Hard Work Trying to Look Like a Prime Minister
Aides insist Ed Miliband speaks at a podium even in this busy Huddersfield factory

Happy Easter!
Ed Miliband and wife Justine spend a wet bank holiday talking to activists in Blackpool

Act of War Ed Miliband challenges the charge that he can't be trusted on defence

Where Are They Now? Ed Balls and Jim Murphy lose their seats after launching their Full Fiscal Assault in the shadow of Edinburgh Castle

One of Five Million Conversations
Activists chat in Crouch End, London – where they snatch the seat from the Lib Dems

Securing A Win
Ed Miliband is flanked by minders on a visit to the target Hornsey & Wood Green seat
– one of Labour's few gains on election night

Smile for the Cameras
Ed Miliband on a campaign visit before taking on Nicola Sturgeon and other opposition party leaders in a TV debate

Brimming With Self-confidence
Ed Miliband on the morning of polling day, expecting to travel from here in Doncaster to Downing Street

Essex Appeal
Far left newspapers are sold outside Jeremy Corbyn's Chelmsford rally

What Have I Done?
Labour's interim leader
Harriet Harman awaits the
announcement of her
successor

The Shape of Things to Come?
Labour's new deputy Tom Watson disagrees with Jeremy Corbyn on key policies
but has a mandate of his own

... And Then There Was One
Jeremy Corbyn's opponents
maintain a dignified silence as
they are told the bad news that
they have lost

You'd Think He Had Lost…
Shadow Chancellor John McDonnell gets emotional at Jeremy Corbyn's victory

Centre of Attention
The press crowd around the newly-anointed Labour leader

Do They Mean Me?
An unassuming Jeremy Corbyn fumbles to find his specs

Matters to Address
Jeremy Corbyn's first speech
as Leader of the Opposition

Marriage of Convenience

18 April

- Ed Miliband is mobbed by a hen party.
- There are unfounded suspicions the encounter has been staged.
- There's a danger that enthusiasm on the street is confused with support at the ballot box.

'IT'S A SET UP. It's got to be a set up.' One of my colleagues was absolutely convinced that those ever so cunning Labour campaigners had arranged for wonkish, awkward Ed Miliband – who in truth seems a lot more assured and confident in real life than on television – to be 'mobbed' by a group of attractive women.

The Labour battle bus had left the Wirral to make its way to the marginal seat of Chester, and was pulling up – appropriately enough – outside the city's Westminster Hotel. Bride-to-be Nicola Braithwaite had been enjoying drinks with friends in the hotel bar when a celebrity who wasn't actually a cast member of locally-set *Hollyoaks* was spotted. Nicola Braithwaite was a solicitor who was opposed to legal aid cuts so was minded to back Ed Miliband anyway, but she told my colleague Callum May she had been surprised to be invited aboard the Labour vehicle:

> We went out to get a picture and I was invited onto the bus to meet him. He was lovely and we had a brief chat then I left and he came to the door to see all of the others.

Two words prove that this was no pre-arranged photo-op. Rachel Kinnock. The women were shouting 'Selfie! Selfie!' and 'hashtag Ed.' One of the group – Anna Heaford – later told commercial radio station LBC that she thought the Labour leader had been 'kind of intimidated by the cackle of all of us screaming at him' and there was a woman 'who looked quite ferocious... saying to security, 'have you got this under control?'

You could see her point. All this emphasis on trying to make him look prime ministerial and already one of the hen party was referring to the Labour leader on Twitter as 'Nicola's stripper.' If any objects associated with such evenings were to be produced in his presence, the benefit of celebrity recognition would be outweighed by humiliation. The genuinely spontaneous incident was brought to a close.

But earlier at the Wirral school, too, Ed Miliband had been asked to pose with members of his audience for selfies. I saw it myself on station platforms, on trains, anywhere where he was briefly exposed to the public. And whatever your focus groups are telling you, it must feel like a real connection is being made with a supportive public. This could lull the most sceptical of us into believing our message was breaking through rather than that random strangers want a picture with someone they have seen on the telly.

A Day at the Races

20 April

- Ed Miliband fails to deploy a new attack on the SNP.
- Scottish trade unionists have been shifting allegiance.
- There is huge frustration that speculation over SNP influence isn't abating.

ED MILIBAND DIDN'T mention the prospect of a second Scottish referendum when he spoke to trade unionists in Ayr. He was giving the keynote address at the STUC conference which was being held at the seaside town's famous race course – home of the Scottish Grand National. The horses weren't running today but that didn't prevent the news coverage from being packed with puns. Indeed Ayr used to be a two-horse race between Labour and the Conservatives but now the SNP were clear favourites.

The make-up of Labour's focus groups had been expanded to include not so much trade unionists but political unionists – Conservatives or Lib Dems who might vote Labour tactically to keep the SNP out in a small number of seats. The prospect of a second referendum hadn't filled them with joy. They had regarded the matter as settled. Better still, they were linking the issue of the referendum to perceptions of SNP hypocrisy. Some of them felt the otherwise trustworthy Nicola Sturgeon looked 'shifty' when she was asked about another referendum in TV interviews and debates. What was she hiding? It wasn't in the general election manifesto but would the SNP put it in their next one? This was proving a more effective 'worry point' than the prospect of Full Fiscal Autonomy.

The Scottish party had been at best neutral, and possibly even a little sceptical, about campaign visits from Ed Miliband. But they had grown to see their value. He was seen as less divisive, and with less New Labour baggage than Jim Murphy. And anything he said was guaranteed national coverage. So he was a useful vehicle for conveying a new line. Murphy's team urged him to raise the fear of another disruptive referendum during his day at the race course. But he pulled up short of the fence and didn't make the leap.

The SNP were launching their manifesto on the other side of the country so it was assumed – correctly – that Miliband's contribution would be reduced to a mere clip in response on the main news bulletins. And he had taken the view that today was an opportunity to talk about what Labour would do, not what the SNP might do. His message to the trade unions was a familiar one: the only way to be assured of getting a Labour government was to vote for it. Every vote for the SNP risked the chance of David Cameron returning to Downing Street.

Perhaps there was another reason for not articulating what would now be a key line of attack from Scottish Labour, and one which Miliband himself did deploy later in the campaign. The allegiance of some Scottish trade unionists – like the population as a whole – had been shifting from Labour to the SNP. Before the September 2014 referendum, the SNP's Trade Union Group had 800 members. At the last count, a year on, it had 16,000. They had their own bright and busy stall right outside the STUC conference hall. Some of the UK media who had made the trip to Ayr had done so in the expectation that Ed Miliband would be heckled, for once, from the Left. But he didn't rile his audience, and spent more time attacking the Conservatives – denouncing David Cameron as 'deceitful' – than his main Scottish opponents. He chose to emphasise common cause, not more recent divisions, saying: 'The battle to build a country that works for working people is the story of our movement.' So he left unscathed, and withdrew to a private meeting with his Shadow Scottish Secretary Margaret Curran and Labour MPs Brian Donohoe and Ian Davidson. It was left to Jim Murphy to argue that it was time to 'rebuild the NHS, not rerun the referendum' at a street rally in Glasgow. Miliband wasn't in attendance.

The UK Labour leader was heading to Manchester, where he was to give a speech on the NHS the next day. But while he had bolted from Ayr race course, questions about what demands he would be saddled with from Nicola Sturgeon if he couldn't win a first-past-the-post election followed him south.

His inner circle were the angriest I have heard them when not only did that NHS speech get very little take up, but Sir John Major's warnings about a minority Labour government – which began being trailed as Miliband left Scotland – were then covered extensively. The former Conservative prime minister said:

> If Labour were to accept an offer of support from the SNP, it could put the country on course to a government held to ransom on a vote-by-vote basis.

Again, Ed Miliband was forced on the defensive, insisting 'It ain't going to happen' (and indeed it didn't – but not in the way he was expecting). The BBC also reported remarks by the Conservative former Scottish secretary Lord Forsyth to *The Guardian*:

We've had the dilemma for Conservatives, which is they want to be the largest party at Westminster and therefore some see the fact that the Nationalists are going to take seats in Scotland as helpful. But that is a short-term and dangerous view which threatens the integrity of our country.

Those close to Miliband felt that the wider media had given this criticism of Conservative strategy scant attention, and had left some of them frustrated over how they could recover the agenda. Ed Milband, however, was once again about to hit the headlines in a quite unexpected way.

The Most Unlikely Cult of the 21st Century

21 *April*

- 'Milifandom' treats the Labour leader like a pop star, but doesn't seem to shift votes.
- Miliband himself calls it 'an unlikely cult'.
- His successor may have to distinguish between engaging younger voters and actually gaining votes.

'SHE THINKS IT'S a case of mistaken identity'. That, Ed Miliband told the *Evening Standard*, was his wife Justine's reaction to the news that her husband had a fandom. Milifandom. For those still unfamiliar with the concept, Wikipedia describes it thus:

> *Fandom* is a term used to refer to a subculture composed of fans characterised by a feeling of empathy and camaraderie with others who share a common interest. Fans typically are interested in even minor details of the object of their fandom and spend a significant portion of their time and energy involved with their interest.

Usually, though, fandoms are reserved for pop stars, not politicians.

Seventeen-year-old Abby Tomlinson and friends had started the Twitter hashtag #milifandom the previous week but today was the day that it began trending and the wider world woke up to it. It became a 'thing'. Abby was 17 and therefore a non-voter but argued there was a serious point to her initiative. It was 'a movement against the distorted media portrayal of Ed' as well as a way of demonstrating 'how powerful young people are'.

There is little doubt she did much to beef up and buff up Ed Miliband's image. His decapitated noggin was photoshopped by followers on to the bodies of – amongst others – James Bond, Ross Poldark, and Rambo – often in a state of semi-undress. The following day Ed Miliband formally recognised the craze, but skipped over the images and stuck to the substance. He tweeted the founder:

> @twcuddleston It's good to hear young people who care about politics speaking up for the things they believe in. Ed Miliband (@Ed_Miliband) April 22, 2015

@twcuddleston There's a lot at stake at this election for young people. I hope more young people will join you & get involved. #VoteLabour Ed Miliband (@Ed_Miliband) April 22, 2015

It was a clever use of social media – largely because the Labour Party hadn't thought of it themselves. So there was no 'trendy vicar' element to it – it was by, and for, young women and teenage girls and the party could simply ooze enthusiasm for it. Abby Tomlinson's followers on Twitter leapt to 11,000 in a week and at last count exceeded 31,000. But many of these may have been below the voting age at the time of the election, and in the end Labour were very nearly two million votes behind the Conservatives. So while first Buzzfeed, then mainstream media, enthusiastically reported the phenomenon, it probably didn't shift significant numbers of votes.

Abby finally met up with Ed Miliband at the Commons in June and, appropriately enough, announced on Twitter: 'They say "Never meet your idols" because they won't live up to expectations. I however completely disagree, @Ed_Miliband exceeded mine.'

They then took, you guessed it, selfies. Miliband in his resignation speech had acknowledged the role Milifandom had played in the campaign, calling it 'the most unlikely cult of the 21st century.' Abby subsequently backed Andy Burnham as his successor.

Milifandom might well have been a successful way of engaging young people in politics. But another rather more blatant, top-down approach designed to achieve the same thing later in the campaign would turn out to be far less successful. In fact if you'll pardon the pun, it may have diminished the Labour Brand.

Blood on his Hands,
Blood on the Carpet

24 April

- Ed Miliband is accused of smearing the Prime Minister.
- But Labour had big internal battles too over Ed Miliband's foreign policy address.
- The new leader Jeremy Corbyn will try to emerge from the shadow of Iraq by apologising for British participation.

IT WAS A SPEECH about conflicts – and it created a few of its own. The idea was straightforward: in order to appear statesmanlike, Ed Miliband had to deliver an address at some point in the campaign on foreign affairs. His whole team agreed to that. It would be at Chatham House in central London. In diplomatic and political circles, 'Chatham House rules' mean you can say whatever you like when you are there, however controversial, and it won't be attributed to you publicly. Sadly for Ed Miliband this otherwise convenient arrangement was put aside when he chose to give a televised speech. Sections of it had been briefed to the press the night before, which Labour spin doctors regarded as relatively innocuous and simply a way of underlining Miliband's far from obvious foreign policy *bona fides*.

This in fact is exactly what was pre-briefed on Libya:

> He (Miliband) will say the refugee crisis and tragic scenes this week in the Mediterranean are in part a direct result of the failure of post conflict planning for Libya. David Cameron was wrong to assume that Libya's political culture and institutions could be left to evolve and transform on their own. The tragedy is this should have been anticipated, it could have been avoided.

Conservative spin doctors, especially those closest to David Cameron, saw these words as an opportunity to turn the tide on Ed Miliband. There had indeed been tragic scenes of migrants from Africa failing to get across the Mediterranean to a new life in Europe. The fortunate ones were picked up at sea, many others drowned. So those close to Cameron picked up on the phrase 'could have been avoided' and called the broadcasters – was Ed Miliband suggesting the Prime Minister had 'blood on his hands'? Miliband was forced on the defensive and asked about this at the press conference which followed his speech. His own failure to raise the deteriorating situation in Libya and at sea at prime minister's questions also came under scrutiny. None of this had been intended. As one adviser said:

> If we had wanted to smear the Prime Minister, believe me, we wouldn't
> have buried it on page three of a press release about a foreign policy speech.

That row was very public, and was widely reported. What got less attention at the time were the rows at the very top of the Labour Party well before the speech was to be delivered. Ed Miliband and Stewart Wood were keen to use the speech as a way for Labour to 'move on' from the Iraq war, but just about every other adviser felt that would be a wasted opportunity so close to polling day as the issue wasn't desperately resonant with voters now. Alastair Campbell, Tom Baldwin and the general election co-ordinator Douglas Alexander all argued that now was the moment to take the battle to the SNP as well as the Conservatives. The concept was to have a 'big speech' which would be about defending the UK's position in Europe – something they would allege that David Cameron couldn't do – and defending the integrity of the UK at home by strengthening the attack on the SNP. It would have accused the Prime Minister of putting party interests ahead of the national interest – caving in to Eurosceptic demands for a referendum, and fuelling Scottish nationalism with his plan for English Votes for English Laws. Campbell had already volunteered to put pen to paper.

What followed – in the words of one insider – was 'an almighty f***ing row.' General election chairman Spencer Livermore and newsman Bob Roberts strongly felt that further mention of the SNP would add fuel to a fire that was difficult enough to extinguish and it should be denied the oxygen of publicity. In the end one of the combatants said the two sides ended up with a 'no score draw' and a much weaker speech was delivered.

There was just one mention of the SNP, in this context:

> The Conservatives are now trying to do everything they can to talk up
> the prospects of the SNP and pit English nationalism against Scottish
> nationalism. Let me be clear: this is incredibly dangerous for our country.

There were six mentions of Iraq, including a reference to learning the lessons of the 2003 war. Jeremy Corbyn would at least be less conflicted about how to handle a foreign policy speech. There is little doubt he would not have heeded advice to 'don't mention the war'. By criticising Britain's involvement, he would at least have cheered his supporters – though it's unclear that 'swing' voters would feel so passionately.

As Ed Miliband left the venue, a silent group of Conservative activists were outside, this time sporting not Alex Salmond but Nicola Sturgeon masks. A senior Conservative strategist told me that, with her heightened profile, she was seen as even more noxious in the seats they had to win than the former SNP leader, so new likenesses had been ordered. It clearly wasn't entirely in Ed Miliband's power to decide when to shut up about the SNP.

New Town Blues

25 April

- Ed Miliband visits the new town of Stevenage – said to be a 'textbook' local campaign.
- Labour activists have a higher number of conversations with voters than ever before.
- The party will fail to win the seat.
- The next leader needs to look at the message, not just the numbers of messengers.

I WASN'T IN the best of moods. Awake from 5.30am, I had to be in Stevenage, the new town in Hertfordshire which was now looking rather jaded, by 7.30am that Saturday morning – and the weather had just turned. Spring seemed to have slipped back towards winter. The wind got up as the rain fell down. Ed Miliband had slipped in an extra 'campaign stop' before his scheduled appearance at the Gallipoli commemorations in central London. The event had been due to be held in the open air but the inclement weather meant that around 100 activists has to crowd into a tiny community hall off the historic high street – the Victorian and Georgian oasis in the desert of 20th century concrete.

As a cloud continued to hang over me as much as the town, I decided to start work on a 'behind the scenes' piece that had been commissioned by the *One O'Clock News*, to be shown later in the campaign.

So before Ed Miliband and entourage arrived, we filmed the full nature of the event – party members arriving and having their names checked off on a list, being issued with badges and stickers and posters, and then awaiting their leaders' arrival so they could cheer him like some returning hero from a battle for the benefit of the TV cameras. No non-party members had been asked along. Too often just a 'clip' of a party leader is shown and it's not always transparent that they are addressing party loyalists and not the public so we had decided to inform viewers of just how controlled and choreographed a campaign can be.

Ed Miliband spoke for around ten minutes and delivered the message we had now heard for many weeks. 'Britain works best when it works for working people. That's what we are fighting for – that's why we need a Labour government.' After an initial reluctance his minders conceded that he would take two media questions, one from me and one from Sophy Ridge, a colleague from Sky.

He was asked about – and promptly ridiculed – Nick Clegg's latest red lines for a coalition deal.

And I asked him about the topic of the day – further warnings over privatisation of the NHS if David Cameron remained in Downing Street and a new limit on the amount of income NHS hospitals could gain from treating private patients. But at the end of a lacklustre week of NHS stories there was little interest from TV or radio programmes to broadcast this.

That's not to say Labour at this stage felt the campaign was going badly. The candidate here – Sharon Taylor – thought there was a 50/50 chance of success. Gordon Brown had campaigned in Stevenage in the 2010 election when Barbara Follett had just stood down as the MP. She hadn't seemed to be a natural fit with the constituency. She was an image consultant, originally from South Africa, who had taught a generation of aspiring female politicians how to 'power dress' – but those garishly bright broad shouldered suits even then looked as contemporary as a New Romantic's hairstyle. She was also married to millionaire novelist Ken Follett. Nonetheless she had held the seat since 1997 and perhaps reflected the aspirational nature of some of her constituents. She had been replaced by Sharon Taylor – the leader of the borough council – who lost by 3,578 votes to the Conservatives.

But now morale amongst the door knockers and envelope stuffers of Stevenage's Labour party was high and their enthusiasm and openness penetrated my earlier gloom as I stayed behind to chat once their leader had moved on. Taylor had been a councillor since 1997 so had fought many local campaigns, and felt that the often under-reported Labour ground war had been going well.

They had contacted 700 voters locally in just one day and 15,000 since the campaign began. While in 2010 doors had been shut in her face, now at least people were willing to listen. Nationally, incidentally, Labour claimed to have contacted in excess of four million voters at this stage – or twice as many than at the last general election.

Richard Henry, the constituency chair, said he had seen a change in attitude towards Ed Miliband.

> He was elected as leader so narrowly and we all knew David much better than Ed. I met him a few times since and I think party members began coming round to him a couple of years ago. I think it's fair to say it's taken members of the public quite a bit longer but in the past few weeks support has been hardening up as they began to see fairer media coverage and see a bit if what he's really like. He did do a public meeting here a few months back and faced some pretty hostile questioning. But he handled it well and some people who were never Labour supporters

thought they might vote Labour now because they had met him. Until then they believed the papers that he couldn't become prime minister.

Some at the top of the party had been urging Miliband to do more of these genuinely open meetings, rather than spending so much time talking to the hand-picked audiences he had addressed today. As well as a target for activists to hold five million conversations, they had wanted Miliband to speak at 2,500 events. But it's not clear that would have been the best use of his time – as what had been regarded as a highly successful meeting in Stevenage wouldn't lead to a successful outcome on polling day.

Indeed, Labour's head office had regarded Stevenage as a textbook campaign. It just culminated in the wrong result. What this highlighted for some of the most senior figures in the party is that however many salespeople you have, however committed they are, they have to be touting a product people want to buy. And in Stevenage and many other seats in the South, where middle income people were struggling with mortgages payments and the cost of childcare not zero hours contracts or with the DWP, the national message had too little to say that it was relevant to their lives – even if they did warm a little to the main messenger, Ed Miliband.

And this experience seems to have been shared by candidates in some other seats Labour failed to win. In the pamphlet *Never Again* – published by the Labour-affiliated think tank the Fabian Society in August – the failed candidate for Northampton North, Sally Keeble, argued:

> We had our targets to achieve in voter contact, and sometimes these seemed overwhelming. A small dedicated team mobilised volunteers to contact many thousands of voters. But the swing voters knew they were electing not just an MP but a government, and the ground war wasn't enough… along with a credible leader we need a big picture that will appeal beyond our core vote.

Generation Rent

25 April

- Labour devises a policy aimed at engaging non-voters and new voters.
- There's another 'retail offer' of a rent cap.
- Fears are raised that Labour has little to say to more affluent voters.
- Labour's new leader is also committed to controlling rents, but will still have a challenge to get transient families to vote.

IT WAS AN ATTEMPT to open up a new front. While we were in Stevenage where Labour's latest NHS 'story' had failed to gain traction, back at Labour HQ in London, Tom Baldwin was preparing to brief on another audacious intervention in the market – one that would make the headlines.

Almost a year previously, Ed Miliband had first talked of 'Generation Rent' and had come up with proposals to introduce more secure three year tenancies in the private rented sector in England. There were plenty of exemptions, including the right for a landlord to regain their property for use as their principal residence. He based this on a similar system which had existed for a decade in Ireland and which had also tipped the relationship between landlord and tenant a little on the latter's behalf.

And despite warnings there, it hadn't led to a dramatic loss of properties from the market. But irrespective of any effect on demand and supply, there was a belief that policies which would point up that Labour at least 'felt the pain' – and would articulate the concerns – of private tenants was good politics on a number of fronts.

First, it would be part of Ed Miliband's project to move his party 'beyond New Labour' – which had too often not done enough to regulate markets – and would underscore his message to stand up for working people. Second, there had been an astonishing explosion in private renting over the past decade or so, with the English Housing Survey suggesting that the number of households living in rented accommodation had almost doubled to 4.5 million since 2002 as house prices in some parts of the country had soared. Third, there could be potentially a source of untapped support amongst private tenants – it had been estimated that, with insecure tenancies, more than 40 per cent of them hadn't registered to vote at the last election.

While Ed Miliband had also raised the issue of rent levels in May 2014 it had been decided to keep the 'retail offer' for the election. Around 4.00pm I got a call from Tom Baldwin to tell me what it was. An incoming Labour government would impose a three-year real-terms freeze on rents. Aware the policy would be controversial, I reported Labour's intentions on the *Ten O'Clock News* that night having swiftly gathered some reaction.

Landlords' associations warned that further regulation would reduce investment in the sector and ultimately the supply of much needed rented accommodation. But Labour had given core supporters another reason to make the trip to the ballot box and had created another dividing line – that tactic much favoured by Ed Miliband's old boss Gordon Brown – with the Conservatives. The swiftness and severity of the reaction from the communities secretary Eric Pickles delighted Labour most of all as they could portray him as out of touch. He tweeted that: 'Rent control appears to be the most efficient technique presently known to destroy a city. Except for bombing.'

Never mind that he was paraphrasing a left-of-centre Swedish economist, Assar Lindbeck.

Critics now say that the policy betrayed an obsession Ed Miliband had with winning the support of non-voters rather than concentrating on getting people to switch from voting Conservative.

And while the policy might well deal with market failure, taken together with more restrictive labour laws, higher corporate taxes and a new levy on high value homes the overall message focussed on helping the poorest at the expense of the better-off.

But what should have been even more worrying for Labour wasn't a critical reaction to their policy on renting; it was the lack of any sustained reaction. Yes, I had 'broken' it on the TV news. But their inability to kill off continued speculation over whether they would need life support from the SNP for a minority government came home to me when I was asked to set out on Radio 4's PM programme what I understood to be Labour's position in a hung parliament. Yet I had been asked to do the same thing for the BBC website – almost a week before. To Labour's great frustration, neither the papers nor broadcast media were growing tired of the speculation. And the next day would begin in much the same way for Labour – with talk not of rent controls, but the degree of control Nicola Sturgeon might exercise over Ed Miliband.

Marred by the SNP Myth

26 April

- The Conservative charge that Ed Miliband would be 'held to ransom by the SNP' is proving difficult to kill.
- Miliband hardens Labour's rhetoric but to no avail.
- The party's strategists feel that post-election speculation is smothering their campaign.

SLAYING THE MULTI-HEADED hydra would have been an easier task than killing off the Conservative charge that a weak Labour government would be 'held to ransom' by the SNP. Ruling out a coalition deal hadn't done it. The creature had come back stronger than ever. So a new weapon was tried on the BBC's *Andrew Marr Show* this morning as the speculation – like the hydra's breath – continued to suffocate Labour's campaign.

What had been implicit was made explicit. That there would be no 'confidence and supply' arrangement as well as no coalition. This type of 'deal' would have meant SNP support for Labour's budget and the broad thrust of its legislative programme, outlined in a Queen's Speech, in return for concessions – but no joint programme for government, and no SNP ministers. So Ed Miliband now extended his familiar mantra from 'no coalitions' to 'no coalitions, no tie-ins.'

Andrew Marr asked him explicitly about 'confidence and supply' – though he used slightly different terminology: 'What about a Supply and Support deal?' To which there was a catch-all response from the Labour leader: 'I have said no deals, honestly.'

Then, for the avoidance of doubt, Ed Miliband continued: 'It's going to be a Labour Queen's Speech, a Labour budget, I couldn't be any clearer than that.'

Ed Miliband had been warned by his close constitutional confidant Lord Falconer not to go quite this far earlier in the campaign, but with the issue not abating even he agreed by this stage that it would be necessary to try to close it down as much as possible by whatever means possible. There was a danger that Labour wouldn't have the luxury of working out how to handle the Nationalists in government – because unless they could prove they could handle them in opposition, Ed Miliband wouldn't be in office.

The word went out to any Labour politician taking part in TV or radio debates with the SNP to keep any off-air remarks to the bland and predictable. Do not talk about anything that might happen after the election, they were instructed.

The many heads of the hydra, however, laughed in Labour's face. Ed Miliband had used one of the most powerful weapons he had kept in reserve – and stab at it as he did, he still couldn't kill the beast.

A Trip to the Theatre

26 April

- Two former Labour leaders who failed to win elections urge support for Ed Miliband.
- The campaign occupies its 'comfort zone' but gains little coverage.
- The next leader will have to broaden the party's base.

'SHE IS LABOUR ROYALTY'. That's how Matthew Laza – the party's energetic broadcasting officer – described Ed Miliband's right-hand woman Rachel Kinnock. Well, today much of the royal family were out in force. Rachel herself had come to recce the venue. Her mother and father, Neil and Glenys Kinnock, were in the front row. And I ran in to a former courtier – or lynchpin of the then leader of the Opposition's office – Neil Stewart in the bar. He was bemoaning Labour's likely fate in Scotland.

The venue was the Almeida Theatre in Islington. The performance wasn't the newly revived David Hare play *Absence of War* – which charts how a Labour leader who fails to be true to himself then fails to win an election. Instead it was something altogether less challenging. It was a rally for international development.

There was mild panic when the disgraced ex-Labour MP and indeed ex-con Denis MacShane was spotted by party staff outside. He was intent on going in and I had a brief chat with him. He had come to praise Ed Miliband, not bury him. He observed that the electorate would normally give an incumbent government a second chance but whatever the outcome Miliband had fought a surprisingly good fight and steadfastly faced down those calling for an EU referendum. Not wishing to cause embarrassment he would take in proceedings from the circle – accessed by a separate entrance – rather than watch from the main body of the hall.

The crowded event got under way hosted by former EastEnder Ross Kemp. Labour were deep in their comfort zone. Or discomfort zone. The Almeida had had a refurb and the seats were certainly softer than before. I remember coming to a performance of Brecht's *Life of Galileo* here some years ago and it felt like I was sitting on a spike. When the Inquisition showed him the instruments, I was praying they would instead finish him off quickly so I could get a nice comfy seat in the pub across the road, which has now become a designer clothes shop. But there were other reasons to be discomfited. Speaker after speaker – such as the Shadow

International Development Secretary Mary Creagh and the former Secretary of State Baroness Amos – set out the horrors of child poverty and the
high rates not just of infant mortality but of mothers dying in child birth
in Sub-Saharan Africa.

The only lighter moments came in a video message from Gordon
Brown who recalled meeting Nelson Mandela along with the late singer/
songwriter Amy Winehouse. 'You have got a lot in common with my
husband' she tells a surprised South African leader. 'How so?' he inquires
politely. 'You have both spent ages in prison'. In another video message
comedian Eddie Izzard observed that just 85 people own as much wealth
as one half of the world's population, and concluded 'this is not good'.

The star turn was, of course, Ed Miliband himself. And he wasn't here
to deliver a counterintuitive message. He wasn't going to tell the audience
that he couldn't promise to defend the international development budget
until he had got the deficit down. Quite the reverse. He repeated that
spending on foreign aid – along with health and education – would be
protected. And he made clear it would be an early priority of his premiership to go to the UN general assembly in September and argue that other
developed nations should raise their aid budgets to 0.7 per cent of GDP.
And all this in the constituency represented by Emily Thornberry, the
shadow minister who had allegedly so provoked Ed's ire that she had to
resign her post for the offence of snootily tweeting a photo of a white van
and an England flag outside a voter's home at the previous year's Roches-
ter byelection.

So now we had the spectacle of a current Labour leader being cheered
by a past Labour leader who failed to win an election, having been praised
on video by another leader who had failed to win an election, surrounded
by Labour luvvies, in a left liberal metropolitan suburb.

It was easy meat for opponents but in fact the event got very little
coverage in part due to the London Marathon, a football match at the
nearby Emirates stadium, and emerging news of a genuine overseas emergency in Nepal – a devastating earthquake. If this had been an event to
reinforce Labour's values and reinvigorate grass roots support, back at
base Ed Miliband's staff had been working on a sixth election pledge
designed to appeal to aspirational voters that hadn't yet decided whom to
back. By mid-afternoon I knew what it was. And it would be unveiled far
away from the reassuringly supportive atmosphere of north London.

Building Non-Traditional Support

27 April

- Labour launches a sixth election pledge.
- It's a late attempt to appeal to aspirational voters outside south-east England.
- Labour's new leader will have to make the party more relevant to those who are striving to improve their lives.

THE VENUE WAS certainly aspirational. It was Stockton's equivalent of the Almeida Theatre – the Arc, an arts centre and auditorium. Bean burgers and bruschetta were on the menu of its cafe. Ed Miliband at last had an answer to those critics who said his policies ignored those struggling to get on in life. It was neither a policy for those on benefits, nor for the metropolitan elite. The short-hand sixth pledge was 'Homes to Buy and Action on Rents' but the substance was the temporary abolition of stamp duty for all first time buyers purchasing a home worth less than £300,000. So it would be of limited help in high-cost London, but potentially attractive here on Teeside, where Labour were hopeful of ousting James Wharton – the Conservative MP who tried to pilot his EU referendum bill through the last parliament – from his Stockton South seat.

Campaign director Spencer Livermore admitted:

> Our policy offer was far too narrowly focused. We all knew it but Ed wanted to campaign on the issues he cared about and that was his prerogative as leader. But we took whatever opportunities we could to broaden the agenda.

Ed Miliband was resistant to using the word 'aspirational' – which would become a staple of some of his potential successors' vocabularies – but the new pledge enabled him to promise to 'restore the dream of home ownership'.

* * *

Since 2011, some close to him had been pushing him to address an erosion in Labour support amongst what were termed 'new homemakers' – and a senior party staffer was shocked to hear that he was indicating that he had little intention 'to do what my brother would have done.' So in reality today's policy was really another 'back of the fag packet' retail offer rather than a strategic broadening of the campaign. It had long been decided to unveil a sixth election pledge at some point in the campaign to inject momentum and ensure that any impression of novelty and fresh thinking didn't die after the manifesto launch. But it had been by no means settled that the pledge would be on housing. To an extent hamstrung by the self-denying ordnance that nothing in the manifesto would require additional borrowing or spending, it was felt that an expensive rabbit – a mink, perhaps – could not be pulled out of a hat later in the campaign. So Ed Balls in particular was said to be sceptical that a low-cost but attractive enough offer on housing could be found. Labour's sixth pledge in 2005 had been on immigration, where it had been perceived as weak but this time there already was an immigration pledge. There had previously been talk of a fuel duty freeze, as this could drive Labour onto Conservative territory, and might even appeal to owners of those vehicles that Islington's Emily Thornberry liked to photograph.

In the end, tackling tax avoidance from landlords – and charging non-EU residents a higher rate of stamp duty for property purchases here – raised enough to offer extra help for first time buyers. Labour had criticised the effect on the market of the government's Help to Buy scheme and plans to extend the right to buy to housing association tenants so now they finally had something more, and more positive, to say to aspiring homeowners. But for some – such as John Prescott, and subsequently Andy Burnham – the policy wasn't radical enough. They would have preferred to build on schemes which enabled renters to acquire an increasing share in their home until they reached, if they wished, complete ownership. But as one strategist put it: 'Look, it gave us a decent headline for half a day. And it fulfilled Spencer Livermore's wish to get us talking about something other than the SNP.'

Labour's Brand Problem

28 April

- Ed Miliband tries to appeal to non-voters by meeting 'Mr No Vote' Russell Brand.
- Newspaper coverage is disastrous.
- Note to new leader: You can be judged by the company you keep.

THERE'S AN OLD adage that there are no shortcuts to electoral success – but some in Labour's top team must have felt they had found one. A third of those registered to vote declined to do so on polling day but some of Miliband's advisers believed it was worth trying to tap this potential reservoir of support. So who better to persuade non-voters to vote than perhaps the best known non-voter of all, apart from the Queen? Celebrity comedian and self-styled revolutionary Russell Brand abstains from alcohol and the democratic process but what if he could be persuaded just to take a tiny sip from the voting well? After years of laying off, would it rush to his head and – who knows what might happen – could he headily endorse Ed Miliband? And he has more than ten million followers on Twitter – more people than, in the end, actually voted Labour. So could he – like a trade union baron of old – move his bloc of (former) non-voters into Labour's camp?

Views on the venture were split. Lucy Powell, Vice-Chair of the election campaign, had been approached by Brand for an interview with Ed Miliband, so she discussed whether this could be a serendipitous key to unlocking potential support that had been hard to reach. She knew it wasn't without risk, but Miliband himself seemed confident that personally canvassing this non-voter could bring benefits. Newsman Bob Roberts was much more sceptical. On balance, it was decided to make the trip – actually Brand doesn't do drugs either – to the comic activist's trendy Shoreditch pad. Miliband recorded an interview for Brand's YouTube channel *The Trews*.

There was clearly a degree of nervousness, as those of us following the Miliband campaign around the country weren't told about it in advance. Neither were very senior members of the Shadow Cabinet. Together, we only discovered it had taken place because the car sent to spirit Miliband away from Shoreditch was delayed and he became a victim of the social media he sought to exploit when this message appeared on Twitter: 'A friend of mine lives opposite Russell Brand and snapped this picture of Ed Miliband leaving his house...'

But on the surface what had gone on inside the house had been a success. And several days later, Brand uploaded an 'emergency' message. Although he acknowledged he was 'Mr Don't Vote', and disagreed with Labour on Trident, he dispensed some very specific advice. If you live in Brighton, back the Greens' Caroline Lucas. If you live in Scotland, as an Englishman he wasn't going to tell you what to do. 'But anywhere else, you gotta vote Labour.'

Had masses of young people flocked to the polls, in retrospect this would have been a masterstroke. But they didn't. Instead, it gave a hostile press the excuse for a field day, delivering what one adviser termed 'Kinnock-type coverage.' One front page pictured the two men beside the headline: 'Do you really want this clown ruling us? And, no we don't mean the one on the left' (ie Russell Brand). Worse, it allowed David Cameron to pour scorn:

> Politics, and life, and elections, and jobs, and the economy. It's not a joke.
> Russell Brand is a joke. Ed Miliband hung out with Russell Brand. He's
> a joke. I haven't got time to hang out with Russell Brand.

So the careful attempts to create a prime ministerial image for Ed Miliband – the avoidance of 'weird' food, the eschewing of factories and premises where health and safety laws might require him to wear a hair net – were all negated by this one encounter, according to some of his closest advisers. One aide called it 'naff and desperate.' Bob Roberts goes further – even rating it as one of the biggest mistakes of the campaign, helping to further alienate older voters:

> People in their 50s and 60s were appalled that a future prime minister
> was meeting someone who was anti-democratic and they saw as not very
> pleasant.

Post-election, Russell Brand posted a video message appearing to show some contrition. Mimicking Miliband he says: 'Thank you Russell Brand for f***ing up the election by getting me to come round your house.'

Dangerous Territory

29 April

- Labour defends tax credits despite some evidence they are losing the argument on welfare.
- Party strategists fear their opponents' plans aren't getting enough scrutiny.
- Private polling suggests Labour's support is lower than in published polling.

IT HAD ALWAYS been planned. A return to the safe but fertile terrain of how Labour would address what it called a 'cost of living crisis' in the final week of the campaign. At one of its few London press conferences – flanked by his Shadow Chancellor and Shadow Work and Pensions Secretary, Rachel Reeves – Ed Miliband announced that tax credits would rise at least in line with inflation. This was consistent with his stated aim of governing on behalf of working people. It might indeed motivate that core vote. But in the past fortnight in English marginal constituencies the Labour leader had been reiterating his message of fiscal responsibility.

It was perhaps too tempting not to be seen to stand up for those in work who still needed state support to help their families. Later that day, the Lib Dem Chief Secretary to the Treasury, Danny Alexander, would release edited highlights of a document he claimed was commissioned by David Cameron in 2012 and which had been presented to the Quad – himself, Cameron, Clegg and Osborne – for their consideration. Alexander said the Lib Dems had vetoed it – the Conservatives that they never considered adopting the contents as a package. But the document did provide a clue as to how the Conservatives' aim of saving £12 billion from the welfare budget might be – at least in part – achieved: limiting child benefit and child tax credits to families with up to two children, and paying child benefit for both children at the lower rate which currently applied to the second child. Though the dossier wouldn't appear in the papers until the next day, Labour knew it was coming.

But in riding to the rescue of working families, Ed Miliband appeared to be ignoring polling evidence from marginal seats.

Focus groups carried out by Lord Ashcroft – the wealthy former Conservative deputy chairman – suggested that swing voters were indeed worried about the cost of living and found austerity – in the peer's words

– 'disagreeable'. But they were every bit as concerned that Labour in government would spend too much and tax too much. Furthermore, YouGov's polling suggested a policy of limiting child benefit to two children would be popular – with two-thirds of voters approving of it, including a majority of Labour voters. And rival polling company Comres was finding that in the 50 most marginal Conservative seats – where Labour had come second in 2010 – three in five voters were concerned about the influence the SNP would have over a minority Labour government. So the message, broadly, was don't tack to the left, and remind voters fiscal responsibility was on the front page of the manifesto.

But Ed Miliband was receiving competing advice. Key aide and Shadow Minister Jonathan Ashworth – Gordon Brown's former political secretary – was a lynchpin in the relationship between his leader and the wider party and he was picking up at this stage in the campaign a difficulty in converting undecided voters in to Labour supporters.

These were people on modest incomes in small and medium-sized towns or living in new housing estates on the edges of towns who had declared themselves Labour in 2010 and who were, at the very least thinking twice now. Although in work, some of these voters relied on tax credits to boost their income. So it was important that something was done to 'scare them off voting Tory.' Warning of risks to their in-work benefits might contain the magic formula.

Ed Balls agreed. Or rather, he believed this whole attack should have begun much, much earlier. He was appearing alongside his namesake for only the second time in the campaign. He had – despite his willingness – only rarely been brought in to strategy meetings to discuss the election. He had been more or less allowed to do his own thing, with the campaign team showing scant interest in the content of his speeches. He had gone round marginal seats warning voters of the risks of a Conservative government but felt his own leader had been too reluctant to do the same.

At its core, Ed Miliband was uncomfortable with the idea of tax credits. He was influenced by the work of the American academic Jacob Hacker who coined the term 'pre-distribution.' He believed that employers, and not just the state, should have responsibility for lifting employees out of poverty, though governments could help provide the skills which would enable workers to command higher wages. Although he had worked for the creator of tax credits, Gordon Brown, Miliband bought the notion that the system subsidised low wages. So he was far more reluctant than Balls to defend it. But for Balls this was really all about taking the fight to the Conservatives, and possible cuts to tax credits – and therefore in some swing voters' incomes – was a way to do it.

So it was agreed between the two Eds to lambast what they would portray as a likely assault by the Conservatives on the working poor. But the Shadow Chancellor was frustrated by how his leader prosecuted the battle and felt the attack had been blunted.

For Ed Miliband, this was more about trust than about benefits.

The Conservatives had set out only £2 billion of their proposed £12 billion reductions to the welfare budget. So while the official line – sent round on social media by Labour – was that 'child benefit was on the ballot paper' at the election, this was about more than the future of one benefit. After all he – along with Ed Balls – had been content to announce what amounted to a real terms freeze in child benefit to demonstrate Labour's ability to 'take tough decisions'. And a Labour government wouldn't be restoring it to those households where one person earned more than £60,000. In the end despite a negative assessment of Gordon Brown, voters hadn't trusted the Conservatives to form a majority government in 2010 and Ed Miliband would argue that – with secret agendas on cuts – David Cameron's party shouldn't be trusted again.

Perhaps each by a different route, both Eds were nonetheless bringing Labour back on to their traditional territory. David Cameron and George Osborne were saying a Conservative-only government, free from Lib Dem shackles, wouldn't increase tax rates and would cut the welfare bill – whereas Labour had already set out some tax rises and were now promising to uprate benefits. More of this was to come – and some in Labour's ranks believe it may well have contributed to keeping a few closely fought marginals blue on 7 May. Although the party's message was aimed primarily at those in receipt of in-work benefits, some candidates believed the leadership instead should have done more to shed its pro-welfare image, however unfairly it had been acquired. Will Straw, who failed to win Rossendale and Darwen in Lancashire for Labour, set out his views in the Fabian pamphlet *Never Again*:

> Wherever I turned there was a palpable sense that the welfare system was devoid of any sense of contribution… People wanted to know what Labour would do about the family down the street on benefits who'd 'never done an honest day's work in their life'. It might make us feel uncomfortable and it might be unfair, but the public thought that we were on the side of people who don't work… Ed Miliband famously forgot to mention the deficit in his 2014 conference speech. He didn't even plan to talk about the welfare system. He should have been saying 'Labour – the party of work – the clue is in the name… I want to teach my kids that it is wrong to be idle on benefits.'

Labour strategists close to both Eds felt there was another reason that not enough of those marginals had been turning from blue to red. And that is the prism though which the press were reporting the election – aided by what turned out to be inaccurate polling. As voters either believed – or believed they were being told – that a hung parliament was a given, they focused on what a Labour government, being dragged to the left by 'Lady in Red' Nicola Sturgeon, would do to their taxes. Had the papers been reporting polls which suggested the Conservatives might be capable of winning a majority then the focus may have been less on taxes and more on tax credits – and George Osborne's plans to restrict them. While Andrew Marr and other colleagues did a masterful job of interrogating the chancellor over his planned welfare cuts and pushed for more detail, Labour felt that this line of inquiry wasn't getting the same prominence as the working assumption that they would lock Cameron out of Downing Street. Tom Baldwin had felt this had skewed the nature of the campaign:

> In the final three weeks of the campaign, the only risk that voters were being told about was that of a Labour/SNP deal. There was very little debate about the risk of a Tory second term, let alone an overall Conservative majority so our stories about what would happen to tax credits or the NHS just did not gain traction.

So Labour could indeed have five million conversations, or more, on welfare cuts but too few people who might suffer from them actually believed they would happen.

Labour's pollster James Morris told me that his own internal surveys tended to put the party's support lower than the published polls. The fact that public polls flattered Labour's position proved damaging because it opened them up to more scrutiny than the Conservatives, with fewer people focussing on what that party would do, freed from the constraints of coalition.

But Labour's treasury team – and Ed Balls in particular – believed the party leadership had to take more responsibility for how the election was being reported. Swing voters in English seats were indeed concerned that a rampant SNP would drag Labour further from the centre ground. Ed Miliband was distancing himself further and further from Nicola Sturgeon, but not leading from the front in implanting the notion of a risk from the right, and not just from the left. There was huge frustration that while Ed Miliband would often make a cursory joke at David Cameron's expense at the start of his speeches, he would then do far too little to warn of the Conservatives' plans. So for many of the 'don't knows' amongst the electorate, the risk of a minority Labour government was playing heavily in their minds with no countervailing threat to weigh up.

No Question of Deals

30 April

- Ed Miliband indicates he would rather not be in office than deal with the SNP.
- Critics say this approach is counter-productive and Jeremy Corbyn may need to revisit it.

'THEY WEREN'T TELLING us whether we were f***ed, or how to avoid being f***ed. All they told us were the different ways that we were being f***ed.' That's verbatim – but an abridged version of a senior official's assessment of what Labour's focus groups in Scotland were telling him.

The switch from trying to win 'soft' SNP support or win back former Labour voters to seeking the support of anti-independence 'switchers' from other parties was having only very, very limited success. The emphasis was now moving more decisively to shoring up the Labour vote in England. With focus groups there showing key voters were still both credulous of, and concerned about, the prospect a minority Labour government being at the mercy of the SNP it was decided to toughen the stance. Douglas Alexander, representing a Scottish seat, knew that even tougher rhetoric towards the SNP might upset former Labour voters who had backed the 'Yes' campaign. But that ship had not only sailed, it was well over the horizon while it was hoped that some support south of the border that was drifting away might yet be steered towards a safe haven. So as general election co-ordinator he sanctioned an even harder line towards the SNP.

The vehicle for delivering the message was to be the final televised encounter of the campaign. It was to be a special edition of BBC *Question Time* – special not least because the participants wouldn't be sitting round the familiar table with veteran host David Dimbleby, and with each other. To accommodate the Prime Minister's demands, David Cameron, Nick Clegg and Ed Miliband would each face the audience separately for a 30-minute grilling. There would be no question of a debate between the three party leaders. Given the now indisputable resonance of the SNP question in English marginal seats, it was anticipated the issue would arise from the audience. And it did when Simon Wilkinson asked Ed Miliband why the Labour party was misleading the country over a deal with the SNP. The Labour leader was fully prepared, though rather disingenuously he suggested his message was aimed at the Scottish electorate when he declared: 'I want to say this to voters in Scotland...' when in fact just about everything which followed was aimed at voters further south: 'Let me be plain. We're not going to do a deal with the Scottish National Party; we're not going to have a coalition, we're not going to have a deal.'

But then he went further: 'Let me just say this to you – if it meant we weren't going to be in government, not doing a coalition, not having a deal, then so be it.'

Just to underline that, he raised two fundamental issues on which he disagreed with Nicola Sturgeon – renewing Britain's Scottish-based nuclear weapons, and reducing the deficit. He could not have had a harder line towards the SNP than to suggest he would rather sacrifice a stint in Number 10 than reach an accommodation on an iota of their policy programme.

Nicola Sturgeon was quick to respond. She said: 'He sounded as if he was saying that he would rather see David Cameron and the Conservatives back in government than actually work with the SNP.' She knew that this approach would chime with those 'No' voters in Scotland who felt that there just wasn't 'enough of a difference' between Cameron and Miliband and who were looking to the SNP to be 'Stronger for Scotland'. Labour expected to take a hit in Scotland, and their focus groups duly delivered quite a whack. What was more surprising is that the tactic wasn't more successful in England. Partly this can be explained by a lack of consistency – a sense that Labour was getting dragged almost against its will towards a tougher position – from a position of no coalition, to no deal of any kind, to no government at all, if need be. In other words the party and Miliband in particular always seemed to be on the back foot and not arguing from a position of principle.

But a senior SNP official felt this move towards the toughest possible stance could have achieved the very opposite of what Labour intended, and cost them support in England. By in effect buying into the Conservative narrative that the SNP were somehow beyond the pale, that they were indeed people with nefarious objectives and with whom you could have no working relationship, voters in English marginal seats were then invited to consider who would be stronger in resisting the demands of these barbaric hordes. And the answer, it would appear, was the Conservatives. Labour privately expected to be able to 'lock out' the Tories from Downing Street but wouldn't publicly extol the benefits of a 'progressive majority.' Labour never challenged the terms of the debate set by the incumbent in Downing Street – that this would be something to be feared rather than embraced.

And the former Labour first minister of Scotland, Henry McLeish, agrees that this approach had been damaging to his party in Scotland:

> Ed should have said from the beginning that he wanted a mandate to govern and that he would speak to anyone to keep the menace of the Tories out – it was a serious error to say in the end he would speak to the SNP over his dead body – it made Labour seem out of touch.

A senior Shadow Cabinet member who was involved in discussions on how to handle Labour's SNP threat came to the conclusion that the stronger line – while worth a shot – ultimately lacked authenticity in the eyes of the electorate:

> We were treating the SNP as being with us to lock out the Conservatives yet we were also saying no deal of any kind. Our problem was that we were being forced into what the public perceived to be an impossibilist position – us saying 'no arrangement whatsoever' just didn't ring true in some way.

There is now a pressing challenge for the next Labour leader on whether to attack or accommodate the Nationalists. Some in the Shadow Cabinet are warning against continuing to treat the SNP 'like the North Korean communist party'. If around half the Scottish electorate believe it's all right to vote for the values espoused by the SNP, Labour will need to prove that their own values of solidarity and social progress are better than the Nationalists – it won't be enough, this line of argument goes, to just 'rail against them'.

A Question of Credibility

30 April

- Ed Miliband answers questions on spending in the worst possible way – according to his own advisers and pollsters.
- Labour pays the price for not being consistent enough on deficit reduction.
- The next leader will have to restore credibility on Labour's ability to manage the economy.

ONE SHADOW CABINET aide almost put his foot through the television screen. Another – close to Ed Balls – was more sanguine. He just had a terrible sinking feeling. And that sensation was pretty much shared by those in Ed Miliband's camp too. They thought they had prepared him well for this, the last television encounter of the general election. *Question Time* was coming from Leeds, where Ed Miliband had spent part of his early childhood while his Marxist academic father Ralph taught at the University.

But there was to be no warm homecoming. Miliband's team had been worried that only one in four audience members would be Labour supporters but in the end the numbers mattered less than the ferocity. Not for the first time, David Cameron had waved around the letter from 2010 in which Liam Byrne had told his successor as chief secretary to the Treasury that 'I am afraid there is no money.' He hadn't realised that there would be a coalition government, that David Laws – briefly – would be in post rather than Philip Hammond and that he would make the wry comment public. Many journalists groaned when the Prime Minister subsequently produced it but clearly Conservative research was telling him it was resonating with the voters he needed to win over.

The very first question – from audience member Elizabeth Moody – seemed to reflect the Conservative attack: 'Five years ago the outgoing Labour treasury minister left a message – "there's no money left." How can we trust the Labour party with the UK economy?'

Miliband referred to the letter as David Cameron's 'regular prop' and he answered in line with his preparations – that he would get the deficit down every year, and would balance the books – and that Labour had learnt the lesson of lax regulation of the banks in the past.

But some in the audience weren't satisfied – the follow-up question was from the owner of a marketing company, later identified as Catherine Shuttleworth. She said Ed Balls had regarded the letter as a joke, but running a business wasn't a joke so if that is how Labour treats the economy, how can they be trusted?

The Labour leader used the stock answer that had taken so long to formulate – how Britain would succeed if working people succeeded – and combined this with reminding her he was offering a cut in business rates for small enterprises. That wasn't good enough – Catherine Shuttleworth wanted Ed Balls sacked.

She denied being a Tory stooge and later told newspapers that she had voted Lib Dem in 2010 and wasn't a member of any political party, though she had worked closely with Andrew Jones – who became the Conservative MP for Harrogate – when setting up her business.

But then the killer blow. A simple straightforward question.

'Do you accept when Labour was last in power, you overspent?'

And an all too simple, straightforward answer: 'No, I don't.'

Chairman David Dimbleby then interjected. 'Even with all the borrowing?' Once again, Ed Miliband said 'No' and got a hostile reception as he reeled off the achievements of the previous government: 'there are schools that were rebuilt in our country, hospitals were rebuilt, there were sure starts centres that were built that would not have happened so I don't agree with that'.

He did go on to say the global financial crisis had caused the deficit to rise and he would reduce spending but the damage had been done. The next questioner said it was 'ludicrous' for Miliband to say he hadn't 'bankrupted' the country – that he was lying. The questioner cut across his response, accusing him of 'spending irresponsibly'. Then a young woman kicked out as he was going down: 'If you can't accept that you overspent in the last government, why on earth should we trust you not to do it again?'

Miliband tried to shift the ground by responding with the dividing lines so beloved of his old boss Gordon Brown: 'You have to make a choice... David Cameron would cut the NHS' while Labour had a 'balanced plan' – 'we can balance the books without sacrificing our public services, without sacrificing tax credits... tax credits are on the ballot paper at this election. I do disagree with Mr Cameron. I have a different plan.'

By now some of his own supporters were coming close to hiding behind the sofa to escape the unfolding horror before their eyes. A Shadow Cabinet aide confided:

Westminster remembers what he forgot last year – that he didn't mention the deficit at conference – but that was way before most voters even thought about the election. When you screw up a week before polling day, that's a different matter.

One of his own advisers said 'getting his answer wrong on spending was the biggest single mistake of the final week of the campaign.'

And another member of his inner team began thinking of paint stripper:

> The gloss we had managed to put on the first few weeks was exposed as just that, and we now knew what the public thought when they saw underneath.

The answer Miliband had prepared earlier – rather longer than the one he gave on the night – to the question 'did you overspend' was as follows:

> I understand why you are asking the question – I take the view that it wasn't Labour's spending that caused the financial crisis. It was the crash that caused the deficit, not the deficit that caused the crash. But the world has changed, money is tight now, there's a premium on every pound, so I'll be straight with you. Did overspending cause the crash? No. But we are going to take a different approach to spending now in difficult times? Yes.

His pollsters believed this wasn't an ideal form of words because he was answering a different question – not had Labour spent too much, but had Labour's spending led to the crash? A senior Shadow Cabinet member told me they had expressed dismay at being given similar advice to 'dodge the question' rather than deal with it if it came up in interviews.

Nonetheless, the pollsters took the view that it was better to say anything, however unconvincing, other than 'No' in response to whether Labour had overspent. Any answer involving the 'No' word had been tested in focus groups, and had provoked horrifically hostile responses.

The pollsters had also tested in advance what Miliband would have said had his memory not failed him at the previous year's party conference. His passage about getting the deficit down, telling people 'there won't be money to spend after the next election' and that he and Ed Balls would be 'taking a tough new approach' to borrowing – along with what he should have said on immigration – had registered by far the most positive response. There was less approval for his attack on the Conservatives for leaving people to struggle on their own and for his 40-plus mentions of the word 'together'. His passage about the 'real' people he had met – such as Josephine and Gareth – and which he seemed to manage to recall verbatim had bombed.

So having subsequently suffered for forgetting the deficit, he should at least have remembered that a downright denial of overspending could also inflict damage – that what he shouldn't say could be as important as what he should have said.

Election campaigns have a way of finding politicians out. Miliband's

aides prided themselves on how he had avoided a 'Gillian Duffy' moment
– when the previous leader was berated by that mouthy supporter on
immigration. Miliband had no such embarrassing encounters, and had
addressed the substance of the incident by telling Labour voters he, unlike
apparently his old boss Gordon Brown, didn't think it was 'bigoted' to
talk about migration. But the bigger lesson of the Duffy incident was that
the former prime minister had said one thing in public and another in
private. In other words we found out what he really thought. So while
Miliband's advisers didn't recognise it at the time, in his own way he was
having his Duffy moment in full view of the *Question Time* audience. He
had previously been offering reassurance on the deficit but ultimately
perhaps he just gave an honest answer on previous spending. But one
which, in the words of a close aide:

> Played into people's anxieties. They felt look, these people were involved
> in the crash and we just don't know if we are ready to trust them. Our
> biggest failure wasn't – as some say we did – to move to the left. Our failure
> was not being able to deal with the damage to our reputation that came
> from being associated with the crash. And I guess it was also a failure of
> leadership. Ed wasn't a big enough figure to transcend our record.

Labour's election director Spencer Livermore reminded me that no one
incident in an election is ever as decisive or quite as iconic as the media
retrospectively suggest. Nonetheless even in well-run campaigns, it's
difficult to hide from reality: 'You can't paper over things during a
campaign. Our core weaknesses were found out and we paid the price'.
And while he hadn't fallen flat on his face in Leeds, the cameras picked up
Ed Miliband's stumble as he left the stage. Quick as a flash, the chancellor
turned Tory spin doctor for the evening, George Osborne, told the *Politics
Home* website: 'I'll leave you to interpret that and find the correct metaphor.'

When Ed Miliband returned to the 'spin room' he was cheered by his
team but the changing expression on the faces of his spokesmen Bob
Roberts and broadcasting officer Matthew Laza gave a more accurate and
very visual verdict on his performance. Their cheery, chummy demeanour
evaporated after the answer on the deficit, their smiles replaced by frozen,
rictus grins.

One of Miliband's aides admitted: 'Leeds lost us momentum. It was
the beginning of the end. Ed was livid with himself. He knew, he knew...'

* * *

For some of those in Labour's inner circle, this performance was the cul-
mination of nearly five years of indecision on how to handle Labour's

economic legacy. Many of those in the upper echelons of the party have, on the surface, reached a consensus – they will use a variation of the following sentence: 'we could have defended the previous government's record. Or we could have conceded and moved on. In the end we did neither.' There is near universal agreement that the Conservatives had been able to pin the blame on Labour for overspending earlier in the last parliament while the party's leading figures were engaged in a summer-long battle over who should succeed Gordon Brown. Few lessons seem to have been learnt here.

The consensus breaks down over what should have been done – and who was to blame for not doing it. Some say it was the Blairites' fault – David Miliband had two opportunities to become Shadow Chancellor. He could have accepted his brother's offer immediately after the leader-ship election, or again when Alan Johnson resigned early in 2011. He could then both have defended the previous government's record and got tougher on future spending commitments. And Alan Johnson – who didn't enjoy his time as Shadow Chancellor – has been criticised for bailing out unnecessarily, making it all but impossible early in 2011 for Ed Miliband to do anything other than appoint Ed Balls.

But it's lot easier to take that view with the benefit of hindsight. Mili-band senior wanted to avoid a 'psycho-drama'. Suppose there had been disagreements on economic policy. Or anything else for that matter – for example, over whether to back air strikes on Syria. The Blair/Brown divi-sions had been bad enough. Labour's opponents in the press would have relished the added spice of brotherly spite.

So let's assume the older brother option wasn't realistic. Ed Miliband didn't appoint Ed Balls instantly as Shadow Chancellor and had a long discussion on economic policy before confirming him in post.

Those close to the Shadow Chancellor would point out that Balls had to do much of the heavy lifting on deficit reduction in the latter half of the parliament and that it was Miliband who either forgot to talk about the deficit or forgot, as in the *Question Time* encounter, how to talk about it because it was never really at the front of his mind. They would also argue that he had to do much to repair Labour's relations with business – even if he famously forgot the surname of the man who had chaired his small business task force, Bill Thomas. Asked on BBC *Newsnight* about where the 63 business leaders who had backed Blair in 2005 had gone and who supported Labour now, he had said 'Bill somebody...'

But those in Miliband's inner circle believe Balls' five-point plan to stimulate growth while the economy was flat-lining was a political error. It may well have worked had Labour been in power and had to deal with sluggish growth but it wasn't focused enough on how Labour should position itself in 2015 when there was a good chance that the economy would be expanding again. And with proposals for a further temporary cut in VAT it looked like Labour hadn't learned the lessons about tax and spending.

I have spoken to various advisers and allies of Ed Balls and this charge uniformly riles them most. They point out in his Reuters speech in the June of 2013, Balls himself effectively called time on the VAT cut and argued instead for productive investment in infrastructure. But he also delivered a warning to the Shadow Cabinet two years before the election:

> I have a tough message for my Labour colleagues. The situation we will inherit will require a very different kind of Labour government to those which have gone before. We can expect to inherit plans for further deep cuts to departmental budgets at a time when the deficit will still be very large and the national debt rising.

And as one of Balls' allies told me:

> It was his idea to change Labour's position on spending. We signalled a much tougher approach. Ed (Balls) caused a huge row by saying winter fuel allowances would no longer be universal. He was booed at the 2014 conference for being willing to take tough choices on child benefit. For almost two years it was the treasury team which was single handedly hammering away at a fiscal responsibility message when it was actually the whole Shadow Cabinet and the leader in particular who needed to say it every day if it was to have any hope of getting through to voters.

But whatever their criticisms of Ed Balls, some of Ed Miliband's own advisers believe he himself missed two opportunities.

Not long after his appointment to advise on strategy and communications, the former *Times* journalist Tom Baldwin – along with his friend Alastair Campbell – assessed that the Conservative attacks on Labour's economic legacy over the summer had been toxic and could in fact become more potent, not less – unless a strong antidote was deployed. Baldwin wanted a bold response early in Miliband's leadership – a counter-attack on the 'Tory Big Lie' – contacting and wheeling out economists and experts to take issue with the idea that Labour's spending caused, or at least significantly contributed to, the financial crisis.

In the end, what was supposed to be a concerted campaign in the winter of 2010/11 was boiled down to one 800-word article by the party leader. It became part of that approach – described over and over to me by several of his confidants – 'to tick a box and move on'. But for others close to Miliband, it was more important to 'move on' than go back. The leader himself did not want – they said – to squander airtime reliving arguments on Gordon Brown's behalf rather than looking to the future. And, actually, lax regulation of the banks was partly to blame for what happened so that should be conceded rather than simply, staunchly defending all that went before. Polling at the time, too, suggested there was little to be gained from defending New Labour's record too prominently.

The second potentially missed opportunity came when George Osborne abandoned plans in 2011 to eliminate the deficit by the end of the parliament.

Some felt at this stage Labour had the perfect cover to go from stimulus to consolidation – to say 'we told you so, you couldn't bring the deficit down in one parliament, you are now accepting that Alistair Darling (the Labour chancellor before the 2010 election) was right.' Tom Baldwin was pressing to go further: 'We needed a clearer and more coherent argument. Big reform without big spending.'

In other words, similar spending to the Conservatives but a clear set of different priorities. It never quite happened. Miliband did use the 'big reform without big spending' formulation closer to the election – notably in a speech to business leaders in June 2014 – but many of those around him felt it was too little, too late.

Jon Cruddas believes that too much complacency had set in following what was being called publicly George Osborne's 'Omnishambles' budget of 2012, and privately the 'clusterf***'. This had included reducing the top tax rate while placing a levy on Cornish pasties, before various u-turns were effected. While it was disastrous in the short-term for the Conservatives – in its aftermath Labour even enjoyed occasional double-digit opinion poll leads – Cruddas believes it was also damaging for his own party:

> Labour had an unearned poll lead that they thought could be banked which disincentivised the heavy lifting that was needed.

When the economy – and the Conservatives' political fortunes – recovered, it then became apparent Labour hadn't fixed their own economic roof when the sun was shining.

Mayday, Mayday… Scottish Labour's Existential Threat

1 May

- Ed Miliband faces resistance in Glasgow.
- Labour unofficially reduces its Scottish target seats to just two.
- The new UK and Scottish leaders will need to 'build a movement' from a much-reduced base.

AFTER LAST NIGHT'S stumble, Ed Miliband needed quickly to regain his balance. A story on the bedroom tax was briefed – it would be abolished on day one of a Labour government. This wouldn't need to await legislation as councils would simply be given enough money to prevent them imposing benefit cuts on tenants who 'under occupied' their home. But it transpired that the Shadow Work and Pensions Secretary, Rachel Reeves, had said much the same thing back in December so it didn't gain much traction, unlike Miliband himself – who covered three countries in one day. With the Conservative narrative that a weak Labour government would be beholden to the SNP, he tried to change the story. He was in favour of unity not division – and would stand up for working people in every corner of the land. He began his day traveling to Cardiff then via a 'campaign stop' in Gloucester, he flew with a press pack in tow from Bristol to Glasgow.

I had gone ahead to Scotland and was awaiting his arrival at the Tollcross swimming pool – a state of the art community facility which had been the previous year's Commonwealth Games Aquatic Centre. Here, of course, the home nations had competed against each other. Polls at the time suggested Scotland's relatively impressive medals haul hadn't significantly enhanced a sense of national identity.

Yet here was Ed Miliband about to enter what used to be familiar territory for Labour only to discover it was growing increasingly dangerous. There was a statistically insignificant demonstration outside. But the imagery was more damaging than the numbers. About two dozen members of the self-styled Scottish Resistance waved saltires and placards denouncing Labour as 'red Tories'. John Scott – who wore a 'resistance' T-shirt – told me he believed Labour was 'finished'. Many on the left would be voting SNP – this was as much about opposing austerity as backing independence.

Then there was a one-man counter demonstration. A five-foot muscle-bound package of anger strode across the venue's car park impervious to the bracing weather in a T-shirt and shorts and made a bee line for the Resisters. 'You f***ers' was his opening greeting. 'You don't feed anybody. My food bank feeds 400. And you don't stand up to the criminal gangs.' There wasn't much resistance here.

My Glasgow based colleague James Cook was amused by the spectacle but the anger-machine suddenly changed target. 'Are you laughing? What are you f***ing laughing at? How many people do you f***ing feed?' With that, he turned on his heels and strode off as though to war.

One of the key members of the Resistance was Sean Clerkin. He had made a name for himself by being a sort of Scottish Michael Crick but with added attitude. Or perhaps Dennis Pennis without the humour would be the better description. He had tried to doorstep Iain Gray, then Labour's leader in Scotland, on a Glasgow street ahead of the 2011 Holyrood elections. The hapless leader – who squandered the double digit Labour poll lead the party had had earlier that year – didn't handle it well and took refuge in a sandwich shop. This provided one of the defining images of the campaign. The SNP went on to win their first ever overall majority... though that's not suggesting cause and effect.

So against this backdrop, Ed Miliband chose to enter tonight's venue by a side door.

On the reasonable assumption this is what he would do, we caught it on camera which probably didn't help Labour's prospects in Glasgow. That said, those prospects couldn't have been much worse.

The rally was held in Glasgow East, the seat of the Shadow Scottish Secretary, Margaret Curran.

The recent history of the seat undermined the convenient untruth that Labour's Scottish woes were entirely related to fighting a very negative cross party campaign with the Tories on the referendum. At the nadir of Gordon Brown's time as prime minister in 2008 Labour had lost the seat in a byelection to the SNP city councillor John Mason. The defeated candidate had been Margaret Curran. Through strong connections to the east end communities and a formidable campaign that involved meeting thousands of her potential voters face to face, she won it back at the 2010 general election. Her tendency to engage in argument rather than avoid conflict meant that of all the speakers at that night's rally she was the only one who wanted to go outside and ask the protestors why they hated the Labour Party. She was persuaded by her highly competent adviser Martin McCluskey that this would be a bad idea which in all probability would steal the headlines from Ed Miliband.

The Tollcross event was hosted by ex-*Taggart* star John Michie and the 300-strong audience was too loyal to suggest he investigate the strange disappearance of the Labour Party in Scotland. The atmosphere was upbeat – 'blitz spirit' as one activist called it – but when Margaret Curran paid tribute to Gemma Doyle, the young MP for nearby West Dunbarton-shire and Douglas Alexander it was like she was reading out a political obituary. Her own seat, too, would be lost once more to the SNP.

In the weekend that followed the rally, some of the Scottish papers suggested that the party had a strategy to save half a dozen seats. In reality that was a little ambitious. You might think the loss of around 30 of Labour's 41 Scottish seats – a 75 per cent reduction – would be desper-ately depressing for party activists. In fact, leading Labour figures confessed they didn't challenge this speculation because the prospect of holding a dozen seats in the most difficult campaign they had waged was in fact a morale-booster for both candidates and foot soldiers alike.

John McTernan, Jim Murphy's chief of staff, said:

> We were facing an existential threat in Scotland. We had a near-death experience but we didn't die. We had to ensure there was a Labour party left. We kept things going with vigour; we have some good organisers and good candidates for the next Holyrood election.

And Bob Roberts – Ed Miliband's near-constant companion – said that his leader's view that night was that 'we were going to go down fighting. We would never look like we were abandoning Scotland'.

By 1 May it was clear that Margaret Curran's career at Westminster was over. Polling was being carried out around every three or four days and it wasn't bringing good news. Some sections of the Scottish press were reporting that she was sucking in resources for what was essentially a lost cause. While she continued to get enough resources to campaign, the decision had already been taken to divert efforts elsewhere. There had been a tense meeting attended by, amongst others, Jim Murphy, John McTernan and the general election co-ordinator Douglas Alexander, who had suggested the shift in resources. Alexander was handed a telephone and told in no uncertain terms to communicate his decision direct to Margaret Curran himself.

By publicly stressing some seats were still winnable, Labour was giving its rank and file the motivation to pull its diminishing core of supporters out to cast their votes – and to try to prevent the SNP getting more than 50 per cent of the popular vote in Scotland. A base from which to rebuild – and the retention of 'good' second places in some contests – was essential. But there was recognition at this stage that seat retention would be minimal.

One of the most senior figures in the party admitted he was waking up each day now worrying about how to save not 12 seats but just two seats – those of Jim Murphy and Douglas Alexander.

Indeed insiders have told me this pair of once-safe seats weren't just fought as tightly-contested marginals. Labour were so desperate to retain them that the party in effect poured in the resources that would be expected at byelections, when there isn't the distraction and cost of a simultaneous national election. This had included moving a regional organiser from Yorkshire to Paisley to try to save Alexander's seat. In a much diminished Scottish party that as recently as 1997 has provided around half the cabinet – including the chancellor, and the foreign and defence secretaries – these were seen as the two remaining top-table talents.

It had been expected that one or two others might limp home – possibly the Shadow Scotland Office Minister, Willie Bain in Glasgow North East, who had seen off the SNP at a by-election as recently as 2009. Surprisingly few thought that Gordon Brown's old seat of Kirkcaldy and Cowdenbeath would be saved following his retirement. Although Ian Murray's majority in Edinburgh South had been slender in 2010, polling suggested he was picking up non-Labour voters who wanted to keep the SNP out. This was aided by the press exposure of an 'unofficial' Twitter account – in the name of a one Paco McSheepie – run by the SNP candidate Neil Hay, in which he had compared 'No' voters in the referendum to Quislings, or Nazi collaborators. And he hadn't been desperately nice about some elderly voters, either.

One of Jim Murphy's campaign team told me there was evidence in his East Renfrewshire seat that non-Labour unionist voters would 'switch' to save him and savage the SNP even in the absence of a Neil Hay. Here in a seat he had won from the Conservatives, even if Labour's Scottish leader insulted the Tories many of them locally would rally round him to keep the Nationalists out, I was told. It didn't work out like that.

His former chief of staff John McTernan said:

> Jim had already halved the Tory vote in the seat over the years. There is a point where you can't squeeze it any further. In the end some people are actually Tories, just like I couldn't be persuaded not to vote Labour.

By 1 May it was clear Labour Day wasn't going to be Labour's day. As he spoke at the Tollcross rally, some of Jim Murphy's closest advisers felt he couldn't hold on. After the last weekend of the campaign they were almost certain. John McTernan observed: 'If you lose on an 81 per cent turnout, people do actually want you to go'.

But I've been told in that other 'target seat' – Douglas Alexander's – even on polling day they felt they were in with a chance against his

20-year-old student opponent Mhairi Black. Although there is plenty of comment on social media about Labour's lack of presence in the seat, insiders insist the 'contact rate' with voters had been excellent.

So what had really been going on?

* * *

Many of the most senior figures in the Scottish Labour Party agree that the biggest single failing was their inability to 'win the peace'. After being in a wartime coalition government in 1945, Labour had a distinctive message and a plan for the renewal of the country.

In 2014 the UK had also been under threat, not of invasion but of disintegration. Labour politicians had fought alongside Lib Dems and Conservatives to 'defend the union.' There is much written elsewhere about whether that campaign had been too negative, whether Labour's role in it had been distinctive enough, and if apparently close association with those in power at Westminster had tainted their brand in Scotland.

Certainly the former Labour First Minister Henry McLeish believed:

> We won the referendum, but we never really had a campaign. We were being punished heavily by being associated with the Tories in 'Better Together' – that was a catastrophic mistake.

But however the referendum was won, there is near-universal agreement that too little thought had gone in to what would happen afterwards. The SNP always had a plan – as the former Labour MSP Des McNulty would tell colleagues: 'we went in to a referendum to win a vote. The SNP went in to it to build a movement.'

And jaws dropped all around Scotland when on 19 September 2014, the day the result was declared, David Cameron declared this:

> We have heard the voice of Scotland. And now the millions of voices in England must also be heard. The question of English votes for English laws... requires a decisive answer.

McLeish believes Cameron 'lit a fuse' that day. Scottish 'No' voters felt patronised and abandoned. Labour, the leading party in Scotland for more than half a century, was left like a rabbit staring in to the headlights of the oncoming Tory juggernaut in England, and if it turned its gaze the other way – oops a pimped-up fuel-injected SNP pantechnicon was coming at it.

Insiders insist that it wasn't until Jim Murphy took over the Scottish Labour leadership in December 2014 that serious polling was undertaken to assess the attitudes of former supporters who had said 'Yes' to independence that September. But almost as saliently while Labour had used social media – and accused opponents of using what felt more like anti-social media during the insult-strewn and intense referendum campaign – they hadn't really known how to exploit its potential as effectively as the SNP.

Facebook v Foot Weary:
Right People, Wrong Conversations

2 May

- The SNP have a more sophisticated social media strategy than Labour.
- Strategic errors by the unionist parties have given the SNP powerful advantages.
- The next Labour leader will have to modernise communications as well as their message.

ED MILIBAND PREPARED to leave Scotland for the south coast, having avoided any incidents that might embarrass or undermine him nationally. But he also took the early-morning flight from Glasgow to Gatwick knowing he couldn't expect to retain more than a handful of seats here and would have to work even harder to reassure voters in England that they could trust his party with his nation's purse strings. So what of those he left behind?

His Shadow Scottish Secretary, Margaret Curran hadn't had an easy ride from some of her SNP opponents but she said the voters themselves had often been civil, polite – even embarrassed. Things hadn't been going well when an elderly constituent invited her into her home to apologise for not voting for her. Others were a little more robust – telling her that Labour had 'let them down'. Scratch beneath the surface and voters who took this view tended to exempt her and sometimes Jim Murphy from that verdict, but they cited other MPs who had been in 'safe' seats for a long time 'and were taking us for granted'. It was becoming an increasingly difficult narrative to counter.

At least the views of these voters were clear if not always logical. The bigger danger which Labour faced was not understanding who amongst their former voters had shifted allegiance, and why. Or as Margaret Curran puts it: 'We could not engage with our potential supporters in a modern way.'

Jim Murphy had appointed Gregor Poynton as head of 'external engagement' in January 2015. Poynton had had hopes of becoming the Labour candidate for Falkirk in 2013 but withdrew over allegations that he had been involved in signing up new members specifically to back him at the selection meeting – allegations he vehemently denied. As well as having a background as a Labour Party organiser, he had more recently run the British arm of the social media company Blue State Digital – blue being the colour used to denote states held by the Democrats in the US. The organisation had been formed by some of those who had pioneered new forms of fundraising – especially the ability to draw in large amounts of small donations – and new ways of communicating with potential supporters when the left-winger Howard Dean had sought the Democrat nomination for president in 2003. The company went on to play a key role in Barack Obama's election campaign in 2007, and his re-election campaign four years later.

Those at the top of the party welcomed his appointment but even at the time felt it may have come too late. One senior politician bemoaned the fact he hadn't been appointed by the previous Scottish leader Johann Lamont: 'we should have had him three years ago.' The SNP appeared to have learnt the lessons of the Obama campaigns rather quicker than Labour – and had developed their techniques during the long run up to the referendum.

* * *

First of all, the SNP had built up what one insider dubbed a 'pyramid of information' on voters. Their door-to-door canvassing was rather more sophisticated than Labour's – and started much sooner. Campaigners would conduct 'surveys' on the doorstep to build up a profile of the voters' interests and level of engagement – and what local issues might be troubling them. In some cases demonstrating this level of interest in a voter played well with long-standing Labour supporters who had felt 'taken for granted' by their usual party of choice. But it also allowed the SNP to send carefully targeted messages to swing voters well before the formal election campaign got under way.

The 'Yes' campaign in the referendum had involved far more people than the membership of the SNP – though some previously non-partisan campaigners were to sign up to the party as a way of feeling they were doing something positive in the wake of a 'No' vote. But the SNP's long-standing activists used the time they spent on Scotland's doorsteps to plan ahead for future campaigns – particularly the Westminster general election that would follow the very next spring. So the activists asked not just about how people intended to vote in the referendum, but about their voting intentions in both the upcoming Westminster and Holyrood elections, and how they had voted in the past. They also queried – crucially – what voters' second preference of party would be. This in particular gave them a useful means of targeting 'Yes' supporters who usually voted

Labour but might consider the SNP as second choice. Winning their support – elevating the SNP from second to first choice – was the key to unlocking Labour's hold on seats in Scotland's central belt. And the SNP tended to know just who they were, and how to reinforce this process.

To some extent the groundwork had already been done. In 2011, when the SNP gained the 'impossible' overall majority at Holyrood, this was because they had won Labour and Lib Dem seats on a first-past-the-post basis and not as a quirk of the more proportional voting system for the Scottish parliament. The aim was therefore to persuade people to vote in the same way at Westminster. SNP strategists felt the phenomenon of what was often called 'differential voting' – where people were more likely to back a UK-wide party in a Westminster election – would erode over time but as one of them put it 'the referendum became a powerful catalyst in that process'.

This exercise of intelligence gathering on voting intention during the referendum campaign was also useful in identifying 'No' voters who might also at least consider voting SNP if there were no threat to the union. It's worth remembering that the former SNP leader Alex Salmond currently represents a seat where voters rejected independence but where former Lib Dem voters – unenamoured with the record of the coalition at Westminster – were looking for a home. Indeed, every one of the half dozen SNP MPs who sat at Westminster failed to persuade voters of the merits of independence in their constituencies, but may have persuaded them that they were hard-working MPs for their area who would stand up for Scotland within the UK and not just argue for separatism. Labour MPs couldn't uniformly convince voters of their endeavours on their behalf.

* * *

Secondly, the Nationalists were peerless at peer-to-peer contacts. The SNP recognised that in an era when politicians had lost so much trust, it was far better to convey messages through families and friends – often on Facebook. As one senior Labour politician put it: 'we had no way of speaking to people in their current mood.'

And shoe-leather was no substitute for smart phones. One of the 40 Labour MPs who lost their seat said:

> While we might have been having five million, five minute conversations on the doorstep people were having maybe a two hour conversation with an SNP supporter, who may be a work colleague or friend, for two hours on Facebook. And quite often people had their own individual reasons to hate us.

But it wasn't just in peer-to-peer contact where the Nationalists had the edge. They were also deploying modern media to disseminate their message from on-high.

We may be on the cusp of a new era in political communication. The SNP held regular Question and Answer sessions with Nicola Sturgeon – and other frontbenchers in the Scottish Parliament – on Facebook in real time. She had pledged when she succeeded Alex Salmond to be an 'accessible' leader and that's exactly what younger people in particular felt she was delivering. While these forums were more about exuding empathy and competence than in disseminating particular policies, the SNP were also picking up voters' concerns that they may have to spend more time addressing – for example, they said more and sounded more sceptical about fracking as a result of these sessions and therefore appeared more responsive than some of their opponents. But what is fascinating is that the Nationalists didn't publicise these sessions by telling the papers 'tonight Nicola Sturgeon will be on Facebook'. So although all this was very public and regular users of social media who had taken an interest in the referendum campaign knew all about these Q&As, those involved in more traditional forms of media – including some political rivals and journalists – either were ignorant of them or ignored them. There was a failure to grasp the creation and maintenance of a self-reinforcing community which was hidden in full public view.

The SNP were also better at creating the impression of activity than their opponents. People tend to break news on Twitter and share it on Facebook. The former is far more used by journalists and politicians. And here the SNP were creating a sense of momentum to match the more targeted or personalised messaging to voters elsewhere on social media.

The freelance Scottish data scientists Gary Short, who is not an SNP supporter, told the BBC during the campaign that the Nationalists were very disciplined at putting out their message in a way which played to Twitter's strengths. He collated every tweet sent using the hashtags #GE2015 or #GE15 – these got pick up amongst those interested in the campaign, and not just party activists. Many political campaigners used only the hashtag of their own party in messages, which meant they were often talking to themselves. The SNP didn't make the same mistake. Gary Short examined the retweeting of official party messages. On one day of the campaign, the SNP – using the #GE2015 hashtag – got 118 times as many retweets than an official Labour message.

* * *

SNP insiders would say that they had two big advantages over Labour – yes, a more sophisticated virtual campaign – but also a much better actual campaign.

Their members' app directed activists to where they were most needed and had details of campaigning – leaflet-runs and canvassing – in local areas which was easy to access and ensured even just the occasionally active supporter could always find out how to join in when they had time. But there's little point having a members' app if you don't have many members who will use it. Labour refuse to break down UK-wide membership figures into the nation and regions of the country. But with around 21,000 ballot papers going out in the contest for the Scottish Labour leader, then that is not a bad approximation for actual membership in Scotland. Once the largest party in Scotland, Labour now isn't even close.

The SNP's membership soared to 90,000 after the referendum and many new members, battle-hardened by arguing for independence on the doorsteps, were keen to find an outlet for their frustrations. There was no need whatsoever to get withdrawal symptoms from the camaraderie of that campaign with a general election just around the corner.

Arguably, it was strategic errors by their opponents which gave the SNP a fair wind. The coalition government had agreed to the Nationalists' timescale on a referendum, and had conceded a question which allowed them to be the more positive-sounding 'Yes', and not the 'No', campaign. The proximity of the general election to the referendum meant their campaign battalions never stood down, while the component parts of 'Better Together' inevitably had to be rent asunder and each party had to do battle with their erstwhile temporary allies.

But the particularly damaging factor for Labour had been the length of the campaign. Although the UK media only really concentrated on the referendum in the last few months – and then hit the panic button when YouGov suggested the 'Yes' campaign were marginally ahead ten days before polling day – the arguments had been conducted over the preceding two years in Scotland. A senior SNP strategist described the phenomenon:

> Labour voters who were thinking about voting 'Yes' became more and more staunchly 'Yes' as the campaign went on – and in inverse proportion became less and less Labour. Had the referendum been conducted quickly – in say a three-month period – I don't think we would have seen a breakdown in party affiliation to that degree.

But despite Labour's own 'No' campaign – fronted by the energetic Anas Sarwar – the more that some Labour voters saw their politicians share platforms with other parties and the Conservatives in particular, the less they felt an affinity with Labour themselves.

And it's impossible to underestimate the contempt in which the Conservatives are still held in some communities many years after the de-industrialisation of the Thatcher era. Jim Murphy tells a story of a voter at the previous election. The prospective supporter set out his logic on the doorstep: 'I was thinking of voting BNP. But I'll probably vote Labour because I don't want to let the Tories in.'

Luvvies for Labour

2 May

- A celebrity rally is trumped by the arrival of the royal baby.
- News of a less welcome arrival – Labour's 'tablet of stone' – begins to leak out.
- Labour falls behind the Conservatives in key seats.

'I HAVEN'T SLEPT. I flew directly from LA to come here and show my support for Labour.' So said a hirsute Jason Isaacs who was hosting a celebrity-packed late-afternoon rally in central London. The venue was the Royal Horticultural Halls, a stone's throw away from Westminster and presumably Labour wanted to show that their support was blossoming. Like the Holywood actor Jason Isaacs, I too had flown in to London, hadn't slept much and felt a bit jet lagged. But I hadn't wafted in from paradise – I had flown here from Glasgow Airport.

It's just that after the longest 'short' campaign in living memory, politicians and journalists were feeling somewhat jaded and perhaps that's not the best time to make big decisions. Labour had almost been saved from themselves, but not quite. Outside the rally I ran in to Tom Baldwin who told me that tomorrow would see the unveiling of what had been dubbed the 'Torstone' – an eight-foot and six-inches-high limestone plinth which would have Labour's election pledges inscribed on it. It had gained its nickname from its creator Torsten Bell, Labour's policy and rebuttal director. The beast had already been filmed that morning in Hastings, but the pictures were under strict embargo until tomorrow.

Now, today you just couldn't give news away. The royal baby had arrived and party politics had been put on hold. Coverage of the celebrity rally had been pulled. Viewers were denied seeing Ronnie O'Sullivan try to snooker the Conservatives, or to hear Paul O'Grady verbally savage – or should that be 'Lily' Savage – the chancellor, combined with the threat or promise (depending on your politics) to move to Italy if the coalition returned to power. So had Labour unveiled their latest initiative today it may well have sunk... like a Torstone.

After the rally I was ushered in to the Green Room by Labour's broadcasting chief Matthew Laza to try to set up an interview with Isaacs for Radio Five Live the next day, as it was assumed normal political service would be resumed once the regal progeny had been given a name, or several. Miliband's inner circle were nibbling on a buffet. I spoke briefly to Ed Miliband himself who asked me how I thought it was going. I answered honestly that it had been a well-run campaign but that wouldn't necessarily determine the outcome. We had a brief chat about Jason Isaacs's speech, which Miliband had missed, and the Labour Party pension scheme (sic). The mood was downbeat as, that weekend, Labour's internal polls were suggesting that it was only '50/50' that Miliband could make it to Downing Street as the Conservatives were likely to be clearly ahead in the number of seats.

Despite what some published polls were saying, Labour's own research suggested they were now falling behind in key English marginals. The SNP issue – despite the Labour leader ruling out any form of deal in the most robust form possible – was still seen to be hitting them hard. But even the comfort blanket of knowing that the party had fought a slick and professional campaign was about to be stripped from him.

Edstone

3 May

- The 'tablet of stone' fiasco highlights dysfunctional decision-making.
- Tensions within the campaign become apparent.
- Labour's hard-fought battle to regain a reputation for competence is buried.
- The next leader will need clearer lines of command and control.

'ALL GOOD DECISIONS are collective decisions'. That was the familiar refrain from Bob Roberts whenever he was asked who was behind a particular initiative. Today I asked a follow-up on the Torstone. 'So was this a collective decision?' 'Eh no.' We were standing in the gymnasium of a school in Worcester – home of course to those 'Worcester women' who helped Labour to power in 1997 but neither they nor their daughters were going to do so in 2015. We were awaiting Ed Miliband's arrival for a Question and Answer session with undecided members of the public. But on one issue the verdict was already clear. What was now being called the 'Edstone' on social media was a disaster, and every Labour official present tried to distance themselves from it. Roberts later admitted: 'We completely underestimated the effect of social media or the reaction it would get on social media'.

And what had that reaction been? Perhaps the most damning came on Twitter from one of the writers of the political comedy *The Thick of It*. Simon Blackwell felt it was beyond satire: 'Ed Miliband builds a policy cenotaph. And you wonder why we stopped doing *The Thick of It*.'

Boris Johnson inquired: 'Who does he think he is? Moses?' and pretty soon photoshopped images of the atheist Ed Miliband as that biblical figure appeared on social media and the ridicule spread like a plague of locusts.

The stone's intended destination was the garden of Downing Street, where Messrs Cameron and Clegg had chummily proclaimed their coalition five years before. But then it emerged that this might require planning permission – from Conservative-controlled Westminster City Council. I inquired why the stone hadn't been brought to Worcester from Hastings. I was told it was 'too heavy' and would 'go right through the floor of the gymnasium'. So where was it now? 'In storage.'

George Osborne had likened the Edstone to Labour's Sheffield rally in 1992 when a hubristic Neil Kinnock declared –in the manner of an overly enthusiastic American preacher – 'we're all right!' before a single ballot had even been cast. Labour insiders don't believe the 'policy ceno-taph' had the same negative impact. But it had stripped away a veil of competence. And it undermined another of Miliband's key messages – he wouldn't take voters for granted, he wasn't 'measuring the Downing Street curtains.' Yet now he had revealed a soft spot for the stone – in the corner of the Number 10 garden – and somewhere where he would be able see it every day to remind him of his promises.

So how had this political albatross been allowed to fly?

*   *   *

'I should have stopped it.' 'It should have been stopped.' 'You would have to been an idiot to say it wasn't a mistake.'

Three Labour strategists. A rare consensus. Yet the limestone was chiselled nonetheless. The concept had come from Scotland where Torsten Bell had been drafted in towards the end of a panicky referendum campaign the previous year. His allies despise how he is apparently now being scape-goated for the Edstone when often his advice and strategic thinking had got the party out of scrapes, not landed them in trouble. And the initial idea wasn't entirely ludicrous. The 'Vow' by the unionist parties to give the Scottish parliament more powers – and carried on the front page of the Labour-supporting *Daily Record* on what appeared to be ancient parch-ment, but was in fact knocked together by the newspaper itself – was considered a powerful intervention in the closing days of the campaign.

The idea of what presentational tools might be necessary to convince a sceptical electorate that politicians wouldn't break their promises was uppermost in Bell's mind but this had also impressed Douglas Alexander. Then, following the referendum, on the day Alex Salmond was about to hand over power to Nicola Sturgeon the far-from-publicity-shy First Minister unveiled yes, an actual stone at Edinburgh's Heriot-Watt Univer-sity commemorating what he regarded as his biggest achievement in office – free tuition for Scottish-based students. His own words had been etched in to it: 'The rocks will melt with the sun before I allow tuition fees to be imposed on Scottish students'.

Now that got Labour strategists thinking. Trust in politicians was pretty much at an historic low. Trust in Labour's Lib Dem opponents in so many seats with high student numbers was even lower, as they had broken their tuition fee pledge once in power. At this stage, despite first announcing it at the start of his 2011 conference, Ed Miliband had still not got his own fee reduction policy through a sceptical Shadow Cabinet or past a Shadow Chancellor who had believed his core task had been to keep the manifesto free from uncosted spending commitments. But there were discussions about taking a chip of Salmond's block and putting a tuition fee cut in England in stone, the better to embarrass Nick Clegg. In the end it was decided to put all the pledges on it.

I have spoken to people at the heart of the decision making process and still can't precisely establish when the stone went from an idea in to action. I'm told it was first discussed in December 2014, that it had been through about ten planning meetings, that initially it might have been – like the Vow – more of a newspaper advert, or poster, mocked up like a stone rather than the real thing. One adviser admitted: 'It was a lack of focus. An over familiarity with an idea.' It had indeed been dubbed the Torstone internally and some staff had a mocked-up version as a screen saver – channeling the opening credits of *2001: A Space Odyssey*. No one was stopping to think of the wider reaction. Certainly there were modifications. Ed Miliband himself didn't want it to be the height of a grave stone, for obvious reasons – so, at eight feet and six inches tall, it was almost on the scale of a mausoleum. There seemed to be incredulity it would ever happen – then, 'Torsten knew this stone mason...' – who turned out to be a Conservative supporter.

Its creation underlined a serious point and an important lesson for Jeremy Corbyn – that very often there were no real clear lines of command. Spencer Livermore, a veteran of the Gordon Brown premiership, was the general election campaign director while another Brown ally, Douglas Alexander, was the election co-ordinator. Though they mostly got on, on some issues they did not see eye to eye. Livermore had been adamantly opposed to the 'Edstone' but somehow mere opposition to an idea at a senior level didn't kill it. He was seen as a talented strategist but Ed Miliband had made clear to him on his appointment in 2014 that he was there to organise the campaign, rather than advise on it. He did so professionally but he wasn't responsible for the structures that preceded him.

Miliband in effect became his own chief strategist. But there were overlapping policy roles, too – between Stewart Wood, Greg Beales and the actual director of policy Torsten himself. Tom Baldwin was the senior adviser (strategy and communications) – while Greg Beales was director of strategy and Bob Roberts – eh, communications. Tom and Bob tried, and sometimes failed, to rub along through a policy of demarcation rather than cooperation. Jon Cruddas – who was supposed to be reviewing Labour policy – recounted how there was never a formal execution of the 'one nation' narrative. Policy teams would talk about it while separate strategy meetings were held on the transition to the 'cost of living crisis.' In the end, he recalls, 'we just ran out of road.'

While those close to the leader had overlapping roles, there were also senior officials in Labour's Brewers Green headquarters who felt they were being left outside the tent entirely. In fact they regarded it as more of bivouac because Ed Miliband tended to consult and communicate with only a small group. As one of the said to me:

> Do you think that bloody stone would have happened if he had talked to us? There were lots of people with experience of several elections, but they didn't talk to us. And I don't even think most of the Shadow Cabinet knew about the stone.

Indeed a senior Shadow Cabinet source confirmed this:

> Senior members of the Shadow Cabinet never really believed he could win so they were distant, but also for the same reason kept at a distance by him. There was no wise old owl to say stop.

Ed Miliband was said to have a mistrust for many of the long-standing party officials whom he knew, or believed, would have preferred to have had his brother lead the party. He had wanted the Labour's former deputy-general secretary Chris Lennie to move up a rung but the former GMB official Iain McNicol was appointed to the role of general secretary in 2011 by the party's ruling National Executive Committee instead. While working relationships between head office and the leader's office improved in the run up to the election – with all the senior staff working from Brewers' Green from January 2015 – there had been a long period of tension and mutual suspicion. McNicol was said to have been incensed when Spencer Livermore told staff they should report to him on his appointment as general election campaign director in 2013. He was soon put right. In truth, while McNicol was the senior figure, Livermore had the leader's ear, and neither was fully in charge. So the simple reason the stone happened is that no-one stopped it – or perhaps felt empowered enough to stop it. As one adviser said more generally about decision-making under Ed Miliband: 'He wasn't weak. He was stubborn. But stubborn in his indecision. His answer to disagreements was to bring even more people into the room.'

The stone wasn't the half of it. The timing of the unveiling was supposed to embarrass Nick Clegg, so it was decided this would coincide with the Lib Dem leader's appearance on the Marr programme on BBC1. Now, never mind that the Twitter storm had already started before the Lib Dem leader faced his inquisitor and so could join in the fun. The idea was that the stone would be a physical symbol of trust. This would be accompanied by an announcement of some substance from the party leader. And we were in Worcester waiting to hear it as he addressed undecided voters who seemed more concerned about the cathedral city's parking arrangements and poor train service.

Ed Miliband finally declared that if he didn't deliver on his pledge to reduce tuition fees in office, then he wouldn't stand again as Prime Minister in 2020. This invited more questions than it answered. Six pledges were on the stone. So if he failed to meet any of those, would he hand back the keys to Downing Street? 'No, the tuition fee pledge is a very specific pledge'. So this was an anti-Clegg gimmick? 'No, it's about restoring trust'.

Now, the stone was pretty big. But not big enough to contain the entirety of the six election pledges. So the tuition fee reduction hadn't even made the cut. In fact the word 'education' appears nowhere in stone. Instead we are promised 'Homes to Buy' – no-one had accused Labour of trying to close down the housing market – 'An NHS with Time to Care' ('time' is unspecified); 'Controls on Immigration'; 'Higher Living Standards for Working Families'; 'A Strong Economic Foundation'; and 'A Country Where the Next Generation Can Do Better Than the Last.' Yes the D-word, and any reference to bring debt and the deficit down, is missing, too. In fact Ed Miliband might as well have promised to throw in the towel if he couldn't meet any of the edited form of his pledges because they were either bland, or difficult to measure in any decisive way.

But one strategist defended the stone because, going into the last week of the campaign, the media were for once – if not always with a straight face – talking about Labour's pledges and not the Conservatives' core messages.

The party's interim leader Harriet Harman did remind me that history is written by the winners. Had Labour achieved a broader political appeal and been on course to win a majority, or the largest number of seats, a risible 'Edstone' wouldn't have formed part of Ed Miliband's political obituary. 'It depends on the prism through which it's viewed,' she said. It could have been seen retrospectively as a masterstroke that helped restore trust in politics had there been a Miliband premiership.

But there wasn't. And it wasn't.

Message, Not Mileage

5 May

- Ed Miliband targets a small number of marginal seats in the last 48 hours – and fails to win any of them.
- The Edstone refuses to die.
- The next leader will need better information on the party's performance.

THE CAMPAIGN WAS either flagging – or extremely well focused. With polling day just 48 hours away, David Cameron was planning to campaign throughout the night. Nick Clegg was embarking on a Land's End to John O'Groats tour to see the strange disappearance of Liberal Britain for himself. And Ed Miliband was taking the train 35 minutes outside London's St Pancras station to Bedford.

I had coined a phrase for that day's *One O'Clock News* – that Miliband obviously regarded his message as more important than the miles he travelled. This was then taken up the following day by our commander-in-chief Simon Lister. A senior and well-respected BBC producer who usually worked on coverage of the royal family, it had been his job these grisly few weeks not just to keep a strong editorial head on his shoulders, but to deal with the incredibly intricate logistics of getting reporters, camera crews and production staff around Britain either with, or in the wake, of Ed Miliband. He had the stamina and demeanour of someone who might feel that being in the Special Forces wouldn't be quite elite enough for him. Rather than being grateful for the limited nature of Labour's last few days on the road, he correctly asked why they weren't matching the travel plans of their opponents. Either my phrase had somehow penetrated his brain or great minds think alike, but he accosted Bob Roberts with the line: 'So are you saying your message is more important than the miles?' By the following day Ed Miliband's chief spokesman had decided to commandeer the words for himself as he made it the closing catchphrase of the campaign. Aware of the media's penchant for alliteration, in the marginal seat of Pendle, he briefed a huddle of journalists with a knowing smile that: 'The message is more important than the mileage.' They say imitation is a form of flattery but this was definitely a form of mickey-taking.

None of the select set of seats Miliband visited in the dying days of the campaign was won by Labour. So if he wasn't putting in the miles, the message wasn't having much traction either.

Miliband's first port of call on his limited-stop tour was a pre-fabricated community centre on the edge of Bedford where the losing candidate in 2010, Patrick Hall, was standing again. He had come to warn a mixture of activists and undecided voters that NHS trusts in England were facing a £2 billion shortfall – and he had a rescue plan. I asked him that if the £2.5 billion he had promised the NHS was going to bail out struggling hospitals, how was he going to pay for the thousands of nurses, doctors and midwives he was promising? His not entirely convincing answer was that these extra recruits would help deal with the crisis in the hospitals.

And that was that. I was all ready to put this on the news, until the Edstone refused to die. One of the key figures in his election team, Lucy Powell, had been on BBC Radio Five Live. Asked if carving Ed Miliband's promises in stone made them more believable, she had said:

> I don't think anyone is suggesting that the fact that he's carved them into stone means that he is absolutely not going to break them or anything like that.

It sounded like she was admitting that, despite chiselling those pledges in stone, Miliband wouldn't necessarily keep them. But she did complain that on social media as well as actual media, she had been selectively quoted. She had also said on the radio that Ed Miliband 'stands by his promises', and the stone 'was just another way of highlighting that, which is that he's a guy of principle, of decency, a guy who is tough and he is going to deliver on his promises he set out, unlike some of this opponents.' She later tweeted: 'Honestly Tories and others desperately misquoting what I said. Anyone who heard the whole interview knows I said the opposite.'

But the hare was running and her comments became the story. So inevitably in a set-piece interview for the main news bulletins, Ed Miliband was asked about the stone all over again. He said:

> I'm absolutely clear, we are going to deliver our policies, we are going to deliver our pledges and that is the reason we carved them in stone.

But soon enough, political obituaries of his time as Labour leader would be published.

Five Million Conversations

6 May

- The Labour leader expands the list of target seats in England – to include some Tony Blair never won.
- It soon becomes clear contacting voters and convincing them aren't one and the same.
- If the next leader wants to get to Downing Street, they will have to pay more attention to what's being said on the doorstep.

I ASKED ED MILIBAND if he was ready to be Prime Minister. After all, not just the Murdoch press with whom he had gone to war were against him. Papers that had supported Labour in the past – the *FT, The Independent* – weren't backing the party under his leadership. Without hesitation, he said emphatically, 'Yes' he was ready to be prime minister. As for the papers:

> In the final hours of the campaign I am going to focus on the thing that matters more than anything – the British people and the choice they have before them.

He was speaking at a packed gathering of activists at the Colne Municipal Hall, in the marginal seat of Pendle, on the edge of the Pennines. The high hills had broken the clouds and outside, the streets of the town were awash amid a heavy downpour. Inside, though, his bedraggled supporters gave him a warm reception. ITN's Carl Dinnen shared my view that Miliband appeared as confident as he had ever done during the campaign.

Labour had done no polling of its own in the final week but the public surveys at least weren't showing a collapse – and Miliband had had some good news from those running his field operation back at HQ, which he lost no time in announcing to those who would soon be braving the elements to try to bring out the Labour vote:

> At the start of this campaign I said that we wanted to have four million conversations in four months. And I am so proud that today, on the final day of campaigning, we will top five million conversations. The Labour Party will have more members, more activists, more volunteers out on the streets tomorrow than all the main parties combined. And you know, I think this tells you all you need to know about where the energy lies in this election… This race is going to be the closest we have ever seen. It is going to go down to the wire.

Of course, as we now know, it didn't. Miliband ended that day's campaigning with a rally in Leeds. En route from Pendle, he was supposed to have stopped off just across the Pennines in Keighley but the ensuing press pack was redirected. While Labour staff campaigning in that seat were telling us how well it was going, I ran in to the candidate at the evening rally, the affable John Grogan, who had previously been the MP for Selby before losing his seat. He admitted 'It's 60/40 we will lose in Keighley. We just don't have the numbers.'

The atmosphere for the final gathering of the campaign wasn't all that upbeat. I spotted the former Leeds MP John Battle in the audience, whom I had known years ago. He wasn't confident his party was on the brink of greatness. 'I think there will have to be a second election' he whispered. So why hadn't these five million conversations made enough of a difference?

Ed Miliband had wanted to give a rallying speech right at the start of the year but had no new message. Lucy Powell asked Patrick Heneghan – the director of field operations at Labour HQ – how many doors had been knocked upon in 2010. It had been approximately two million. Powell suggested doubling it to four million. She said this wasn't a 'back of the envelope' figure – rather it was an attempt, at the beginning of election year, to set 'an ambitious but achievable target'. So speaking in Salford on 5 January Miliband said:

> We will win this election, not by buying up thousands of poster sites, but by having millions of conversations. I am going to be leading those conversations in village halls, community centres, workplaces right across the country, starting this very week and every week from now until the election... Our campaign is setting the goal of holding four million conversations with people in just four months about how we change our country.

One senior party insider – not Heneghan – described this as a 'gimmick.' He added:

> It was a way of getting a headline. Yes, we had targets seat by seat for door-knocking but the five million figure, or indeed the four million figure which preceded it, had no strategic significance whatsoever. And Ed Miliband didn't seem to give it another thought from January until the campaign got under way.

Labour had invested £18 million – £3 million more than has previously been reported publicly – in organising in its key seats and in contacting voters. By historic standards, this was a huge amount – though less than was spent when Labour last won in 2005 and the party had paid for expensive billboard sites. By Election Day, 700 permanent or temporary

Labour organisers or what were called 'mobilisation assistants' were in place, along with an impressive number of volunteers. So what was the nature of the conversations that party activists were having – and why did their party leader appear to assume that by merely contacting voters, you were convincing them? One of those officials back at Labour's HQ was particularly frustrated that a leader could place so much store on a 'process story.' As he put it: 'Policies on immigration, on schools, on jobs, that's what wins you elections. Conversations aren't ends in themselves.'

In fact the total number of 'conversations' came closer to six million. But these were – what were called by party members – 'Voter ID conversations'. Everything was geared towards pulling out the Labour vote.

This 'priority list' – circulated to party members in one marginal seat – shows the relative lack of importance assigned to those who hadn't made up their minds:

If you don't have voter ID for enough Labour voters to be confident of winning, you could add the following to your target voter pool:

- Uncontacted voters in Labour households.
- People who voted Lib Dem at the last election but were Labour voters previously.
- Former Labour voters.
- Undecided voters.

Throughout the UK, canvassers were encouraged to ask up to five questions on the doorstep but in some cases they simply established if someone was intending to vote Labour and had done so in the past. Some campaigners ratcheted up apparently high contact rates but acquired little useful information – for example if someone was doubtful, they should be asked if they preferred a Conservative or Labour government to assess whether there was 'soft' support there that could later be hardened up, and they should be interrogated on whether they had voted Labour in local government elections. Little, if any, time was wasted on those who said they were opposed to the party.

Labour's general secretary Iain McNicol said:

There is a question to be asked if these conversations should have been more detailed – in other words 'Persuasion conversations' – my guess is that would have been more useful. The reason you build up voter ID is to identify your Labour supporters and turn them out. This time, there were too many don't knows or those who were against. The 'don't knows' were really important. There should have been more detailed analysis of where the 'don't knows' were thinking of going.

Shadow Women and Equalities Minister Gloria de Piero – along with Harriet Harman – had met a whole range of voters as their pink bus toured Britain. Three years previously De Piero had conducted her own 'Why Do You Hate Me?' tour to find out what was turning people off politics, and politicians. She had had plenty of genuine – and frank – interactions with voters and indeed non-voters. But now she said:

> The 'five million conversations' weren't real conversations. Very little time was spent on the doorstep. It was like talking to people through a glass partition – like you have in banks. We were saying something but they weren't really listening. It wasn't really a two-way conversation. But even when you could get useful information, there wasn't an easy way to act on it. I visited voters on a Barratt housing estate who mainly backed us in 2010 but who were now saying 'No' or 'Don't Know'. I fed that in nationally but I don't think it made a difference. A post-election analysis showed we did very badly amongst this group of voters – known in the jargon as 'new homemakers' – who lived in towns rather than cities and amongst families with small children. When I mentioned our free child care offer it was the first many of them had heard of it.

And the former head of party relations for Ed Miliband – and member of Labour's ruling National Executive – Jonathan Ashworth, told me:

> As the operation was about getting out the Labour vote we just didn't talk to the high number of don't knows after the Monday before polling day. And they were quietly and decisively heading towards the Tories when we were making assumptions at the time that some would come to us. They were worried about Ed's leadership but also we hadn't convinced them on the economy.

Anecdotally, from talking to some defeated candidates and those who campaigned for them, they were indeed encountering a high number of 'don't knows' – and there wasn't much of a system to feed the concerns of undecided voters back to their HQ.

Stella Creasy, who contested her party's deputy leadership and outperformed the national trend in her Walthamstow constituency in two consecutive elections, wrote on the *Labour List* website in June:

> Often on doorsteps, people will tell you how they are voting, or not, and also why and what else concerns them. In the main, such information – if recorded – is then passed onto councillors or candidates to act on separately. Some local parties have proactive systems for following up issues locally, but this information is seldom used beyond this initial action. There is no culture of 'two-way' traffic – of issues gathered at the grassroots being fed back to the centre to shape campaigns and vice versa...

From talking to those in marginal seats I think there are also lessons we can learn from how our opponents focused their efforts on targeting specific, often localised messages at small groups of people.

Labour organisers concede that the Conservatives' targeting and messaging was more sophisticated but are very brittle at the suggestion they somehow failed to pull out the numbers. To some extent, insiders say, they were lulled in to a false sense of security. The election had proved divisive, so many long-standing Labour voters were easily persuaded to go to the polling station. And unlike in 2010, after the crash and the expenses scandal, the 'don't knows' were often polite if uncommitted, whereas five years previously more hostility had been encountered. But that didn't mean these voters were necessarily softening to the Labour message.

Party officials maintain that good organisation can tackle the problem of 'differential turnout' – in other words, there is a greater the tendency for Labour supporters not to cast their ballots than Conservatives. Jon Mellon and Chris Prosser have been analysing data from the massive British Election Study of voters and they suggest that differential turnout was indeed a problem for the party as 'considerably fewer of those saying they were going to vote Labour are likely to have actually turned out to vote'.

But to make a difference, Labour organisers insist the party needs to be within shouting distance of their main opponents – one, or two points. To be six or seven points behind is just too much of a gap to plug.

And this time they didn't even know how far behind they really were. From January, Labour's field operation had been concerned about the 'retention rate' – that is, the number of people who voted Labour in 2010 and who would stick with the party in 2015. There were reports that this rate was falling, and in the past some Labour defectors would go, perhaps, to the Lib Dems. This time the Conservatives were the beneficiaries, but with a high number of 'don't knows' being recorded on the doorstep, that wasn't immediately clear. There wasn't the budget for Labour to poll in every constituency – so they often relied on the work done by Conservative – supporting Lord Ashcroft who of course made available his results to all and sundry and that research had tended to point to the vote was holding up in marginal seats.

There was another reason why they were foxed into complacency. The most active and committed often sign up for postal votes since it's no longer necessary to prove it would be impossible to get to a polling booth in order to obtain one. These are regarded as votes 'in the bag' if you can ensure supporters cast them nice and early. Agents from the parties can then attend the opening and verification of postal votes before polling day to ensure correct procedures are followed. They are not supposed to peek at how the votes have been cast, but some do. And from what they had seen, certainly in many marginal seats those who had voted early – if not often – had been putting Labour in the lead. Those who voted on polling day turned out to be less enthusiastic.

Labour's final private polling had suggested the party had slipped to one or two points behind the Conservatives in marginal seats, but that information wasn't shared with everyone involved in the campaign – even at very senior levels.

And the British Election Study identified another problem – public polls, which the organisers did see, tended to overstate Labour support because the party's lead grew most strongly between 2010 and 2015 amongst those who were the most unlikely actually to cast their ballots.

But even if the organisers had realised that they were both falling behind in marginal seats and amongst those most likely to vote, it would have been difficult to move people and resources around late in the day.

* * *

There was another – political – problem. Party organisers had drawn up a list of 80 key seats. Ed Miliband's slogan at the time, in 2013, was 'One Nation' and he wanted his list of target seats to match the narrative. So he ordered an expansion to 106 seats. While, logically enough, 88 of these seats were ones which Labour had lost in 2010, 15 had last been won in 2001 – and three had never been held even in the Blair landslide of 1997.

So already resources were having to be devoted to some areas where all the conversations in the world were unlikely to lead to the election of a Labour MP. And because every candidate was told if they were in a key seat or not, diverting funds proved difficult as some were not being taken kindly to being 'written off'. From January – subtly then more blatantly – there had been a *de facto* narrowing of the target list without any formal recognition of the fact, and more organisers moved to where they could potentially have most impact.

But the more fundamental, over-arching point was that structurally the system was better at identifying, than growing, the Labour support.

The Strange Disappearance
of Arnie Graf

6 May

- Senior figures feel they are missing the advice of veteran US community campaigner Arnie Graf as polling day approaches.
- There are suspicions he fell victim to internal feuds.
- The new leader will have to examine how best to build as well as identify the Labour vote.

'YOU CAN'T PULL out the Labour vote' – unless you have built it up in the first place. That is the uncontroversial view of one of the most senior people in Labour's ranks. How to build up that vote proved far more controversial. And the failure to do so cost seats Labour had targeted to win. Some organisers were regretting not having one man around as polling day approached.

The party machine is, as we established, geared up to identifying the Labour vote and getting it to the polling station, or at least to completing a postal ballot. This is the internal advice, for example, which one constituency circulated to its members: 'The aim of any operation is to increase the turnout of Labour votes to ensure that Labour wins in key areas.'

What was needed in addition was to expand that vote in marginal seats. And Labour initially looked to someone who was said to have inspired Barack Obama – the American community organiser extraordinaire Arnie Graf.

He was introduced to Miliband by Lord Glasman in 2010 who had taken his advice in *London Citizens*, the grassroots group that campaigned for the living wage. Graf agreed to conduct a 'root and branch' review of Labour's structures following field work in 14 different locations.

His report was completed in time for Labour's 2011 conference but it wasn't widely circulated. Some of the ideas were subsequently taken up, though in most cases not until after the Falkirk debacle – for example, building up a network of supporters. These cut-price 'members' voted amid some controversy in the recent Labour leadership contest. There was a restricted take-up for the idea of 'open primaries' where everyone who says they share Labour's values – and not just party members – can vote for parliamentary candidates. Miliband wanted to limit this to areas where the local Labour Party organisation was moribund.

But his supporters inside Labour HQ say Graf's true worth was sharing his expertise in community organising gained over three decades in Chicago. After his report was completed, he visited the UK every few months to dispense advice. As one insider put it:

> His work was crucial to how we should rebuild for the future. What he did was show that you can pick up issues that affect people's everyday lives even when you are in opposition and make a difference. Then, it becomes easier to get them engaged and involved, and you know you can count on them come polling day. You are expanding your activity and your base.

That 'crucial work' was undermined when in January last year *The Sun* ran a front-page story with the headline 'Ed Aide Illegal'. It said that Graf had a business visa, which allowed him to travel regularly to the UK but not to accept a salary. Labour insisted there was nothing illegal in the arrangement, and that they had lawyers' letters and correspondence with the Home Office to prove it. He was merely reimbursed for wages foregone in the States.

But the damage was done. One of his allies said:

> After the furore over his immigration status – and as he is not an immigrant it should have been irrelevant – but after the fuss, Arnie felt he couldn't really come here very often.

He did make a week-long trip in June 2014 to meet Labour officials and politicians but he wasn't out and about in communities where his work was more valuable.

There is still immense bad blood within Labour HQ as it is assumed that the leak to *The Sun* could only have come from an insider in an attempt to take out a rival for Miliband's ear. But while one man can provide inspiration, it's hard to believe that an American in his early 70s could single handedly have delivered crucial marginals. Labour organisers say that despite Graf's absence, similar ideas were put in to action in some areas, and this was reflected in better results – for example Wes Streeting's successful overturning of 5,500 Conservative majority in Ilford North. And Stella Creasy's work in taking on loan sharks in her community and pay day lenders more widely had helped strengthen Labour's majority in her seat without the need for Graf's advice.

Even if Graf had moved permanently to this side of the Atlantic, he could not have waved a magic wand in those areas where local Labour parties are moribund or don't work with their wider communities.

Graf himself penned a post-election missive to party supporters, posted on 4 August on the Labour List website which at least diagnosed the problem he was originally supposed to have helped to cure:

The party's failure in the last election had very little to do with the organisers in the field. The fault lies with their job assignments, expectations, and with the limited regard that too many of the national leadership hold them in. The organisers are not expected or assigned to grow the party. They have no time to develop meaningful relationships with people in the communities where they are assigned to work; therefore, the party remains out of touch with the vast majority of people throughout the country.

Labour's membership has surged since the election defeat – up by a third to a little less than 300,000 – and there are also about 112,000 'registered supporters' too, who have signed up at a cut-price rate and may choose to get more actively involved by the time of the next election. So with a potentially larger army of foot-soldiers, or 'persuaders', Labour may well have the option of running more campaigns alongside conducting more sophisticated canvassing if it can hold on to those who have joined as members or supporters over the summer of 2015. The party's new leader may never have a better time – or reason – to look at a root and branch reform of the party's organisation – and its purpose.

A Little Less Conversation:
Food, Drink and Fun

6 May

- The Conservatives' polling shows them consistently ahead of Labour, and proves more accurate.
- David Cameron may have fewer troops fighting his ground war – but they appear more mobile.
- Much of the Conservative campaign exists 'beneath the radar'.
- Jeremy Corbyn will have to look at the more sophisticated techniques of his party's opponents.

THE CONSERVATIVES were having trouble getting people to canvass for the Prime Minister. That was Ed Miliband's constant refrain at his rallies and public meetings. 'I am not surprised', he would joke, 'I wouldn't want to knock on doors for David Cameron either'. But with an ageing Conservative membership, and one which party insiders have told me is smaller than their published figures, Labour really did feel they were winning the ground war.

The trouble is that unlike an 'air war' – on television and radio – a ground campaign is carried out under the radar. Conservative sources say Labour under-estimated the scale of their operation and that left them with a 'blind spot' in seats where they were vulnerable. Certainly, there had been clues to the Conservatives' capability. Less than a year before the general election, the Conservative Patrick Mercer resigned as MP for Newark, due to a BBC Panorama investigation in to his role in setting up an All Party Parliamentary Group apparently for a paying client. UKIP's tails had been up, having gained the largest number of UK seats in the European Parliament. The Conservatives were desperate not to lose the constituency to a defector from their ranks, now the UKIP MEP for the area, Roger Helmer. So the seat was used as a test bed for techniques developed by the then party chairman Grant Shapps. *Team 2015* consisted of highly motivated volunteers who flooded the constituency on a daily basis, disseminating messages to target voters. The Conservatives retained the seat. Their candidate Robert Jenrick won with a majority of nearly 7,500 on a turnout of a little more than 50 per cent.

Both Labour and sections of the Conservative hierarchy agreed on one thing – they both doubted that an operation could be mounted on the same scale at the general election. It had never been attempted before. A decision had been taken to fight the constituency targeted by Nigel Farage – South Thanet – like a byelection but as the Conservatives were trying officially to gain 40 seats and defend 40 that were vulnerable – though I am told that privately this was in fact a 50/50 strategy – it was felt resources might be stretched.

But the party chairman was confident and deliberately never responded to Labour barbs about how difficult it would be to mount a campaign. Grant Shapps had been working on the idea since 2012. A ministerial source recalled the reaction when Shapps presented his plans to a 'political cabinet' of top-table Conservatives:

> We had never done this before and to be frank, we were sceptical. If you had a safe constituency the idea of mutual assistance was to put five or six people in a car and send them to a nearby marginal. When Grant Shapps said he had 1,000 volunteers we said wow, that's really strong. But in the end the party had 100,000.

In the party chairman's office there were two whiteboards – with the 50 target seats and 50 that were being defended and well before the formal campaign there would 'superSatudays' and 'superSundays' declared when certain constituencies would be inundated with volunteers. Their *Team 2015* volunteers could only sign up via head office and were surveyed on their interests. 21 separate steps to make people turn up were deployed – and a 'chivvying, team' some of whom were drawn from a big accountancy house, would ring people up days in advance to get them to go along to these marginal seats.

People would be told that food drink and rewards would be available, there would always be a social element to the day and campaigning would be made to sound like fun. But the chivviers would also appeal to a sense of purpose and patriotism – what the volunteers were doing was in the country's interest, they would be told. And the chivviers would try to extract commitments from the volunteers. As one insider put it 'when we got them to commit to a specific train, we knew we had them.'

In the last two weeks the Conservatives narrowed the seats targeted down to just the 24 that they saw as crucial and sent their buses of volunteers there. Some people had signed up to spend one or two weeks in the campaign, staying in hotels around the country and being bussed to wherever they were needed. Party insiders were delighted and a little surprised to be attracting a lot of women and people from ethnic minority backgrounds that hadn't signed up for party membership.

The difference between being in a target seat and one outside, Conservative insiders say, was worth millions of pounds. Before the campaign got under way for the first time every single seat was polled. This would have counted against election expense limits once the formal campaign started so groups of seats were then surveyed and Conservative strategists had access to daily tracking polls. This helped to put resources in the right places. By contrast Labour could only muster three tracking polls during the whole of the 'short' campaign.

So from the start of the year, two seats that hadn't been targeted came in to play – both of them held by the Lib Dems. Vince Cable's Twickenham and David Laws' Yeovil looked possible and the Conservative campaigns there were scaled up. In the end a dozen extra Lib Dem seats were added to the Conservative target list this year. Yet the extent of the Lib Dem collapse seemed to catch Labour and the Liberal Democrats themselves by surprise.

The Conservatives' tracker polls were discussed at senior management team meetings attended by strategist Lynton Crosby, co-chairman Andrew Feldman and campaign manager Stephen Gilbert and these were pointing to around 300 Conservative seats for much of the campaign. There was some evidence of a late swing, though from a higher base than many public polls were suggesting. In the last week the polling suggested the party could gain 324 seats and an overall majority was possible, with a near-wipeout of Labour in the south and east.

Grant Shapps offers his own theory on why Labour apparently had more conversations with voters but gained fewer votes. He points out that in Lord Ashcroft's polling, consistently more voters said they had heard from Labour than the Conservatives. But he puts that down to poor intelligence.

> Labour couldn't win my seat of Welwyn Hatfield yet they still spent money sending eight pieces of generic direct mail – not about the candidate – into my constituency. We would not have wasted money like this. It was very old fashioned campaigning, spraying the message round everywhere. So Labour loved those Ashcroft polls that told them their contact rate was great but it didn't win them seats.

A Labour insider agreed:

> Our operation was tiny by comparison – the Tories knew more than us on how to target individuals, and then they had the organisational capacity to link that knowledge to specific communications with voters. Labour's approach was different, with millions spent on direct mail that focussed heavily on national messaging. It was filling gaps in the 'air war'. If we weren't saying much about immigration on the airwaves, then it would

be covered on a leaflet. But it gives you no connection locally, compared to the stuff the Tories were doing.

Shadow Minister, Jonathan Ashworth paints a similar picture:

We did Royal Mail postal drops which sometimes obliterated whole constituencies or postcodes with leaflets. The ground war was only a means of delivering a national message and the Conservatives' message motivated more people than ours.

And as Labour's pollster James Morris told me:

The most fundamental thing is if you have a problem of brand identity – on immigration, the deficit, whatever – you cannot solve it just by sending everyone the political equivalent of a pizza flyer, no matter how well written it is.

In some areas, candidates went 'off message' but had to pay for the literature themselves, or from local fundraising. Internal critics say Labour spent too much of its targeting effort – such as it was – using Experian's 'Mosaic' Group classifications. These place people into 15 different groups, often based on tenure or household, and then further differentiates them in to 67 different 'types'. For example, the 'foot on the (housing) ladderers', the 'settled ex-tenants', the 'brownfield pioneers'. It's a sophisticated and successful marketing tool, and many companies use the system to decide, say, where to locate a new store but as one strategist bemoaned: 'unfortunately for politicians, the type of house you live in correlates only very weakly to what you really care about.'

Labour and the Conservatives – and indeed the SNP for that matter – all used the same, powerful NationBuilder database. As with all systems, the old adage 'rubbish in, rubbish out' holds true. The Conservatives managed to exploit its full potential by carrying out vast surveys, sometimes sent by professional staff by post where they simply didn't have the volunteers on the ground to deliver them. The detailed information which came back was used to better target their messages. So far fewer voters would have received the very general mailshots that Shapps got in the post from Labour. By contrast, Labour tended to use the database to direct volunteers to where they were most needed, and to connect those who had been in touch with the national party with local campaigns. The first priority of the incoming general secretary Iain McNicol had been to pay down Labour's large debts – so money for the database wasn't available until 2013, and the Conservatives had a considerable head start.

Jonathan Ashworth believes the party should have invested in the database sooner – 'we had the capacity to do better targeting, with very talented data analysts just like the Tories. But we hadn't put in the money early on, and we had made a strategic decision to do what the Tories couldn't – and flood individual constituencies with volunteers.'

Incidentally, in one parliamentary term, Labour cut their own debts by £12 million and are on course to be debt-free by mid-2016. Perhaps they should have made more of their financial rectitude during the campaign.

Breakfast in Doncaster

7 May: Polling Day

- Ed Miliband expects to reach Number 10.
- He is given elaborate instructions on how to avoid the local livestock that might make him look less than prime ministerial.
- The new leader will need more reliable, up to date, polling.

IT IS THE MOST middle-class object. Ever. Don't take my word for it. In a vast study of British social attitudes conducted by Gordon Brown's former pollster Deborah Mattinson for her BritainThinks project the cafetiere was the object most people believed typified a middle-class lifestyle. So I betrayed my humble origins by squeezing down on the one resting on the table in Ed Miliband's conservatory before the coffee was remotely ready to pour in my desperate desire to get a caffeine fix.

The Labour leader and his wife Justine had voted early – though not often, as the traditional motto of the voter-riggers goes – in his Doncaster North constituency and they had invited the press pack that had pursued them for the past six weeks in for breakfast. Joining them was the gang with which we had become familiar – the affable communications chief Bob Roberts, broadcasting guru Matthew Laza, 'second brain' Stewart Wood, and the cool and competent *chargé d'affaires* Rachel Kinnock.

The house, Justine admitted, wasn't regularly used as the kids were at school in London but wouldn't have been a bad place to let them run free with a generous garden backing on to open countryside at the edge of the constituency.

Earlier in the morning, though, the proximity of a rural hinterland very nearly posed a problem. Ed Miliband shared with us the map which Bob Roberts had drawn for him, demonstrating the best route to the local polling station. Surely he wasn't so unfamiliar with his own constituency that he required a map to cast his vote? No, not at all. The Labour leader then pointed out to general amusement a stick-like object scrawled on the piece of paper and took guesses as to what beast it purported to represent. It was in fact, a horse. Bob Roberts said:

> Yes I know my lack of artistic skill became the butt of jokes but we had constructed a route to the polling station up a country road – we knew the cameras would be interested. So the image was sunlit uplands. But when it was recced, we found out we had a problem with an aggressive dog and a horse kept sticking its head over a wall.

The last thing we wanted was the pictures of a possible prime minister being bitten by a hound or looking as though he was having a conversation over a fence with a rather sleepy-looking nag.

So an approved route was chosen to minimise risk, though it hadn't become entirely possible to avoid a 'vote UKIP' poster. Someone wondered aloud whether the now prime ministerial security detail surrounding Miliband wouldn't just take the unfortunately curious equine out. Ed Miliband had his own tale to tell about security. He had left the previous night's rally in Leeds in an armoured vehicle but had intended to join up with his loyal band of campaigners aboard their 'battle bus'. The burly security men had driven them to the rendezvous point, an almost deserted car park near Leeds United's Elland Road ground. The only sign of life was a courting couple in another vehicle who got spooked at the sight of Ed Miliband's chisel-jawed minders. The Milibands patiently waited for the bus for nearly half an hour then gave up. One of those aboard the bus later told me 'we detoured to get a few beers in'.

I joked that sitting in the deserted car park must have been like a scene from A Very British Coup – the thriller by the former Labour MP Chris Mullin in which a left-wing leader is ousted from office subtly but effectively. Miliband said, 'Yes, I was worried they were about to open their "in the event of a Labour government" envelopes'.

The mood that morning was relatively upbeat. Ed Miliband wore casual clothes and said there was no point worrying about the result as little could be done to change it. He certainly believed he could be prime minister at that stage. He was under orders to do some canvassing then rest for the long night ahead. The published polls were still suggesting it was too close to call and one insider said: 'Look, one things for sure. Cameron is just not going to get an overall majority.'

The Loser Always Wins?

7 May: Polling Day

- Ed Miliband is prepared to become prime minister even if Labour is a long way behind the Conservative in seats and vote share.
- Labour's top team discuss various possible outcomes – no one is allowed to write down 'the secret scenario'.
- Labour's new leader could face questions over legitimacy.

IT WAS TIME TO tell the truth. Labour had made clear, degree by degree, that they wouldn't do a deal with the SNP to gain power. But Ed Miliband time and again had managed to avoid – or, frankly, evade – questions over whether he thought it would be legitimate to become prime minister with fewer seats and votes than his main opponent.

On polling day, what journalists and politicians assumed was implicit finally became explicit. Back in 2010 Labour 'big beasts' such as David Blunkett and John Reid spoke out against attempts to form a 'coalition of the losers' and for Gordon Brown to stay on in Downing Street with fewer seats and votes than David Cameron. Five years on and that was – if necessary – exactly what Ed Miliband intended to do.

The former Lord Chancellor Lord Falconer was tasked with calling political editors and commentators to quote – and then explain, and indeed interpret – paragraph 2.12 from the Cabinet Manual, the document drawn up by the then Cabinet Secretary Gus O'Donnell. It had been commissioned by Gordon Brown but completed under the coalition and was to codify the 'conventions and rules that affect the operation and procedures of the Government'. The relevant paragraph read:

> Where an election does not result in an overall majority for a single party, the incumbent government remains in office unless and until the Prime Minister tenders his or her resignation and the Government's resignation to the Sovereign. An incumbent government is entitled to wait until the new Parliament has met to see if it can command the confidence of the House of Commons, but is expected to resign if it becomes clear that it is unlikely to be able to command that confidence and there is a clear alternative.

Charlie Falconer's expert opinion was that it was perfectly legitimate for the leader of the second largest party to become prime minister. Ed Miliband gratefully accepted this advice, as it was just what he wanted to hear. Both Falconer and Miliband believed that even if there were to be an absence of deals with the SNP, in a hung parliament Sturgeon's party – for the sake of their reputation in Scotland as well as their prospects at the 2016 Holyrood elections – would have to be true to their words and agree to 'lock out' David Cameron from Downing Street. Therefore, in these circumstances there was a likelihood that Ed Miliband could command the confidence of the House, so Cameron shouldn't cling on in a minority position and put forward a Queen's Speech only for it to be defeated. He should be put under immediate pressure to clear off.

There was only one very slight flaw in this grand plan. It was bollocks. Or rather it was based on false assumptions. Charlie Falconer would admit privately later that from Labour's polling and from its ground operations it was assumed Cameron would struggle to get into Downing Street even with the help of the DUP. Labour's policy supremo Jon Cruddas said: 'We were told we couldn't lose… People were saying we couldn't get less than 35 per cent of the vote'.

Lying beneath this assumption was that the Lib Dems would not be reduced to single figures. Labour simply didn't have adequate research or enough doorstep conversations in Lib Dem/Tory marginals to assess that the Conservatives would sweep the Lib Dems from their south-west heartland. The Lib Dems woke up late to the scale of their impending defeat. And what is fascinating is that while the polls in the end understated Conservative support, they did point to a Lib Dem collapse. One senior Labour figure tried to explain the delusion:

> We saw in the Eastleigh by-election where the previous incumbent, Chris Huhne, went to prison they still clung on so we just assumed where they had the benefit of incumbency they would somehow hold on.

So Labour had more faith in the Lib Dems than either the pollsters – or their recent coalition partners in government. Another working assumption was that even if the number of Labour gains were disappointing in England, there wouldn't be a net loss of seats.

So what scenarios did those at the centre of Labour's campaign consider? Some newspapers have suggested only two possibilities were given any serious consideration. In fact, four were discussed.

The first involved the Conservatives gaining around 290 seats. Under these circumstances it was felt Labour and the SNP together would probably fail to be able to 'lock' Cameron out of Downing Street. Attempts would be made to woo Nick Clegg, but the working assumption was that if it was possible for the Lib Dems to form another government with the Tories then Clegg would take it. A senior figure who would have negotiated for Labour in the event of a hung parliament said:

Clegg felt we hated him far more than we actually did. And he didn't want the humiliation of admitting that the last five years had been wrong so if he kept his seat (which Labour targeted but failed to take) he was more likely to go in with the Tories if that was at all possible.

However, there may only have been enough seats together for a minority coalition.

David Cameron would then be expected to stay in Downing Street and put forward a Queen's Speech and could then possibly get 'over the line' with the backing of the DUP. But it would be a volatile arrangement. In the run up to the election, some newspapers suggested Labour had been talking to Sinn Fein which had been denied. In fact very informal overtures had been made to the DUP who had declared themselves opposed to the 'bedroom tax'. Nonetheless under this scenario it was accepted that Miliband would fail to make it Downing Street – or at least not quickly – but the assumption was that he would remain party leader for the foreseeable post-election period.

The second involved the Conservatives getting about 280 seats. It was felt at this number, together Labour and the SNP could affix that lock to Downing Street's door and keep Cameron out. But also that Cameron would have too few seats to form a coalition with the Lib Dems, who were (wrongly) assumed likely to pick up 20–30 seats. So under this hypothesis, Labour plus the SNP plus a few others – a Green or two, the Northern Ireland independent Sylvia Hermon – would be able together to defeat any Queen's Speech Cameron could put forward. As Labour were therefore more likely to 'command the confidence of the House', the pressure would be on the Conservative leader to vacate Downing Street and give Miliband the keys. The strategy would then be to present a Queen's Speech – with measures designed to be attractive to the SNP and which they would would feel compelled to back – but that it might also be possible for Labour and the Lib Dems to form a government. It would be easier if Clegg had been defeated in his Sheffield Hallam constituency – and if Vince Cable clung on in Twickenham – but not essential. In fact, some advisers felt it would be better to have the existing Lib Dem leader *in situ*.

There had been a debate about whether to 'get to' Clegg before the Conservatives could make a counter-offer. Ed Balls had argued strongly against an early approach and it had been decided, under these circumstances, not to lift the phone to the Lib Dem leader straight away. Instead, they'd plough on with Labour's minority programme with Miliband installed in Downing Street then invite the Lib Dem leader to join in the interests of stability, and to save the country from an overly-influential SNP. But what Labour wanted to avoid was the possibility – as had happened in 2010 – of the Lib Dems running from one camp to the other to produce the best deal. This time they wanted to ensure that Miliband would be ensconced in Number 10 with or without Clegg. The Lib Dems would get something out of a political relationship but they wouldn't get a veto over a Labour government. And Clegg, who had in effect ousted Gordon Brown in 2010, would not be allowed to play kingmaker this time.

The third scenario involved the Conservatives getting perhaps 270 seats. Under this scenario Labour might have slightly more votes than the Conservatives, but slightly fewer seats. The argument would be that effectively there was a draw, but the momentum was with Labour and there was a 'progressive' majority in Parliament. That cabinet manual which Charlie Falconer was interpreting for the commentariat would be important. Senior Labour figures had been discussing the whole question of legitimacy and how far behind the Conservatives it would be possible to be and still have credibility in forming a government. One source close to the discussions said:

> Ten seats behind would have been a slam dunk. Fifteen less and it would depend on what it felt like – had we made iconic gains from the Conservatives? Twenty was borderline.

Others felt that it would indeed have been perfectly legitimate for Ed Miliband to govern without the aid of other parties despite falling 50 or so seats short of a working majority.

One of Ed Miliband's closest advisers, Tom Baldwin, felt in office Miliband would have allowed himself to be a 'builder' not a 'soldier' and would have successfully constructed a consensus to stay in government:

> Look, it would have been tough. It would have been messy. But I think Ed would have made a better prime minister than leader of the opposition. I believe he would have returned to the One Nation message because that would have been the only way to govern without a majority. That part of his character that sought to bring people together, that listened to arguments, that tried to build a consensus, that would have come to the fore.

Labour insiders say Ed Miliband would have stuck to his campaign promise not to do deals with the SNP. There would be much to Nicola Sturgeon's liking in his legislative programme and of course much discussion with SNP MPs over the individual bills as they went through parliament to ensure they passed, but there would be no prior discussion on the programme itself.

While Lord Falconer was open to some arrangement later in the parliament to sustain Labour in power, the thinking within Miliband's inner circle was that possibly a five year programme of government would have been just too difficult to maintain. Certainly the Conservatives would be challenged to vote with Labour against the SNP on Trident renewal well in to the next parliament – but ultimately if Labour were to deliver on the pledge to clear the current account deficit by 2020 at the latest, tensions with the avowedly anti-austerity SNP – probably returned to power at Holyrood in 2016 – might prove difficult. So even before polling day 2015, there was already talk of an early election in the event of a minority Labour government. But not before Ed Miliband could convince the public that he could make a difference. As one insider put it:

> Ideally we would engineer a situation where the SNP and Tories brought us down – that would give us a way back in Scotland where the SNP said they wouldn't vote with the Tories.

But none of these scenarios really required further discussion. Because in the end it was the 'secret' scenario which prevailed. Some of Ed Miliband's strategists had been pressing for a proper discussion of it – and were told under no circumstances was it to be written down. That is perhaps understandable. The papers had had various stories on the parties 'game plans' for a hung parliament. If this had leaked, the front page of papers not known for their Labour sympathies would have declared something along the lines of 'The Game's Up! Miliband throws in the towel!'

The unwritten scenario was a result so bad that Ed Miliband's resignation would be required – that the Conservatives could form a government with a working majority with no need of other parties. Some in Miliband's inner circle didn't find the idea ludicrous – there had been that leadership crisis the previous November but which had fizzled out for the lack of an alternative candidate. But the official polls and the less optimistic private polling – which had shown the Conservatives ahead, but not massively – weren't pointing to certain defeat. And a senior strategist pointed out that their Conservative equivalent believed there was 'only a one per cent chance' of an outright Tory victory so there simply hadn't been as much prior discussion of this scenario as there might have been. Views had been split on whether Miliband should go quickly, or stay on as caretaker and let the party rebuild without too much shock therapy. This had – like so many other issues – never been resolved before polling day, so when the actual result came there was no consensus on what to do next.

Ed Miliband's willingness to form a government with fewer seats and votes than his main opponent might make matters all the more difficult for a successor trying to clear a deficit of nearly 100 seats with the Conservatives. Unless it looks like they can achieve this mighty task in one fell swoop, then they are now likely to be under greater pressure in the media and in parliament to rule out forming a government from a runners-up position.

Moment of Truth

7–8 May

- Miliband and his inner circle share some chilli con carne as they await the results in Doncaster.
- The exit poll is worse than expected and Miliband's message needs to be redrafted.
- The Labour leader's first instinct is to resign.

ONLY ED MILIBAND'S inner circle saw his reaction to the election results. On the morning of polling day, the Labour leader had invited the media in for breakfast. With polls about to close, the croissants have been replaced by chilli, and the broadcasters were being kept at bay outside the Miliband residence, clustered in the cul-de-sac of recently built homes on the edge of Doncaster.

Inside, amongst those joining Ed and Justine were Anna Yearley, Ed Miliband's fiercely loyal political secretary and gatekeeper; and his 'on the road' team of Bob Roberts, Rachel Kinnock and Stewart Wood. Greg Beales, his strategy director, had travelled up from London to help with speech writing. He was to have been the 'angel of death' who would only make an appearance if it had been assumed Miliband wouldn't make it to Downing Street. He was there to deliver home truths but only made the journey because the regular speechwriter Marc Stears was dealing with a more pressing issue of delivery – the arrival of a new child. Beales in fact had been quite optimistic about the outcome when he headed north.

While all four scenarios had been discussed, the bulk of the speech-writing effort had been devoted to two: either the coalition losing its combined majority and David Cameron losing his momentum but 'clinging on to power' – or to Ed Miliband's right to lead a minority government with the Conservatives 'locked out'. Contemporary reports that Miliband was writing his 'victory speech' were wide of the mark. In fact he hadn't fully completed his speeches before the close of poll.

When Beales got a four-minute warning of the broadcasters' exit poll, he knew either speech probably wouldn't do, and radical redrafting might be necessary. But he didn't blurt out the poll result before it appeared on television.

Perhaps as a way of coping with the tension, Ed Miliband had gone round the room and asked some of the people to whom he had been closest what they would do if Labour lost. He apparently volunteered that he would travel and continue to campaign for action to mitigate climate change.

But there was about to be a dramatic shift in the more immediate political climate. As the entire team gathered round the television at 9.55pm awaiting the BBC election programme, they were braced for second place – but not for the dramatic gap in seats between Labour and the Conservatives which the exit poll revealed as the clock struck ten. The poll suggested David Cameron would fall just short of an overall majority with 316 seats but Labour would lag well behind – and well short of being able to form a government with just 239. The Lib Dems would be reduced to a rump of 10.

In fact the end result was better for the Conservatives – 330 seats – and worse for Labour – finishing on 232. The Lib Dems were reduced to single figures with just eight. The SNP got 56, instead of the predicted 58, though there was no disappointment in the Sturgeon household.

Ed Miliband said, 'if the poll's right, I have to go'. But this wasn't the last word on the subject. Not by a long chalk. He asked the assembled group if this could be correct. Head office was on the line saying this was out of kilter with results from their field operations. The advice was to remain 'sceptical' – either all the previous polls had been wrong or the exit poll was awry.

Back in the Brewer's Green HQ, the press team decided to disseminate this advice more widely. Within minutes of the decision, one text I received reflected the wishful thinking: 'We are sceptical of the BBC poll. It looks wrong to us.' But another was almost delusional:

> The coalition came into the election with a majority of 73, and even if the
> BBC exit poll is right, that has been all but wiped out. Who forms the next
> government is who can carry the confidence of the House of Commons.

Let's examine this more closely. *Even IF the exit poll is right...* That poll put the Conservatives 77 seats ahead of Ed Miliband, and with a higher share of the vote. Labour's official line at that point was that it would still be legitimate for Ed Miliband to move in to Downing Street. The position was untenable and of course subsequently changed, but it does betray Labour's approach on the night – to argue swiftly that the 'loser' could become prime minister.

Those in Doncaster with Ed Miliband reported no dramatic meltdown – rather, as one put it, 'We felt the sand drifting away from under us.' Although Labour won both seats in Sunderland, the first city to declare, they could see the swing to the party was less than they were expecting. Stewart Wood had told journalists at breakfast that Nuneaton would be the litmus test – this West Midlands marginal would reveal whether Ed Miliband could be prime minister or if Labour would remain in opposition. So at 1.52am the *coup de grâce* was delivered.

After the election, I asked the Prime Minister when he knew he would get an overall majority. Despite the upbeat assessment of his strategists who had believed for days that outright victory was possible, David Cameron said he remained 'sceptical and cautious... until Nuneaton'.

Nuneaton is the New Basildon

8 May

- Labour's result is worse than in 2010.
- The party was failing to gain seats it had won when the Conservatives last had an overall majority.
- The new Labour leader is likely to look at why the party is still popular in many big cities but isn't winning in 'market towns'.

THE EXIT POLL broadcast in 1992 – the last time the Conservatives had formed a majority government – pointed to a hung parliament. The decisive blow to the poll's credibility was delivered when David Amess – the outspoken MP with a New Romantic haircut – retained Basildon in Essex. Tony Blair's return to Downing Street was assured when Angela Smith retook the seat for Labour in 1997.

But now Basildon – or Basildon and Billericay as it's currently known – wasn't even on Labour's target list. Neither were seats just across the Thames Estuary in North Kent – seats which the party had held from 1997 until 2010. So, in truth, it was always unlikely that the party was on its way to an overall majority in 2015.

But even the hope of a good second place evaporated when the scale of the defeat in Nuneaton was revealed. This market town near Coventry had seen its traditional industries such as textiles replaced by retail and distribution centres. But Labour had succeeded in winning it from the Conservatives in 1992 despite the overall election result.

Now, not only had Labour failed to regain a key constituency – 37th in its list of target seats – the result was worse than in 2010. The Conservative incumbent and former council leader Marcus Jones more than doubled his majority from 2,069 in 2010 to 4,882 – registering a swing of three per cent *from* Labour to the Conservatives. Worse still, Labour hadn't seen it coming.

* * *

So what went wrong in Nuneaton? Fast forward a month. I spoke to Labour supporters and activists when I was in town to report on the leadership hustings hosted by BBC *Newsnight*. There were factors that were peculiar to the town.

A young, relatively inexperienced candidate who had been selected in controversial circumstances. Vicky Fowler grew up in Nuneaton and was favoured by the former MP Bill Olner. But not everyone in the party had been happy. Local member Jackie Graney told me:

> Marcus Jones was a good MP – we had the wrong candidate, that split the local party. We had the chance of choosing Miriam O'Reilly, who used to work for the BBC – a powerful woman who could have taken on Marcus Jones blow by blow.

O'Reilly had successfully taken the BBC to an employment tribunal over what she alleged was 'ageism' towards female presenters in particular, when she had been bumped from the popular *Countryfile* programme just before it was moved to a prime time slot. Some local activists felt that she was being 'parachuted' into the seat because of her closeness to the party's deputy leader Harriet Harman and she failed to be selected. Jackie Graney said she and others went to work for the former Labour MP Mike O'Brien who was trying to win the nearby seat of North Warwickshire and Bedworth instead of canvassing locally. But he too lost. So were there wider lessons to be learnt from the failure to take Nuneaton?

Jake Croft – a first-time voter and canvasser – told me:

> I am left of centre – I agreed with freezing energy prices. But Labour didn't capture those aspirational things that Blair did, Miliband missed the mark there. There was complacency, and the party concentrated on 35 per cent of the electorate and missed middle-class voters who had backed Blair before.

But he suggested that there was a palpable 'late swing' to the Conservatives from the conversations that he held with voters:

> There was a lot of suspicion of politicians on the doorstep but last minute things moved people to the Conservatives – the stigma of the SNP combined with Tory rhetoric on the economy. There was a fear Labour would ruin the economy – as well fear about the role the SNP might play.

He also suggested some of his fellow canvassers misread voters' moods. They had spent time contacting people who had previously voted Labour but hadn't really been listening to them. If these contacts were counted as part of Ed Miliband's five million conversations, the interaction was simply too cursory to be useful. 'There was a lot of assuming going on. They were assuming some people would vote for them but actually voted UKIP.'

This analysis was reinforced by an older voter, Sally Chater. She said:

> Traditional Labour supporters I know were either staying at home or voting for other parties – some of it was personality over policies – they weren't a fan of Ed's, they didn't like him and didn't look behind the leader to the party as a whole.

But she argued that the campaign in such a key marginal seat had been lacklustre. 'A few leaflets went through the doors but I didn't feel the party was talking to the people I was talking to.'

It's clear one of the challenges for Labour's new leader is how to win back aspirational voters that have drifted away to the Conservatives while also rekindling enthusiasm from long-standing supporters that felt even Ed Miliband wasn't distinctive enough. Alan Baxter told me he was disillusioned:

> I'm a socialist at heart – I didn't back Labour this time. They didn't seem to engage to win over the local people. I still blame them for letting Rover Group go to the wall and introducing work related assessments for people on benefits – they didn't support good working-class jobs in the factories or support the common people when they became unemployed.

Exit

8 May

- Ed Miliband resigns as Labour leader.
- He had been urged to stay on as 'exhausted parties take bad decisions'.
- The starting gun on the Labour leadership election is fired.

I BROKE THE NEWS of Ed Miliband's impending resignation on the BBC election programme around 9.15am. The BBC would rather get it right than get it first – though ideally it would like us to do both. So I was interrogated by some colleagues before broadcasting the news – 'Are you sure?' while others were urging me to get in front of the cameras. With the official Labour line denouncing my well-sourced news as 'speculation', once I emerged from the studio, I was met with the encouraging phrase: 'I hope you're right.' I was – but it hadn't been straightforward.

Ed Miliband had been given competing advice. The general election co-ordinator Spencer Livermore, Lord Falconer and Tom Baldwin had been urging him to stay on while the party recovered from the shock. Baldwin sent an email for him to read on the journey of defeat, from Doncaster to London. He had plenty of time to do so – the victory helicopter had been chopped and he was making the journey by road. Baldwin's missive made the following arguments – that exhausted parties make bad decisions; that the Conservatives had defined Labour negatively after the 2010 election, blaming them for the financial crash and overspending while Ed, his brother and the other Ed had been distracted by slogging it out with each other in a leadership contest; and that no fullterm Labour leader of the Opposition had gone on to become prime minister. In other words, whoever they were to elect quickly was unlikely to make it to Downing Street. So he also argued that it would be better for the country as well as Miliband's own reputation if he stayed on as caretaker leader for six months – rather as Michael Howard had done following the Conservative defeat in 2005. He urged Ed Miliband to 'Tell the party to take a holiday over the summer' – then transform the autumn conference in to a leadership hustings with the candidates beginning their campaign at that point, rather than ending it there. Spencer Livermore called Miliband from London during the night urging him not to rush a decision. But Greg Beales, who was with Ed Miliband, felt the scale of the defeat pointed to the need for a clean break. His adviser Stewart Wood agreed.

Miliband began the first draft of his resignation speech on his laptop. One of his companions noticed that he seemed less tense, almost serene. He said – perhaps not entirely humourously – 'That's because they can't get me any more'.

The final decision to go wouldn't be taken until the morning, after Miliband addressed shell-shocked staff at the Brewers' Green HQ. Then in a conference room with his circle of advisers and his wife Justine, he listened to advice. 'Resilient' is a word Miliband uses about himself but those present were certainly impressed with his composure after one of the worst nights of his life.

It was Justine who vetoed his staying on – raising the cruel and unusual punishment of having to face a triumphant David Cameron over the despatch box at PMQs for an extended period. But those close to Ed Miliband say she simply articulated what he had already decided – that while he would listen politely to contrary arguments, the scale of the defeat would mean he would have to stand down. Spencer Livermore brought matters to a close and Miliband asked for 'five minutes' before thoughts turned again to the resignation speech. He would formally resign just after attending that day's VE Day commemorations. For him, the war was over. David Cameron was later overheard to say he had fully expected to be delivering his resignation to the Queen that day.

Miliband bade his formal farewell at lunchtime in the wood-panelled splendour of the Institute of Civil Engineers, ironically enough against the very prime ministerial backdrop that he and his advisers had wanted to achieve throughout the campaign. Those in the room – apart from the scurrying and fussing of TV crews – largely sat in shocked silence, while some of his staffers showed their emotions on their face. Tom Baldwin had eyes as bloodshot as a white rabbit.

I was there to cover his departure for *The World at One* which, despite the name, had been brought forward to noon. As I entered the room a long-standing Labour official said 'It's like '92 all over again'.

But it wasn't. For Labour it was much worse. A five per cent swing could have taken them to victory in 2015. But the loss of seats and ground – and with new and less favourable constituency boundaries in the offing – they face a bigger task in 2020 than Neil Kinnock faced against John Major. It's been calculated that a five per cent swing at the next election could leave them 47 seats short of an overall majority.

Ed Miliband graciously accepted his own role in Labour's downfall: 'I take absolute and total responsibility for the result and our defeat at this election.'

And he had accepted the argument for an early exit: 'I want to [resign] straight away because the party needs to have an open and honest debate about the right way forward without constraint.'

Then, a final attempt to rally the troops before heading for the Cenotaph and a stiff and formal encounter with the victor, David Cameron:

> You need to show your responsibility. Your responsibility, not simply to mourn our defeat: pick yourself up, and continue the fight. We've come back before and this party will come back again...The course of progress and social justice is never simple or straightforward. Change happens because people don't give up, they don't take no for an answer, they keep demanding change.

But the question was asked instantly whether with a change of leader, Labour would have fared better.

Views varied even amongst those closest to him. A former senior minister in the previous Labour government who had been offering advice to the Labour leader only days before, spat out the phrase 'f***ing Ed Miliband' and told me on this day 'I should have done more' to topple him when the half-cocked coup had been discussed the previous autumn. At the other end of the scale was Bob Roberts who had worked closely with Ed Miliband every day. 'I genuinely don't think we would have done any better if we had a different leader. People forget the big challenge was to move on from both Blair and Brown in 2010 and keep the party unified – of the five candidates, he was the best choice.'

Others say they were stuck with him no matter his shortcomings. The attempted putsch was put down when Alan Johnson declared he wasn't running for leader and was backing Miliband. But what had been a moment of crisis had been resolved, too, by a lack of a grassroots rebellion. Indeed some members were writing to their MPs seeking assurances that they weren't involved in a plot to oust Miliband. So the idea of a clean decapitation rather than a messy fight was probably always fantasy.

For others, Ed Miliband neither needed to go, nor needed his brother at the top table – he was just required to present a different version of himself to the public:

> He was three things at one and the team he had round him often reflected different parts of his character. At his core he was decent, principled, a unifier – very 'one nation'. But part of his self-image was to see himself as a class warrior, attacking vested interests, a divider. Then part of him, like Gordon Brown, was very tactical. Increasingly he looked divisive, that was getting the upper hand, he didn't seem to have clarity of purpose – big ideas were reduced to a series of retail offers. He put very reasonable ideas in very scary wrappers.

But perhaps the words of one former adviser are the most poignant:

> Ed never really knew where he wanted to go. Tony Blair knew where he wanted to end up, and an adviser's job was to provide the evidence, the backing, and the ballast for what he wanted to do anyway. Ed, like his old boss Gordon, almost seemed to like discussing the evidence more than settling on a direction. And in the end the public sniff that out, they just know. This guy isn't a leader.

AFTERMATH

A Question of Leadership

- The contest to find Ed Miliband's successor is transformed by Jeremy Corbyn's inclusion.
- Underlying divisions – from welfare to weapons – come to the surface.
- Shadow Cabinet unity is shattered.
- Labour figures denounce colleagues as 'morons' and 'criminally negligent'.
- Trying to avoid the mistakes of the last leadership contest leads to new errors.
- Former Labour leaders despair – but have they misread the public mood?

IT WAS THE ELECTION they hadn't wanted. Some of Ed Miliband's closest advisers had tried to persuade him to stay on as a caretaker leader. They thought it would be careless for candidates and activists alike to career into a leadership contest in a state of shock.

It soon become clear that the party was trying to correct the mistakes of the previous leadership contest rather than face the future with confidence. When Ed Miliband had won in 2010 he had put his energies in to his campaign, not his victory. He had to give his keynote conference speech just 72 hours after narrowly seeing off his brother for the top job – and didn't have it prepared.

It was decided to save his successor similar difficulties. There would be a 'special conference' on 12 September – ahead of the annual conference later in the month, giving the winner a couple of weeks to get their thoughts, and their new team together before subjecting their main speech to unforgiving and intense scrutiny. Never mind that the media wouldn't be content with an 'Oscar winner' approach on the first occasion, with a new leader simply thanking those who had been involved in the campaign. So in effect the leader's stall would have to be set out twice in the space of a month.

Other options had been available. NEC member Jonathan Ashworth had argued that the regular annual conference should be transformed into a hustings event for candidates and the election of a new leader should follow. Harriet Harman was initially tempted by a shorter timescale, settling the issue before parliament rose for the summer. She was well aware that the length of the previous contest – stretching from May to the very end of September – had allowed the Conservatives to set the agenda in 2010, and along with their Lib Dem allies successfully accuse Labour of at least contributing to – if not causing – the financial crash. But the compromise of a special conference was agreed by the ruling National Executive on 13 May, less than a week after the crushing election defeat. The majority of those present felt the scale of that defeat precluded the leadership contest from being rushed – but equally, there was a reluctance for it to drag on for most of the rest of the year.

Harriet Harman – now the party's interim leader – would resign from her post as deputy, and her replacement would also be elected on 12 September. Announcing the timetable, she said:

> We want as many people as possible to take part. More than 30,000 new members have joined the party in the last few days and I hope many more members and supporters will take this opportunity to have their voice heard.

She should have been careful what she wished for. Little did she know at the time how painful a process it would be, with accusations of infiltration and mischief-making as the party membership soared by a third, and, under rules introduced by Ed Miliband, more than 112,000 'registered supporters' would sign up at a cut price rate of just £3 to have a say on who should be Labour's next leader.

* * *

At first it had seemed pretty straightforward. On Sunday 10 May the Shadow Business Secretary, Chuka Umunna, sat alongside Lord Mandelson on Andrew Marr's BBC sofa – the furniture transported to a temporary pod constructed on college green, the strip of grass where many political reporters hold forth to camera against the backdrop of the Houses of Parliament. Umunna didn't quite say he'd stand for leader but gave strong hints. Later that morning, the Shadow Care Minister, Liz Kendall, didn't stand on ceremony and told the BBC's Andrew Neil she would throw her Blairite hat in the ring. She later told me she simply gave an honest answer to a straight question. It was expected Yvette Cooper would join the race, and I rang Andy Burnham – widely believed to have the best laid plans – to check when he would make an announcement. 'I'm shattered and in shock, to be honest,' he said – and indeed took almost a week before making a formal announcement. He could take his time as he already knew he had sufficient support to launch his bid.

Two days later I took the train to Swindon, when Umunna decided he would announce his candidacy in an unconventional way. He posted a ropy video – complete with wind-battered audio – on YouTube, shot on the town's main shopping street. If he wanted to undermine his slick image and look like an insurgent it wasn't a bad way to do it, though there is a fine line between trying to innovate and lacking gravitas.

I caught up with him amid low-rise industrial units on the edge of town, where the Labour Party had its local campaign headquarters. He was already acting like a leader in waiting, insisting on doing what's called a 'pool clip' – a couple of answers to a journalist from one broadcaster for dissemination to the others. In this case, the honoured recipient would be Sky's Joey Jones. But I, along with ITN's Libby Wiener, persuaded him to take questions from each of us. Libby was definitely 'bad cop', reminding him he 'wasn't royalty'. He had had – and would have – much tougher encounters than this and three days later he would pull out of the contest, citing media pressure. Sources close to his campaign suggested he had the firm support of fewer than ten of his colleagues and it would be an uphill battle to get on the ballot.

But that day I decided to follow in his footsteps and visit the pedestrianised street where he had shot a video which would have been regarded as a professional embarrassment by most terror groups.

I wanted to assess how difficult the challenge would be for Labour's hopefuls and on an iPad, showed various voters pictures of the likely leadership contenders. Unlike some, Umunna was recognised by almost everyone, even if his full name was a mouthful for a voter or two. And he was regarded pretty positively. What jolted me like an electric shock was how much the local shoppers were keen to talk about Labour more widely, without the slightest prompting. Sometimes getting an opinion from random people on the street was about as easy as finding a rap song without a profanity.

This time they held forth and had any of Labour's five million conversations been with these voters, the party might have known Swindon wasn't swinging their way. And some of their opinions could have been scripted in Conservative Campaign Headquarters.

Whack! 'I don't want that Spurgeon in charge!' said a middle-aged man, just one consonant away from the SNP leader's real name.

Pow! 'Well none of these candidates can be as bad as the last leader! He was useless!'

But – ouch! It was how the party was perceived on welfare that really hurt. Despite a slogan which featured working people, Labour was seen on the side of the 'scrounger' not the 'striver' – this despite the fact that the perceived abuse of the welfare system was going on under a Conservative–Lib Dem government.

This comment from a well-spoken woman in late-middle age was not untypical. 'It's the unfairness of it all,' she began, ambiguously. 'My father always voted Labour. I am from a Labour family. But it's so unfair to see people that don't do a day's work have everything – sitting at home watching their colour TVs when everyone else goes out to work.' And it was Labour, not the government that was getting the blame. She wouldn't vote for them unless Labour faced up to this.

And in a sense face up it did – but by again fighting the last election not the next one, the party almost spectacularly split over the welfare issue during the long and not so hot summer of the leadership campaign.

* * *

That split seemed some way off on a searingly hot Saturday, 16 May, when more than a thousand people crowded in to a harshly lit basement beneath the TUC's London headquarters, just round the corner from the throngs of shoppers going about their business in nearby Oxford Street. This had been the venue for the first 'hustings' of the campaign, hosted by the Blairite Progress group – an odd choice of location given that some trade unionists had denounced the group as a right-wing 'party within a party' and had wanted it banned. The warm-up acts ahead of the leadership contenders included the deputy leadership candidate Caroline Flint and newly elected MP Wes Streeting – an east London councillor and former education officer for the LGBT charity Stonewall. Each got the event off to a punchy start, with denunciations of the 'political, not organisational' failings of the previous Miliband regime.

Then the main cast. It wasn't quite the final line-up of the contest as each contender was still seeking the nomination of 35 MPs. Two of those present – Shadow Education Secretary Tristram Hunt and Shadow International Development Secretary Mary Creagh – would subsequently fail to do so. While the remaining candidates – Andy Burnham, Liz Kendall, and Yvette Cooper – tried to emphasise, initially politely, points of difference, it looked at this stage that there was an emerging consensus on some policy areas.

The word that Ed Miliband had been reluctant to utter – 'aspirational' – was to become *le mot de nos jours* in Labour circles. All that emphasis during the election on those on zero hours contracts meant Labour had to broaden its appeal and, in the words of Yvette Cooper, not just move either 'a bit to the left or a bit to the right'. Andy Burnham felt that the proposed levy on high value properties – the so-called mansions tax – had been seen as anti-aspirational. And all three felt the party hadn't been pro-business enough. Now the party's own pollsters have suggested that

Labour's attitude to business wasn't much of a vote winner or loser – it wasn't one of the main factors that would drive someone to cast a ballot. But the candidates clearly felt it was the first baby step toward regaining economic credibility, as well as being a straightforward way of distancing themselves from Ed Miliband's legacy.

It's not surprising the aspirational message was being delivered by all the candidates thus far. An internal Labour analysis by shadow ministers Jonathan Ashworth and Gloria De Piero suggested that while Labour had done well in cities, the party had generally done less well in smaller or medium sized towns, amongst families with young children and with 'suburban professionals' – or what the Mosaic data refers to as 'New Homemakers' who live in modern, private housing estates on the edge of urban areas, and who tend to say they want to 'get on in life'. Around 50 per cent of voters, incidentally, fell into those categories in the seat that Ed Balls lost.

Commentators at the time ruminated on how dull and uninspiring the struggle for the succession was likely to be. The Shadow Justice Minister, Dan Jarvis, gave a speech after the Progress hustings, specifically ruling himself out of the running. Some MPs have been 'parachuted' into safe seats with which they have little connection. So unconventional was Jarvis's background for a Labour politician he had been an actual para-trooper and army officer. So despite Andy Burnham's denunciation of Westminster elites, the three candidates who would get on the ballot paper would all have previously been political advisers to frontbench Labour politicians – Andy Burnham himself had been a special adviser to Chris Smith at the Department for Culture Media and Sport, Liz Kendall advised both Harriet Harman at the DWP and Patricia Hewitt at the DTI while Yvette Cooper had simply served Harriet in opposition.

Those around Ed Miliband believed the candidates at this stage had made an error by 'fishing in the same pool' – leaving another candidate free to trawl for more left-wing votes. Or to mix metaphors, all three candidates – Andy Burnham included – shifted the centre of gravity further to the right of Ed Miliband and crucially – though they didn't realise it at the time – to the right of many new members. By moving away from some of Miliband's positions, they enabled someone further to his left to exploit the political space. Or as Miliband's former aide Stewart Wood described it:

> They made a pitch to the centre during a Labour leadership contest. I can understand why Andy Burnham did it – he felt he had to show he wasn't the prisoner of the unions. Had someone closer to Ed's politics filled that space, that might have been more of a challenge to the Left. But also there

was a feeling that politics had to change, and – I am not saying I agreed with this – but there was a feeling that all those Labour leaders were the same.

All that was indeed about to change. Spectacularly.

* * *

Only three candidates were in the race to be Labour leader at 11.00am on 15 June. Under the new rules introduced by Ed Miliband, in order to get on to the ballot paper, candidates needed to be nominated by 15 per cent of the Parliamentary Labour Party. The threshold had risen from 12.5 per cent under the old rules as MPs and MEPs were no longer guaranteed a third of the vote between them in the actual contest.

The former Labour Party General Secretary Ray, now Lord, Collins – who knew the trade union movement inside and out – had had the tricky task of negotiating the demolition of the old electoral college which had also guaranteed the unions – and what are known as 'socialist societies' – a third of the vote too. The new rules had been agreed at a special conference in 2014 – but the GMB union would only give up the unions' share of the electoral college if the MPs surrendered their special privileges at the same time. So now the votes of Westminster politicians would not have any more weight than the vote of ordinary Labour members (and indeed party supporters who could sign up for just £3) or rank and file trade unionists, who were to be known as 'affiliated supporters'.

The MPs' role now was to be gatekeepers in the process. Clearly, if a politician didn't have the backing of even one in seven of his or her colleagues, they might have trouble leading the parliamentary party – so probably best not to put that MP on the ballot paper. But it didn't quite work like that. The gatekeepers took the gate off its hinges and erected a great big welcome sign instead.

Again, many MPs were really re-fighting the previous contest. In 2010, left-winger Diane Abbot had struggled to meet even the lower threshold to get on the ballot. But confining the contest then to four white males in their 40s would not have been the best publicity for Labour's avowed inclusivity. So some of those to her right – including her fellow leadership contender, David Miliband – 'lent' Abbot their nomination and the result was as expected: she finished last. It was assumed this year's left wing hopeful Jeremy Corbyn would suffer a similar fate now.

Between 11.00am and the high-noon deadline on 15 June, six MPs who didn't share Jeremy Corbyn's politics nominated him to be leader of their party. That got him to 36, exceeding the minimum criteria by one, with moments to spare. A well-organised social media campaign – the official #Jeremy4Leader, and on Facebook JeremyCorbyn4Leader, along with the supportive but unofficial #Jeremy4Labour – had been extolling his parliamentary colleagues to do so. Oxford East MP Andrew Smith was credited with making it possible by getting him over the hurdle of 35 nominations. Tom Watson was prepared to do so *in exteremis* but in the end his nomination wasn't required. But another half dozen MPs who didn't agree with many of Corbyn's policy positions had signed his nomination papers even earlier. Many stated quite publicly they would not subsequently vote for him.

For example, the Ogmore MP Huw-Irranca Davies:

> I think Yvette Cooper is a very strong candidate, but so are others as well. But we are not a cult, we are a broad church – we need to have these broad voices.

And Tottenham MP David Lammy:

> While there is enough that Jeremy and I disagree on to mean that I won't be voting for him, I believe the choice of who becomes Labour's next leader should be made by Labour members and supporters, not by MPs.

In fact only 20 of the MPs that put Corbyn on the leadership ballot said they would vote for him as leader – fewer than one in ten of Labour's Parliamentary Party. But the following month, on 21 July, a bombshell dropped. On BBC *Newsnight*, presenter Kirsty Wark read out the results of a survey of Labour Party members and supporters by internet pollsters YouGov – and it put Corbyn 17 points clear of his nearest rival Andy Burnham. John McTernan – Jim Murphy's former chief of staff, and who had also been Tony Blair's political secretary – was on hand to provide an instant reaction. He questioned the intellectual credentials of those who had lent temporary support to the left-winger:

> The moronic MPs who nominated Jeremy Corbyn to 'have a debate' need their heads felt. They need their heads felt! They should be ashamed of themselves. They're morons.

The motivations of the 'morons' who had put him on the ballot paper had been manifold. There were those – such as Jon Cruddas – who had indeed wanted to 'broaden the debate' after such a setback at the polls, and felt it would be wrong to suppress some views at the very outset. He was also pretty confident Corbyn and, more importantly, his arguments would be defeated fair and square. Frank Field, on the right of the party, wanted to use Corbyn to shake the other candidates out of any complacency and make them confront and criticise Corbyn's anti-cuts agenda. Writing in the *Mirror* a month after nominating Corbyn (22 July 2015) he conceded it was not going well:

I nominated Jeremy Corbyn in the belief that what we in Labour most needed was to debate our future. Instead of rising to this challenge, Jeremy's presence seems to have frightened the other candidates into silence... Jeremy is quite open on the deficit. He doesn't believe any cuts whatsoever should be made. I do not believe the Labour Party will be elected to govern on such a programme. I was therefore hoping one of the other candidates would challenge this deficit denying. Time is fast running out for them to do so.

Margaret Beckett – Labour's interim leader following John Smith's death in 1994 – admitted on Radio 4's *World at One* that she had indeed been one of those described as moronic. She said:

We were being urged as MPs to ensure that the party had a field of candidates and that I thought was a perfectly legitimate point of view. If Jeremy had been a long way behind, I don't think the thought of nominating him would have crossed my mind. But then when it looked as if he might almost be able to stand but then not be able to, I was concerned that people would feel that they had been deprived of the opportunity for their point of view to be aired... But yes, I'm beginning to wish that I hadn't, to be quite honest about it.

A former Labour Party official who wasn't keen on Corbyn's leadership ambitions said that Lenin had had a better term than John McTernan for those who had given what he regarded as an 'ultra-left' candidate a platform: 'useful idiots'. There is some debate over whether Lenin ever uttered the phrase but its contemporary use was a measure of how Corbyn's candidacy had provoked strong feelings.

One figure at the centre of the Ed Miliband election campaign said the MPs who nominated Corbyn had been 'criminally negligent'. But hadn't Ed Miliband taken his eye off the ball when the new leadership rules had been agreed?

* * *

Failure, as they say, is an orphan, and when it comes to the rules for electing Labour's new leader few even admit to knowing the parents. The final proposal emerged from Ray Collins' review after seven months of negotiations held in every region of the country behind closed doors, in what are now smoke-free rather than smoke-filled rooms. It was endorsed at a half-day conference called for the purpose in London's Docklands in March 2014 – at the ExCeL centre. Not many would use superlatives now to describe what happened.

Speak to most senior people in the Labour Party and they will tell you they issued dire warnings at the time. Were the new rules cock-up or conspiracy? Some senior figures believe the former, some the latter but they were very possibly a product of both. One senior Shadow Cabinet member told me:

> These rules were absolutely crazy and I regret not having more of an argument about this. We as Shadow Cabinet members hadn't been consulted. I found out they were taking away MPs' votes and tried to contact Ed Miliband's office to complain. I got a text back from him saying 'It's too late to raise objections'.

He said that many of those now denouncing the rules had actually been initially supportive. 'Blairites' close to David rather than Ed Miliband saw the new rules as a way of diluting union influence:

> In 2010 David won the election amongst members but they only had a third of the overall vote. So the argument was take MPs out if need be, just so long as you weaken the unions – and if you strengthen the party members' role, you shift any future contest to the right. But they sacrificed the stabilising influence of the MPs and didn't factor in the potential politics of these new registered supporters.

So perhaps a conspiracy that became a cock-up, then... again, some of those involved had been looking to the past, not the future. It had been assumed that the views of the rank and file membership would somehow remain static. But in fact while the overall membership figures looked incredibly stable until Labour's election defeat and the surge seen in the leadership election, there had in fact been considerable churn. Indeed by 2015, barely one in three members had actually voted in the previous leadership contest. As Ed Miliband had 'moved on' from New Labour, it's possible some New Labour members moved away. So the membership itself couldn't be relied upon as a stabilising or moderating influence. And while some union leaders played the part scripted for them, warning of a weakening of the trade union link, the general secretary of Unite – the largest affiliate to Labour – Len McCluskey seemed remarkably sanguine. Four days after the special conference to introduce the new rules, his union's executive council resolved to:

> rapidly prepare a plan to ensure that we maximise the number of our political levy paying members who express support for our continuing collective affiliation, and who take advantage of the possibility of becoming associated members of the party.

Under the new rules members had to say explicitly that they wanted the union to pay a £3 'affiliation fee' to Labour on their behalf and that they genuinely wanted to be supporters of the party – so, roughly translated, what Unite's executive was pledging to do was devote considerable resources to the task of signing up these 'affiliated supporters'. What McLuskey realised was that union influence need not be confined to one-third of the vote for a new leader in an electoral college – the more of these new 'affiliated supporters' his union could sign up, the more influence his members would have.

In a briefing note dating from March 2014, the union makes it clear it can see advantages in the new system:

> The new proposals fit in with Unite's political strategy, which is to encourage as many of our members as possible to join and get active in Labour... That is why Unite will not walk away from this – we will be standing and fighting for what we believe in, which is a Labour party of and for the ordinary, decent people of this country. Labour, remember, is OUR party. We – the trade unions – started it and this is a chance for six million ordinary men and women to really make their voices heard.

And it successfully signed up far more supporters than any other union when the leadership contest got under way – around 112,000. The union had used an outside organisation to set up call centres to ring members and tell them about the new rules, and targeted those members who had voted in previous Labour leadership elections as they would be most likely to sign up. One insider said they had spent about £18 per affiliated supporter to do so. The union's executive backed Jeremy Corbyn for leader, and recommended a second preference for Andy Burnham.

Under the new rules voting papers were distributed by Electoral Reform Services, who were conducting the ballot, not by the unions. That meant – unlike in 2010 with Ed Miliband – trade unions couldn't send out leaflets supporting one of the candidates with, or alongside, election material. But Len McCluskey did write to all members urging support for Corbyn, and when members of Andy Burnham's team pointed out that he had been endorsed by the union leadership too, McCluskey 'clarified' that the first choice of his executive was very much Jeremy Corbyn.

In the end, though, supporters who had joined Labour through their trade union didn't dominate the contest – there were 148,000 of them, compared with just under 290,000 fully-paid party members, and 112,000 'registered supporters'. Overall these trade unionists accounted for slightly over a quarter of the total eligible votes – so less than the third of the votes the unions had been guaranteed under the old electoral college system. And in the event, only around half of those entitled to vote did so.

The real innovation – and what turned out to be the biggest headache for Harriet Harman – was the introduction of the new 'registered supporter' who could join up directly for just £3 to take part in the contest. Around one in five of those eligible for a vote in the leadership election were in this category. There had been muddled thinking on this from the outset. The Conservatives had selected some candidates – including the outspoken and independent-minded GP and now MP Sarah Wollaston – by 'open primary' allowing anyone who wanted to take part to do so, not just party members.

Labour could have decided that if their next leader was to have broad appeal, the decision was too important to leave to the activists. Instead they went for a halfway house allowing a wider range of people to participate but only if they 'support the aims and values of the Labour party' and are 'not a supporter of any organisation opposed to it'. Examining what was going on in people's minds would prove difficult. And that task became trickier with Jeremy Corbyn's entrance into the race, as this gave at least two groups of people not normally supportive of Labour an incentive to sign up.

First, those on the right. As Corbyn's campaign appeared to be taking off in mid-July, *The Telegraph* comment page suggested that a victory for him in the leadership contest would be:

> dreadful for Labour, the sort of political disaster the party last suffered in 1983 when Michael Foot's left-wing views saw the party lose by a landslide to Margaret Thatcher's Conservatives.

But it went on:

> Not everyone thinks it would be a bad thing if that was to be repeated at the next general election in 2020. Indeed, some people joke about voting for Mr Corbyn, hoping to saddle Labour with a bearded voter-repellent as a leader. Thanks to Labour's new leadership rules, it doesn't have to be a joke. Anyone can vote in the Labour leadership election.

It then gave a 'handy five step guide' to doing so.

The leader of the Scottish Conservatives, Ruth Davidson, tweeted:

> I seem to have a lot of traffic in my timeline saying that for a mere £3, I can change Labour's future and vote for Jeremy Corbyn. Bargain.

The former Conservative minister Tim Loughton was successfully 'weeded out' by Labour officials who were on the lookout for 'known' opponents who were trying to get a vote. The former Conservative MP and columnist Matthew Parris tried to sign up his llamas. Andy Burnham reported a Conservative councillor turning up at a public meeting to brag that he had a vote. But concerns grew that some of the weeds were not being spotted for the trees. Labour staff had to – at the very least – 'verify' that these new supporters were on the electoral register and were initially overwhelmed by the work involved. Extra staff were hired, and the party's Newcastle offices went in to a 24-hour working pattern to process the new recruits.

Yet they also had to check if an applicant had stood against Labour at an election, signed an opponent's nomination papers, or denounced the party on social media. Not every infiltrator was necessarily well-known or vocal so the national party had to rely on local constituencies to flag up potential problems, with two panels drawn from the ruling national executive committee charged with overseeing the process – and sitting as judge and jury on eligibility.

But Labour insiders always thought that once Jeremy Corbyn was on the ballot paper, the bigger danger would be infiltration from the left, not the right. This proved particularly tricky to police.

Certainly the website run by Trotskyists Socialist Action – which features pictures of Fidel Castro and Hugo Chavez on its home page – was urging a vote for Corbyn within two days of his appearance on the ballot, and provided a link to the Labour Party website to enable supporters to sign up. The website said:

> The left, both inside and outside Labour, are encouraging people to register their support for Labour to participate in the elections. Those unwilling to join the Labour Party, because its policies are so right wing, can instead become registered supporters, as long as they agree with Labour's aims and values and do not support any organisation opposed to Labour. It is hoped that many will register and pay the necessary £3 to vote for Jeremy...

Socialist Action's view was that Labour had lost ground in the run-up to the election when it tried to sound more fiscally responsible, and as a result had become less distinguishable from the Conservatives. This is an extract from their post-election analysis:

> Opinion polls running up to the election overall underestimated Tory support and overestimated Labour's. If this polling bias operated for the past five years, it still remains the case that Labour established a commanding poll lead over the Tories by May 2012. That lead eroded rapidly when it shifted to an explicitly austerity-lite agenda. Labour anchored its general election campaign firmly on the right; with vague pledges, emphasising a commitment to spending cuts, an anti-immigrant message and joining in the right-wing attacks on the SNP... When the Tories shifted their own campaign tactics to making public services spending promises, including an extra £8 billion on the NHS, Labour attacked the Tories from the right, for making 'unfunded' commitments. In effect Labour did snatch defeat from the jaws of victory.

Socialist Action has its roots in the International Marxist Group, which infiltrated Labour in the early 1980s... though since then there have probably been as many splits as there were amongst the anti-Roman liberation groups in *Monty Python's Life of Brian*: 'So whatever happened to the Popular Front for Judea? – He's over there!'

Socialist Action supporters participate in much bigger umbrella organisations such as the People's Assembly and were active in the Stop the War Coalition which Corbyn chaired. But they probably have only around 500 adherents so even if all of them had been successfully signed up to Labour (if they hadn't done so already, without being too explicit about their views) and hadn't been sifted out by officials, their votes would hardly have been proven decisive for Corbyn. More influential would have been their encouragement to people not party-politically aligned but involved in campaigns to join Labour, at least temporarily – but it's perfectly possible many people didn't need that encouragement.

But there were some signs that the degree of 'infiltration' – organised or spontaneous – was much higher than assumed. Ben Bradshaw, the former culture secretary who was a 'Blairite' candidate for the party's deputy leadership, said data from his Exeter constituency suggested that many of those who had applied for a vote in the Labour leadership contest hadn't been historically supportive of his party. From his local activists' contribution to Ed Miliband's five million conversations on voters' doorsteps, they had built up extensive records of which party people had supported in 2015 – and how some of them had cast their ballots in previous years, too. He told me:

> We have cross referenced all the new registered supporters against our canvassing records which are amongst the best in the country and we have found consistently around ten per cent of people have been extremely hostile to Labour and have always voted for other parties.

The issue also arose at what is called Labour's procedure committee – made up of representatives from the party's ruling national executive. On 19 August, *The Guardian* published leaked notes of a meeting where the interim leader, Harriet Harman and the party's General Secretary, Iain McNicol, had supported a proposal to check potential supporters' voting records against canvass returns nationally, in a similar process to the work carried out in Exeter. While someone's stated intention not to vote Labour would not be enough on its own to debar them, Harman favoured emailing or writing to them again to ask if they really did share her party's values. If they didn't respond within 72 hours or provide an adequate explanation for their previous voting intention, they would be struck off. One of her aides admitted to me 'there's not much we can do if people lie', but it was felt that this additional layer of verification would at least contribute to the case that the party was trying to do everything in its power to enforce its own rules. It was believed that this would also make it less vulnerable to a legal challenge by one of the candidates if they were to lose by a small margin. But the vote on the issue was deadlocked on the committee. One member was on a summer cruise and had their lifeboat drill interrupted to be asked their view. The phone signal was dodgy but enough of the conversation made clear that this member would not come to Harriet's rescue. It was felt that those who had perhaps voted tactically could have been denied a say. The committee chair, Jim Kennedy, was an official of the Unite union – which was backing Jeremy Corbyn. One member of the committee said to me that 'he is just doing Corbyn's bidding. Or at least Len McCluskey's.' In any case Harman – at this stage – didn't get her way.

The left had been trying to move the debate away from infiltration on to talk of a 'purge' – the hashtag #labourpurge began trending on Twitter to emphasise it wasn't just those in the centre or right of the party that could question the contest's legitimacy. The arguments against conducting the extra checks weren't entirely partisan or spurious. Some of Kennedy's supporters on the committee weren't against local parties using their data – as Ben Bradshaw had done – to flag up problems but didn't want the party nationally to take on the burden. But the argument was also put forward that the information collected from the election could be out of date. Minds can change.

Now, it's not that difficult for Labour officials to refuse a ballot paper to well-known people that it regards as being on the far left – they did so when Mark Serwotka, leader of the non-affliliated PCS union, tried to become a registered supporter. But many who hold views to the left of Labour might never have stood against the party at an election, or have a record of activity which suggested that they didn't – admittedly, as perhaps the least worst option – want to see a Labour government.

If they said they had been disillusioned with Labour over, say, Iraq, or nuclear weapons and had considered voting Green, that in itself couldn't disqualify them. After all, Labour hadn't expelled Jeremy Corbyn for his anti-nuclear, pro-nationalisation views, so if voters were now being attracted back to Labour's banner and away from other parties on the left because he was on the ballot, how could they be denied a vote?

Matters came to a head in a most bizarre way on 25 August.

* * *

'Follow that car!' That's not a phrase you expect to hear very often, if at all, in political journalism. But BBC producer Sally Heptonstall uttered it to a cab driver as she saw Andy Burnham being bundled in to the back of a Vauxhall Corsa.

So sensitive had Labour become to charges that their leadership contest was descending into farce, they somehow decided not just to descend further, but to plunge headlong off the mountain of ridicule. Some of the leadership teams – spearheaded by Burnham's – had asked for a meeting with Jim Kennedy and Labour officials to discuss fears over infiltration, and to seek reassurances that the party had robust systems in place. A meeting had been granted then cancelled. Harriet Harman had decided that she – rather than just the officials and the NEC's Jim Kennedy – would meet the candidates herself.

That day they were all due to be in Stevenage, the marginal Hertfordshire seat where a good campaign hadn't resulted in victory. Harman had chosen the town as the first stop on her 'pink bus' tour of Britain before the election. But its significance today was that BBC Radio 5 Live was hosting a hustings there – at which Jeremy Corbyn brushed aside concerns about infiltration:

> There's been a lot of nonsense in the papers. Large numbers of people got involved in politics for the first time. A few Tory MPs tried to join, got rejected, end of story.

Harman hadn't wanted to hold her sensitive meeting in the full glare of publicity. So party officials hadn't told the candidates where the meeting would be held. Instead, they would be picked up after the hustings – from the Stevenage Arts and Leisure Centre – and be conveyed to a secret venue elsewhere in the new town. But Burnham had been tailed, though his car tried to shake off pursuers at one of the town's many roundabouts. Having failed to carry out the more elaborate car-chase manoeuvres – such as shooting across a level crossing just before the barriers come down, or zooming across a swing bridge just before it opens – it soon became impossible to conceal the venue and the infrastructure of the mass media pulled up outside the Business Technology Centre.

Harriet Harman then made herself available, and offered reassurances about the process. But within 48 hours further checks on those wanting to become registered supporters had been given the green light.

Labour officials ended up rejecting 57,000 applications – largely because many of these applicants hadn't even been on the electoral register. Some people, though, had joined via their trade union and then had also tried to sign up as registered supporters or members. The new system – unlike the old – is far more effective at identifying and stopping 'multiple voting'. Before, if you straddled all three classes of membership in the electoral college – for example if you were an MP and a trade unionist as well as – naturally enough – a party member, it would not have been impossible to have been issued with three ballot papers. This time it really was supposed to be 'one member, one vote'.

But on the day of the not-so-secret Stevenage meeting it was revealed that only 3,138 applicants had been struck off for political reasons – 1,900 because they had been candidates for, or prominent supporters of, the Greens – and 400 because they apparently had indeed been Conservative 'infiltrators'. Though a definitive official figure wasn't provided, at least 110 refuseniks had been involved in parties or groups to Labour's left, such as the misnamed Left Unity (though arguably they were now trying to unite with mainstream Labour) and the Trade Union and Socialist Coalition. In the end more than 4,000 were denied a vote because of their politics.

The leadership teams stressed they now wanted to be seen to be talking about policies not process, but privately all but the Corbyn team felt the party had probably underestimated the extent of infiltration on the left and right. That said, under the old system when ballot papers were issued to any trade unionist whose union was affiliated to Labour, 2.7 million voting papers had gone out. Polling by Unite suggested only around half their members supported the party, so some ballot papers for the last leadership contest had undoubtedly gone to Conservative, Lib Dem, Green and no doubt SNP voters, too – and without very much fuss.

* * *

The question is why Labour left itself open to the risk of infiltration at all in a brand new system. Clearly Ed Miliband had wanted a swift 'off the shelf' solution to the mid-term Falkirk fiasco – proposals that would appear to be watering down union influence. Some around him saw it as a means of taking up community campaigner Arnie Graf's ideas and reconnecting Labour with those who had lost trust in politics, or didn't take well to the existing bureaucratic structures of political parties but wanted to signal their support.

But even those broadly backing the reforms had warned of potential problems and had been ignored. The general secretary of the GMB union, Paul Kenny, had raised concerns about the low price attached to Labour support – and said a £3 fee risked 'entryism' – in other words those who didn't share Labours values might be tempted to take part in the leadership contest.

So the GMB had pushed for a higher fee of £15–20 but union sources say Labour's leadership rejected this. The Vice-Chair of the election campaign, and former Deputy Chief of Staff to Ed Miliband, Lucy Powell called for a higher threshold for MPs to enter the race – support from 20 per cent not 15 per cent of the parliamentary party, with the aim of having a 'run-off', as the Conservatives do, between just two candidates. This would almost certainly have killed the Corbyn campaign stone dead. But according to those close to Ed Miliband it had been those on the Blairite wing of the party which had been most vociferous in calling for a lower threshold in case they themselves would struggle to get the support of one in five colleagues to mount a leadership bid in future.

The idea of 'registered supporters' had been proposed first in 2011 by the former Cabinet Minister Peter Hain as part of his *Refounding Labour* project on how to modernise the party's organisational structures. It had concluded:

> In order to safeguard the membership offer, there should be no formal rights for Registered Supporters, only local members and affiliates are to be involved in selections [of Labour candidates].

And while supporters would potentially get a vote on a new leader, this would only happen if they exceeded 50,000 in number and – under the old 'electoral college' system – their influence would also be limited. Under the new rules, their vote is on a par with MPs and fully paid-up members.

Views are split on whether Ed Miliband hadn't thought through the potential consequences of the new rules, and was pleased just get out of the Falkirk fix, or whether he was thinking more strategically.

Lord Mandelson warned of the dangers of infiltration at the time. But he got the impression that far from being horrified, Ed Miliband embraced the prospect of more rank and file trade unionists and left-wing supporters signing up for membership as a means of moving the party further away from New Labour. Miliband's inner circle would say this was nonsense. The biggest supporters of the changes were Blairites – if not Mandelson himself, certainly those who admired him as they saw the reforms as a way of watering down union influence.

Miliband had appointed Simon Fletcher as his trade union liaison officer early in 2013. Fletcher – a pivotal figure in the Corbyn leadership campaign as well as the former chief of staff to Ken Livingstone when he was London Mayor – was involved in drawing up the new rules. But so too was the solidly mainstream Roy Kennedy and strategist Tom Baldwin, friend of Alastair Campbell and admirer of Tony Blair. Those who worked with Fletcher at the time didn't find him factional and didn't believe he was trying to devise a system that would one day propel a more left wing candidate into the top job. Instead he was there to reassure the unions that Miliband would 'mend, not end' the union link. He was also, some suspected, there to try to help Miliband see off any leadership challenge he might face either before the election, or if he had wanted to stay on afterwards having failed to gain an overall majority. He would in all probability have required union support to do so. But had Miliband been in the unions' pockets, it's unlikely the Falkirk fracas would have been allowed to escalate in the first place, with party officials willing to involve the Scottish police in an internal row over the selection of a union-backed candidate. The consensus at the time was that the new rules would be a challenge not a sop to the unions, and Fletcher's role was to help keep the support and funding flowing.

A bad worker is said to blame his tools and some think the same was true of Labour's modernisers when it came to the leadership election. Miliband's former strategist, Tom Baldwin, said Labour politicians shouldn't blame the new rules for the apparent rise of the Left. MPs opposed to Jeremy Corbyn shouldn't have nominated him – and if people signed up to support him, well his opponents should have been inspiring others to join the party to oppose him. Writing in *The Guardian* (28 August 2015) he said:

> Those in despair about this process must learn how to galvanise more of those millions of voters who desperately need Labour to be a party of government again, just as much as Corbyn has inspired those who fancy another five years of protest. Any fightback to reclaim Labour must begin by reaching people outside the party and bringing them in – just as Tony Blair did 20 years ago – rather than looking for someone else to blame.

* * *

The event was chaired by a comedian but the message was deadly serious. Stand-up comic and radio presenter Matt Forde hosted what was billed as An Audience with Tony Blair, which had been organised by the modernising group, Progress. Forde jokingly enquired if the former leader had voted for Corbyn but Blair gave a withering rather than witty response. He said 'No, I was a Labour leader'. It was the Conservatives who would want to see Corbyn succeed.

He went on to say:

> After the 1979 election the Labour party persuaded itself of something absolutely extraordinary. Jim Callaghan had been Prime Minister and the Labour party was put out of power by Margaret Thatcher, and the Labour party persuaded itself that the reason why the country had voted for Margaret Thatcher was because they wanted a really leftwing Labour party.

And he offered this analysis of Labour's defeat, suggesting a further move to the left would be 'other-wordly':

> We lost in 2010 because we stepped somewhat from our modernising platform. We lost in 2015 with an election out of the playbook from the 1980s, from the period of *Star Trek*, when we stepped even further away

from it and lost even worse. I don't understand the logic of stepping
entirely away from it.

Perhaps his most controversial advice was that those voting with their
hearts not their heads in the leadership contest should 'get a transplant'.
This was later denounced as 'stupid' by his former deputy, John Prescott.
Indeed, in not endorsing any of the candidates opposed to Corbyn in the
contest, Blair recognised his intervention might prove counter-productive.
He said he doubted his endorsement would help.

If people were signing up for a different type of politics, if they had –
like Corbyn – been involved in the Stop the War coalition, then the views
of the 'Start the War' prime minister wouldn't necessarily be shared.

Senior figures in the party then had a better idea. Rather than a series
of 'drip, drip' warnings of a lurch to the left, wouldn't one big intervention by all the extant former leaders be preferable? It proved impossible
to reunite the band, but both Gordon Brown and Neil Kinnock did
conduct their own solo projects.

On 16 August, Blair's successor at Number 10 was the star attraction
at London's Royal Festival Hall. Clearly visible through the bank of
windows behind Gordon Brown was the former home of the GLC – now
a luxury hotel – once inhabited by Ken Livingstone and other supporters
of Jeremy Corbyn in the '80s. And right outside it was a merry-go-round.
Rather like the objects on that fairground attraction, it had looked for a
while like Labour's left wing had been moving further away from prominence only to come round again into full public view.

Brown had discussed his contribution to the debate over lunch with
close friends in Fife two days earlier. The party nationally and the press
had little advance warning of his remarks. As he delivered them from
memory, he paced up and down with the urgency and stress of a caged
beast longing to be free. Indeed, cameras would need a wide-angle lens to
capture him. Some of the speech was highly personal, suggesting he hadn't
quite got over his own ejection from Downing Street five years earlier when
he talked about being 'heartbroken' and sympathising with activists who
were 'grieving' after the latest serious setback. He said 'I know what it's
like to feel rejection and defeat'. But in many ways the speech was classic
Brown – praying in aid the great Labour and progressive figures of the past,
including Aneurin Bevan, Keir Hardie, John Smith – and Nelson Mandela
– to make the case that Labour needed to remain mainstream – 'desirable,
popular, electable' – and relevant. He made a point of not denouncing
Corbyn by name but appeared to characterise his foreign policy thus:

> Don't tell me that we can do much for the poor of the world if the alli-
> ances we favour most are with Hezbollah, Hamas, Chávez's successor in
> Venezuela and Putin's totalitarian Russia.

Earlier in the month, on 2 August, the leader who knew most about Opposition – Neil Kinnock – had warned:

> In the leadership election, we are not choosing the chair of a discussion group who can preside over two years or more of fascinating debate while the Tories play hell with cuts.

And he criticised what he called the 'malign purposes' of the 'Trotskiyte Left and the *Telegraph* Right.'

In a subsequent intervention on 29 August – two weeks before the new leader would be announced – in the pages of *The Observer*, Blair conjured up an image of what a joint appeal against a Corbyn leadership might have looked like – though he seemed sceptical of its chances of success:

> Neil Kinnock, Gordon Brown and I have collectively around 150 years of Labour party membership. We're very different. We disagree on certain things. But on this we're agreed. Anyone listening? Nope. In fact, the opposite. It actually makes them more likely to support him. It is like a driver coming to a roadblock on a road they've never travelled before and three grizzled veterans say: 'Don't go any further, we have been up and down this road many times and we're warning you there are falling rocks, mudslides, dangerous hairpin bends and then a sheer drop.' And the driver says: 'Screw you, stop patronising me. I know what I'm doing.'

Ed Miliband, meanwhile, had gone 'down under' and largely disappeared from view – but for a snap of him sporting Corbynesque facial hair. He was on a family holiday to the Great Barrier reef, in another country where a Labour party had failed to win a recent election, while Corbynmania raged at home. Perhaps he couldn't be expected to fly back from Australia to issue warnings about the future of the party he so recently led. But his reluctance wasn't just based on logistics. And it wasn't simply whether to deliver a joint message – but any message. He said he was 'unlikely' to get involved. Partly that could be out of humility as he had just delivered a worse result than expected for Labour. While he would make it clear after the leadership election that he had no intention of returning to the front bench, he also had no intention of lecturing the people who had signed up under new rules to the Labour Party about how they should vote. He regarded getting more than half a million people involved in an internal party election, and opening the door to new supporters, as positive. Friends say, like his strategist Tom Baldwin, he believed that all leadership candidates should have made these rules work for them and if they lacked support, they should have been campaigning to increase it.

After all, for all the talk of 'entrysim' and 'infiltration' into Labour's ranks, the radical Left in some European countries weren't trying to sneak into parties in order to change them – they were out and proud and in some cases making an impact, while the more traditional social democratic movements had been struggling.

* * *

In national elections in 2009 under the 'Syriza' banner, a coalition of parties to the left of Greece's 'Labour Party' – the Pan-Hellenic Socialist Party, PASOK – polled less than five per cent of the vote. Following years of post-crash austerity, in 2012 most of the disparate group of ecologists, feminists, communists and ultra-left Trotskyists in the volatile coalition decided to solidify into a political party – 'Syriza, United Social Front' was formed. In January 2015, it scored 36.3 per cent of the vote in parliamentary elections, becoming the largest party in parliament, while PASOK – a party of government as recently as 2012 – was reduced to a rump of 13 MPs and with a derisory vote share similar to Syriza's in 2009.

Had Ed Miliband polled as well, he would have been in Downing Street. Of course in Britain austerity was nowhere near as severe.

But in Spain, too, the mainstream party of the left – the Socialist Workers Party – has been polling less well than Podemos, the radical movement to its left whose bearded leader Pablo Iglesias wants to extend public ownership and leave NATO. Sound familiar?

The 'movement' has gone from being a small collection of economists, Trotskyists, and Trotskyist economists with a prominent social media presence in 2014 into a fully-fledged membership organisation, with 350,000 people signing up within a year – becoming the second largest party in Spain, behind the right-of-centre People's Party.

It's not just on the continent that anti-austerity parties are flourishing. The SNP are no Syriza – but at the general election they had a different, slower trajectory for deficit reduction and stood on an anti-austerity platform. Just as Germany was blamed for the scale of the cuts in Greece, Westminster was whacked for allegedly imposing a financial straitjacket on Scotland.

The message from Athens to Andalusia to Aberdeen was that old established parties of the left were not standing up for 'their' people.

So Labour MPs who nominated Jeremy Corbyn to 'broaden the debate' certainly succeeded on that front – those who wanted to test his ideas to destruction were less successful. It soon became clear that rather than facing an external threat, Labour was in the process perhaps of having its own Podemos created from within. Indeed the Spanish party's leader Pablo Iglesias said he 'saluted and supported' Corbyn.

That's not to say what became known in the media as 'Corbynmania' was manufactured by the far Left to capture Labour. But in an era of disillusionment with conventional politics – the Conservatives gained an overall majority on a bit less than 37 per cent of the vote – a simple, distinctive message can cut through the background noise.

I attended one of the first hustings of the candidates that included Jeremy Corbyn. It was a lively affair. Bizarrely it was held in Dublin. That's because it was hosted by the GMB union which has members in the Irish Republic – and which had also got a very good deal by holding their conference at the massive Citywest hotel and conference complex which had been built without full planning permission, and had been taken in to receivership after the financial crash.

The hustings were chaired by the *Daily Mirror*'s Kevin Maguire and he decided he wanted to obtain straight 'Yes' or 'No' answers to some questions. Each candidate was asked if they backed the Conservatives' benefit cap. Liz Kendall said 'Yes', and Jeremy Corbyn gave an equally straight answer – 'No'. There were jeers from the audience when both Andy Burnham and Yvette Cooper attempted to give more nuanced responses.

This was no love-in for Corbyn – the GMB, unlike other big unions such as Unite and UNISON, didn't endorse his candidacy. One senior official denounced him as 'a bit of a hippie' and that many of the union's members who were working hard in a supermarket and needing tax credits wouldn't take kindly to his support for those who didn't do a 'a hand's turn'. But there is little doubt that the clarity of message won some of the audience over. As one of them said to me: 'He may be unrealistic, but at least he is clear on what he stands for.'

Unconstrained by Shadow Cabinet collective responsibility, he could say what he liked. And he was doing just that. The seeds of the 'Corbyn effect' had been sown. But Harriet Harman was about to pour some Baby Bio all over them.

* * *

So determined not to repeat the mistakes of the previous leadership contest, with the best will in the world Labour's interim leader Harriet Harman made some new ones.

Travelling around the country in her pink bus, she had heard what I had heard in Swindon – people were worried about Labour overspending, but some were less concerned about the totality of public expenditure and more about how it was being disbursed. In short, they feared that too much would be spent by Labour on those who 'deserved' it least and who weren't willing to work. So she was not prepared to let the Conservative narrative on welfare take hold – just as it had on the economy in 2010 – because Labour was too pre-occupied with a leadership contest.

But every silver lining is ensconced in cloud.

George Osborne delivered the first Conservative-only budget in 18 years on 8 July. It was, of course, as much a political as a fiscal event. Labour jaws dropped as he announced a National Living Wage for the over 25s. His critics say it was really an enhanced minimum wage – nonetheless he had stolen Labour's clothes. He had wanted to do this since 2013, but his Lib Dem coalition partners had vetoed it because they wouldn't sign up to the other part of the package – a reduction in spending on tax credits. And it would be this which would cause a problem for Labour leadership candidates in the midst of a contest. The Chancellor was proposing to speed up the withdrawal of tax credits as incomes rose – making three million families an average of £1,000 a year worse off, according to the independent Institute for Fiscal Studies. But, in a welfare bill – separate from his budget – he was also proposing to limit child tax credit to the first two children.

On 12 July, in an interview for BBC's *Sunday Politics*, Harriet Harman declared:

> We can't simply say to the public you were wrong... we're not going to do blanket opposition because we've heard all around the country that whilst people have got concerns, particularly about the standard of living for low income families in work, they don't want just... blanket opposition to what the government are proposing on welfare... for example, what they've brought forward in regards to restricting benefits and tax credits for people with three or more children. What we've got to do is listen to what people around the country said to us and recognise that we didn't get elected – again.

And she commented on the qualities voters should look for in her replacement:

> I do say to all those people who are going to be voting in the leadership election, think not who you like and who makes you feel comfortable – think who actually will be able to reach out to the public and actually listen to the public and give them confidence, so that we can have a better result next time than we did last time. The point is not to have somebody who we can feel comfortable with, the point is to have somebody who can command the confidence of the country and that's what they should have in their mind. There's no point doing choice in a disappointed rage, we've got to be doing choice for the future.

But disappointed rage is precisely what some supporters of Andy Burnham felt when they heard this. And Yvette Cooper's camp were very nervous. While it might have been right, had the leadership election been settled, to then 'reach out' to those who hadn't voted Labour, both Cooper and Burnham's supporters knew that those who had backed the party wouldn't be impressed with apparently failing to oppose Conservative cuts. And they knew Jeremy Corbyn would not only rebel against this position but enhance his standing with members who already liked his plain-speaking, anti-austerity message.

Harman said she had consulted the Shadow Chancellor, Chris Leslie – who was backing Yvette Cooper – and Rachel Reeves, who was widely expected to be Shadow Chancellor if Andy Burnham were to win. But the leadership candidates themselves insist they had no advance warning. And they felt if there had been a better way to grow Corbyn's support nobody had yet discovered it.

The following evening, I took up position in the gaudily carpeted committee corridor of the House of Commons, along with a small but hardy band of newspaper and broadcast journalists. Harriet Harman was to address a meeting of her parliamentary party behind closed doors, with no media access, in Committee Room 14.

So we took turns to listen at the door. Thankfully Harriet has a crisp, clear voice which carries quite some distance, so we weren't entirely reliant on second-hand accounts of the meeting. Turning up a little late, she had walked past the waiting hacks, telling us 'It won't be very interesting.' It was.

Inside, she argued strongly for the party to abstain on the welfare bill when it came before the House in just over a week's time. She said she didn't want to tie the next leader's hands on the detail of welfare reform so abstention was the best option.

She also floated the idea of backing the benefits cap – but with a review after a year – which was something of a concession on her part, as she reminded her fellow MPs that the party had backed a cap in principle in the manifesto. She argued: 'We can't campaign against the public – we want to campaign with the public against the government', adding that blanket opposition makes it difficult to be heard on the things you do oppose.

Her wider argument was not to fall into a Conservative trap on welfare. No vote was taken at the end of what proved to be a stormy meeting. Neither Burnham nor Cooper attended but one shadow minister told me 'Harriet suffered a backlash in there – we were quite split.'

She had gained support for setting out opposition to some of the budget measures on Employment Support Allowance and maintenance grants but when it came to abstaining on tax credits, she faced the one thing colleagues felt she wasn't giving the government – fierce opposition. While her supporters were pleased that five MPs had spoken up in her defence, a clear majority had been critical – with one comparing the cap on child tax credits as 'a form of eugenics'.

The debate was resumed at the next meeting of the Shadow Cabinet the following morning. Both Andy Burnham and Yvette Cooper had argued for what in parliamentary terms is called a 'reasoned amendment'. Though doomed to fail because the Conservatives have an overall majority, it is a device for setting out the Opposition's differences with the government. But that wasn't the full scale of the top-table split. Instead, there was more of a splintering. Andy Burnham explained it to me like this:

> I argued twice in Shadow Cabinet that we should oppose the welfare bill.
> In the second discussion Harriet asked for everyone's views. There were
> a range – abstain; a reasoned amendment then abstain; and a reasoned
> amendment then oppose. I supported that. But too late in the day it
> looked like we were just going to abstain.

What helped concentrate minds was an amendment put down by Helen Goodman, a former shadow minister, which would be a rallying point for Labour rebels. So on 16 July – four days after her TV appearance, and two days after the acrimonious Shadow Cabinet meeting, Harriet Harman met ten of her senior colleagues – and conceded that there would indeed be an amendment to the government's proposals. But in the words of one shadow minister, 'It was tabled with just 20 minutes to spare. It was a dog's breakfast'.

This is what it said:

> That this House, whilst affirming its belief that there should be controls
> on and reforms to the overall costs of social security, that reporting obli-
> gations on full employment, apprenticeships and troubled families are
> welcome, and that a benefits cap and loans for mortgage interest support
> are necessary changes to the welfare system, declines to give a Second
> Reading to the Welfare Reform and Work Bill because the Bill will
> prevent the Government from continuing to pursue an ambition to
> reduce child poverty in both absolute and relative terms, it effectively
> repeals the Child Poverty Act 2010 which provides important measures
> and accountability of government policy in relation to child poverty, and
> it includes a proposal for the work-related activity component of employ-
> ment and support allowance which is an unfair approach to people who
> are sick and disabled.

It avoided mentioning entirely the controversial 'two-child' tax credit policy. And Harriet Harman was still insisting that once the amendment had inevitably been rejected, her MPs should abstain on the welfare bill, and not vote against. Andy Burnham told me he had made progress, but not as much as he would have liked:

Under the pressure I applied, the party moved to the position of a reasoned amendment. In effect this was opposition. Having forced the change I then had a decision. Did I resign from the Shadow Cabinet and walk my supporters through the opposite lobby from the rest of the Shadow Cabinet – or abide by a collective decision that was a compromise. It's different for Jeremy – he is not in the Shadow Cabinet and isn't bound by collective responsibility. It's frustrating.

Liz Kendall had praised Harman's courage in trying to teach the party some hard lessons but even she wouldn't explicitly back the limiting of child tax credit to the first two offspring. She told me she took a more sophisticated approach:

If we are going to oppose something we have to show how we would pay for an alternative. So on tax credits, I say to govern is to choose – we spend £100billon on tax reliefs, many of which are good, but I have asked Margaret Hodge (the former chair of the Commons Public Accounts Committee) to do a big review of those reliefs to come up with the money we need.

But for Cooper and Burnham, they were forced to abstain on measures that they opposed. They knew that when politicians were mistrusted they had just been given a difficult task in arguing that they were really, really against Tory welfare changes – they just weren't prepared to vote against them. Corbyn's campaign – which had already by now taken off – had just been given rocket boosters. Burnham puts it like this:

It was a turning point in the campaign, definitely. It was a no win situation for me – but had I resigned over the welfare and possibly won the leadership at that moment, it wouldn't have been me.

Yvette Cooper didn't quite put it like that but that the welfare row had hindered, not helped:

To be honest it was a complete mess. I always felt we should oppose the bill. It included the abolition of child poverty targets that I had worked hard to establish in the first place. It also included what I call 'the children's tax' – if you have three children and are in work, then – with withdrawal of tax credits – you can be worse off. But we ended up with this messy compromise. We ended with people being confused about what we stood for.

At least some of those divisions have already been reported. But not the full scale of them. It wasn't just leadership candidates who were worried about the approach. Mainstream members of the Shadow Cabinet who weren't competing for the top job felt that Harriet Harman hadn't fully appreciated that Labour could oppose some of the welfare reforms and still be on the side of the 'strivers'. One of them said 'Are we really telling someone working all hours at their local Aldi that they can't have a third kid?'

And while the welfare row broke through on to the front pages of the papers, other tensions remained beneath the surface. So keen was Harman to avoid knee-jerk opposition, even some Blairite frontbenchers were concerned that she might be over-correcting. A majority at the Shadow Cabinet had to nip in the bud the idea that Labour might sign up to George Osborne's flagship measure of raising inheritance tax thresholds. Harman didn't want to alienate aspirational voters in the south-east of England, where property prices were high. But the prevailing view was that the government was being anti-meritocratic, and if Labour wanted to show it too was serious about getting the deficit down, a measure costing almost £1 billion a year by 2020 was not the best way to do so. Plus Jeremy Corbyn – who would almost certainly rebel – might as well install himself in the leader of the Opposition's office there and then.

But Harman was trying to douse any Corbyn effect in her own way. She was concerned his presence would encourage a 'leftwards drift' amongst more mainstream candidates – who had already rejected her, and Shadow Chancellor, Chris Leslie's overtures not to oppose automatically a one per cent cap on public sector pay. Ultimately though she didn't have to stand in another internal election and the leadership candidates were in a tougher battle than they had anticipated which meant now perhaps wasn't the best time to sound too right-wing.

There is little doubt there was 'a Corbyn effect' which frustrated those close to Liz Kendall, who felt she had to do the heavy lifting of opposing his agenda without too much backing from her mainstream colleagues. A little late in the day for some, Yvette Cooper chose to oppose rather than appease the left-winger, denouncing his policy of quantitative easing – effectively a device to fund infrastructure – as risking runaway inflation, and his plan for rail renationalisation as a waste of money which could be better spent on improving child care. She also suggested unnamed others – with Burnham in mind – were 'pandering' or 'copying' Corbyn. But she still staunchly defended Labour's spending record while in government.

At a rally in Manchester, Andy Burnham spoke of Corbyn's energy, and with a month to go in the campaign, extended an olive branch to Corbyn's supporters. A week later at another well-attended rally – this time at a church near London's St Pancras station – Burnham ran through a list of crowd-pleasing policies from ending charitable status for fee-paying schools to opposing the right to buy for housing association tenants. And with just ten days to go until the leadership poll closed, he made 'five promises' to Jeremy Corbyn's supporters if he became leader – which included his opposition to the welfare bill.

But, as we know, party members chose Corbyn over, arguably, what they might have seen as Corbyn-lite. I asked Andy Burnham if he had fallen victim to the Corbyn effect or indeed, had been pandering to the man who had by then become the front runner. He responded:

> I don't see it that way, for obvious reasons. The party hierarchy have been misreading the mood amongst members – they want a different kind of politics to the insipid stuff Labour has been serving up in recent times. We can't lecture people. It's not a case of me veering completely to the left, or whatever. The substance of what Labour was saying has been too shallow. I'd already felt that. Jeremy has come in, of course, and really spoken to that.

But was the nature of the leadership contest moving Labour further away from the voters that the party needed to win back?

* * *

If a week is a long time in politics, then Labour's four month leadership contest felt like an absolute aeon. That cosy consensus amongst candidates and potential contestants at the Progress hustings had – on the surface – been shattered.

But Labour's pollster James Morris isn't entirely convinced that voters concerns can't be addressed from the Left. For him the main lesson from Labour's campaign and Ed Miliband's leadership is this:

> The most important thing is to have strong, clear decision making. It's better to be strongly in the wrong place than to be weakly wobbling from side to side.

With the chopping and changing of Labour's message over the preceding five years: 'Voters seldom had any idea of what the party was saying. Jeremy Corbyn had at least been clear – and used language voters would understand.'

Beyond a lack of clarity, voters were worried about Labour's spending and needed to know they would do something to grow the economy, rather than just move resources around. Corbyn certainly espoused policies for economic growth and his approach – if not his leadership ambitions – gained the endorsement of 41 economists. The list including a former member of the Bank of England's Monetary Policy Committee, David 'Danny' Blanchflower. In a letter to *The Observer* on 23 August, they said:

> The accusation is widely made that Jeremy Corbyn and his supporters have moved to the extreme left on economic policy. But this is not supported by the candidate's statements or policies. His opposition to austerity is actually mainstream economics, even backed by the conservative IMF. He aims to boost growth and prosperity.

Corbyn has, however, railed against austerity and championed borrowing for investment. Morris believes he could argue for his radical agenda in a way which appears to address voters' concerns – for example, portraying his opposition to nuclear weapons as also opposition to 'wasteful' spending, and identifying his very different list of savings from the Conservatives – lowering the inheritance tax threshold, and spending less on defence – to get the deficit down.

But for all the apparent energy of a leadership campaign that was initially being seen as dull, this period of well-publicised Labour introspection could prove there is such a thing as bad publicity. A poll towards the end of the contest by ComRes for the *Daily Mail* suggested the Conservatives had broken through the 40 per cent barrier for the first time since the election – 14 points ahead of Labour – who were languishing in the 20s. This was more than double the six and a half point gap between the parties at the general election.

The poll also suggested that the installation of *any* of the leading leadership candidates was likely to make matters a little bit worse, not better:

> Jeremy Corbyn 22 per cent, Andy Burnham 22 per cent and Yvette Cooper 21 per cent – all had similarly low proportions of respondents saying that they would vote for Labour if they were leader.

The challenges for Jeremy Corbyn are immense. Party management and discipline will be difficult, especially as he himself has been a serial rebel.

But there is one lesson for any leader to learn from Ed Miliband's time in office. To be more inclusive. During Labour's election campaign, the most senior and prominent pair of Labour politicians, the two Eds, hardly met. Ed Balls wasn't prevented from doing what he wanted to do by Miliband, but his allies say he was rarely involved in campaign strategy. The party's general secretary – the most senior official – had difficulty in getting access to the party's own polling regularly. Despite health being one policy area where Labour had a lead over the Conservatives, the Shadow Spokesman, Andy Burnham often felt shut out of his leader's plans. One insider – who was genuinely 'in' – put it like this:

> You need better decision-making processes. Keeping decision-making in a tiny little circle and basically shutting out most of the Shadow Cabinet from doing almost anything is certainly one way of running a campaign but not one I would recommend. The political management operation was fantastic in the past five years – that is, keeping Ed in place – there were ructions, but they managed to hold the whole thing together. But at the cost of overall direction. You need slightly weaker political management – and to do more to bring people in, to share information and create a

leadership team. Although people think of Blair as almost presidential, in opposition prior to 1997 you had that approach.

If the first task of the new leader is to unite a party that was polarised over a long contest, they may have little choice but to embrace opponents. If not, one shadow minister warned:

> There is a very real danger of splits – the parallels with the mid to late '80 are very, very strong right now. Labour must have one eye on its history all through this.

The pages of that history tell the story of the SDP split on the right, and the expulsion of Militant on the left.

Labour's victory song in 1997 was 'Things Can Only Get Better'. A more appropriate phrase – often used in adverts from that era – might now be 'The value of your of investment can go down.'

* * *

So what are the lessons for Labour?

Those closest to Ed Miliband will point out he had a difficult task in trying to create enough distance between his party and the financial crisis for which Labour was seen to be responsible. He had, they argue, little choice but to steer between the two dangerous rocks of difference and credibility. If he went too far left and emphasised his distinctiveness from the government by abandoning austerity then any attempt to restore post-crash economic credibility would be holed below the waterline. But veering right, and signing up to the government's deficit reduction strategy, albeit with different policy priorities, would sink any hope of motivating many traditional supporters who were looking for clear blue water between Cameron and Labour.

But Miliband's strategists would concede that in avoiding some risks on the left and right, too few voters were clear about what forward course he was charting.

Overall, though his hand on the tiller did move the party further left from the centre. The Conservatives gave those thinking about backing them a reason to do so when they successfully argued that the SNP would stick a small outboard motor to the Labour vessel and propel it even faster in that direction, and the economy into stormier waters. But Ed Miliband's main strategists would argue those who sought but failed to succeed him perhaps sought to jerk the tiller back slightly – or more dramatically – while in a state of shock, without a hard headed assessment of the conditions.

Miliband was not relaxed about what he saw as increasing inequality and was proud to have raised the issue of whose interests a growing economy should serve. But his advisers have consistently denied there was a '35 per cent strategy' – a focus on winning just enough votes to get into government, with the help of disillusioned Lib Dems, and those disillusioned with politics more generally.

In fact, nothing riles them more than this charge. They targeted Conservative-held seats and wanted to win back people who had backed David Cameron in 2010. Those around him would, however, concede that they didn't have a compelling enough answer to the question of how to improve living standards for those who had higher incomes in some parts of the country – but who, with little reliance on the state, often felt they were struggling with high costs. Labour performed particularly badly in the south of England, outside London.

The man put in charge of Labour's election campaign Spencer, now Lord, Livermore – felt himself that the focus had been too narrow. As I saw day-by-day on the campaign trail, while Labour had plans to tax those at the top and improve employment rights for those at the bottom, it didn't even emphasise policies it already had – from reducing childcare costs to help to get on the housing ladder – for those in the middle nearly as much. As Labour in the end failed to get anywhere near 35 per cent of the vote then it is obvious, to say the least, that they must broaden their appeal.

While Labour lost seats, however, Ed Miliband's allies don't believe they lost all of the arguments. The Conservatives' adoption of the Living Wage – for over 25s – is a measure Ed Miliband would call 'pre-distribution' – and didn't feel quite bold enough to offer himself. Those vying for the US Democratic nomination for president, including Hillary Clinton, are all following their own version of 'the country succeeds when working people succeed.'

But Ed Miliband has departed front-line politics. And just as Tony Blair was the future once, the new recruits – encouraged in by new rules – can shape the future now. In many ways, it is a very different party to the one which was in government for 13 years. Little more than a third of its 2010 membership are still active.

So it's now for the 550,000 or so members and supporters to draw lessons from the election, not former leaders – and certainly not me.

* * *

Covering both the election campaign and the leadership contest which followed, there do, however, seem to be some very clear pointers to what issues need to be addressed – though many of the lessons drawn from this tumultuous year in the party's history will depend on the political prism through which they are viewed.

To broaden necessarily its appeal, the party will have to decide whether it will put serious political effort and organisational resources into trying to 're-engage' non-voters for whom Russell Brand proved to be no magic wand, or to spend more time winning back people who consistently vote but have drifted leftwards to the Greens, and rightwards to UKIP as well as to the Conservatives. Labour will also need to examine closely why, with a small overall swing to the party despite the loss of seats, older voters seem to be moving in the other direction. But the policies designed to appeal to a wider electorate will depend on the politics of those who develop them.

During the leadership campaign, Liz Kendall argued that reassurance, especially on public spending, was necessary to win back voters in English marginals in particular – Nuneaton, Reading, Stevenage – who hadn't forgiven Labour for being in power during the financial crash. But as the pollster James Morris points out, it isn't impossible to broaden Labour's appeal from the left, too – with caveats: that the party is seen to address key concerns about the economy and about immigration rather than ignore them. A battle would have to be won to make a distinction between borrowing to invest while eliminating the day-to-day deficit. But on the latter it's not, the pollsters would argue, as unpopular as some may think to raise taxes on business to help do this, so long as there are other policies that would convince voters the economy would grow, and not go into reverse under Labour.

But the bigger lesson, the pollsters suggest, is that clarity of message is almost more important than the message itself. 'One Nation Labour', 'Rebuilding Britain', 'The Promise of Britain', 'Squeezed Middle' – the list goes on. A cabinet minister under Blair and Brown said to me: 'Those around Ed Miliband never convinced him that he didn't need five strategies when one strategy would do.' Rather than Labour being regarded as too left- or too right-wing by most voters, they were never really sure what it stood for at all. The other striking aspect of the election campaign is how little of it was spent attacking the Conservatives head-on. Conventional London press conferences – usually the vehicle for denouncing opponents, complete with dossiers suggesting all sorts of horrors would await if you vote the 'wrong way' – had been ditched. As Ed Miliband toured the country he would set out his vision for change – he was, as a senior aide put it, his own strategist. But the team around Ed Balls felt the party leader hadn't conveyed the risks of a majority Conservative government to voters, so Labour's plans were subjected to far more demanding scrutiny from the media.

The difficulty for Labour over the summer was not whether but how to oppose. Harriet Harman's decision to abstain on the welfare bill boosted

Jeremy Corbyn's campaign as he could distance himself from the Conservatives *and* the Labour establishment. That issue is now resolved, but the
underlying dilemma isn't. If you are in opposition, will you be regarded as
a credible party of government if you simply come out against just about
everything the present administration does – including apparently popular
measures? Labour's membership shot up in the wake of the defeat – but the
party leadership can't just speak to their half a million and more members
and supporters but to the ten or 11 million voters Labour will need to win.

Labour is very nearly 100 seats behind the Conservatives – it will
need, on paper at least, to take constituencies it has consistently failed to
win in the past if it is to have a majority in 2020. That's not impossible
but given the scale of the task, it's also likely that the new leadership will
face the same questions as the old. It is now clear that Labour would have
attempted to form a government from a very poor second place. So they
are almost certainly going to be asked again about legitimacy. But fundamentally they will be interrogated on this point: Would they do a deal
with the SNP to get into Downing Street? And they will need a convincing
and consistent answer.

And as for Scotland, Labour's private polling suggested the party
never neutralised the impression it would put Westminster first. A senior
Labour strategist told me that he was frustrated that too many of his
colleagues hadn't accepted that Scotland was lost to them sooner. Just
before the formal campaign got under way, at a tense meeting in London,
Jim Murphy was refused extra resources for his already well-funded
campaign and told to better prioritise what seats he actually thought he
could hold. That strategist's advice is that Labour needs now to accept it
will be 'a long road back' in Scotland and the party must address the 'the
English question'.

Scottish Labour has a new leader – 34-year-old Kezia Dugdale. She
said on the day of her election in August that she was of a new generation,
unburdened by the baggage of the past and that voters should 'take
another look' at her party. Under her leadership, 'Nobody will be in any
doubt about what the Labour Party stands for and who we stand with.'

Former First Minister of Scotland Henry McLeish believes the lesson
Labour should learn from the election is that the only way to convince
voters it won't put Westminster before Scotland, and to be free of the need to
go cap in hand to Labour in London for cash, is through independence. No,
not for the nation, but for the party. Scottish Labour would become a sister
party of what is now the UK party – like the relationship between Germany's
Christian Democrats and Bavaria's Christian Social Union. He argues:

An independent Labour Party could say it's the voice of Scotland. But with rights, would come responsibilities. We would have to raise our own funds but the benefits would be substantial. It would be clear we were sending MPs to Westminster to represent Scotland. We need to display deep patriotism, not cheap patriotism – and not narrow nationalism.

It will be an interesting debate.

Apart from facing political challenges, Labour will also need to look at organisational changes. Several senior people have stressed that a field campaign, or 'ground war' – knocking on doors, delivering leaflets – is designed to 'get the party over the line'. It's no substitute for lacklustre leadership or a political offer people don't want to purchase. Nonetheless, there is evidence that Labour didn't target voters as effectively as the Conservatives or the SNP, didn't put resources into vulnerable seats they needed to defend, were blindsided by the scale of the Lib Dem collapse, and their five million – or more – conversations gleaned little information of use in identifying why some voters were reluctant to support them.

If Labour gets itself into a competitive position again, it will need to carry out reforms. There is every chance it will be less well-resourced in 2020 following reforms to trade union funding, so it may have to be more radical. Its new leader may have no less a task than transforming the Labour Party into a community-based campaigning organisation that puts its new members to good use and continues to grow. That will require a lot of perspiration – but also perhaps more inspiration than was evident during the past five years.

APPENDIX I

Clause 4 – Aims and Values

1. The Labour Party is a democratic socialist party. It believes that by the strength of our common endeavour we achieve more than we achieve alone, so as to create for each of us the means to realise our true potential and for all of us a community in which power, wealth and opportunity are in the hands of the many not the few; where the rights we enjoy reflect the duties we owe and where we live together freely, in a spirit of solidarity, tolerance and respect.

2. To these ends we work for:

(a) A dynamic economy, serving the public interest, in which the enterprise of the market and the rigour of competition are joined with the forces of partnership and co-operation to produce the wealth the nation needs and the opportunity for all to work and prosper with a thriving private sector and high-quality public services where those undertakings essential to the common good are either owned by the public or accountable to them

(b) A just society, which judges its strength by the condition of the weak as much as the strong, provides security against fear, and justice at work; which nurtures families, promotes equality of opportunity, and delivers people from the tyranny of poverty, prejudice and the abuse of power

(c) An open democracy, in which government is held to account by the people, decisions are taken as far as practicable by the communities they affect and where fundamental human rights are guaranteed

(d) A healthy environment, which we protect, enhance and hold in trust for future generations.

3. Labour is committed to the defence and security of the British people and to co-operating in European institutions, the United Nations, the Commonwealth and other international bodies to secure peace, freedom, democracy, economic security and environmental protection for all.

4. Labour shall work in pursuit of these aims with trade unions and co-operative societies and also with voluntary organisations, consumer groups and other representative bodies.

5. On the basis of these principles, Labour seeks the trust of the people to govern.

http://www.labourcounts.com/constitution.htm

Labour Party Leaders

Leader	Took Office	Left Office	Prime Minister?
Keir Hardie (1856–1915)	17 February 1906	22 January 1908	
Arthur Henderson (1863–1935) (1st time)	22 January 1908	14 February 1910	
George Nicoll Barnes (1859–1940)	14 February 1910	6 February 1911	
Ramsay MacDonald (1866–1937) (1st time)	6 February 1911	5 August 1914	
Arthur Henderson (1863–1935) (2nd time)	5 August 1914	24 October 1917	
William Adamson (1863–1936)	24 October 1917	14 February 1921	
J. R. Clynes (1869–1949)	14 February 1921	21 November 1922	
Ramsay MacDonald (1866–1937) (2nd time)**	21 November 1922	1 September 1931	1924 1929–1934
Arthur Henderson (1863–1935) (3rd time)	1 September 1931	25 October 1932	
George Lansbury (1859–1940)	25 October 1932	8 October 1935	
Clement Attlee (1883–1967)	8 October 1935	14 December 1955	1945–1951
Hugh Gaitskell (1906–1963)	14 December 1955	18 January 1963	

Leader	Took Office	Left Office	Prime Minister?
George Brown* (1914–1985)	18 January 1963	14 February 1963	
Harold Wilson (1916–1995)	14 February 1963	5 April 1976	1964–1970 1974–1976
James Callaghan (1912–2005)	5 April 1976	10 November 1980	1976–1979
Michael Foot (1913–2010)	10 November 1980	2 October 1983	
Neil Kinnock (1942–)	2 October 1983	18 July 1992	
John Smith (1938–1994)	18 July 1992	12 May 1994	
Margaret Beckett* (1943–)	12 May 1994	21 July 1994	
Tony Blair (1953–)	21 July 1994	24 June 2007	1997–2007
Gordon Brown (1951–)	24 June 2007	11 May 2010	2007–2010
Harriet Harman* (1950–) (1st time)	11 May 2010	25 September 2010	
Ed Miliband (1969–)	25 September 2010	8 May 2015	
Harriet Harman* (1950–) (2nd time)	8 May 2015	12 September 2015	
Jeremy Corbyn (1949–)	12 September 2015	Incumbent	

  * Acting leader pending election of new leader
 ** Expelled by Labour Party National Executive in August 1931 on formation
    of the emergency National Government

APPENDIX 3

Selected quotes

KEIR HARDIE

Half a million of the people of this country benefit by the present system; the remaining millions of toilers and business men do not. The pursuit of wealth corrupts the manhood of men. We are called upon at the beginning of the twentieth century to decide the question propounded in the Sermon on the Mount, as to whether we will worship God or Mammon. The present day is a Mammon-worshipping age. Socialism proposes to dethrone the brute-god Mammon and to lift humanity into its place. I beg to submit, in this very imperfect fashion, the resolution on the paper, merely promising that the last has not been heard of the Socialist movement either in the country or on the floor of this House, but that, just as sure as Radicalism democratised the system of government politically in the last century, so will socialism democratise the country industrially during the century upon which we just entered. (Moving a motion calling for a Socialist Commonwealth in the House of Commons, 23 April 1901.)

ARTHUR HENDERSON

Another essential to a universal and durable peace is social justice.

One of the first essentials is a policy of unreserved political cooperation with all the nations of the world.

Whatever we do or fail to do will influence the course of history.

The vast upheaval of the World War set in motion forces that will either destroy civilization or raise mankind to undreamed of heights of human welfare and prosperity.

RAMSAY MacDONALD

We hear war called murder. It is not. It is suicide.

It is not God but the Devil who is in charge of the international situation and those who are working for God in it are poor servants if all they do is worship God and neglect their duty to circumvent the Devil.

Yes, tomorrow every Duchess in London will be wanting to kiss me! MacDonald to Philip Snowden the day after the formation of the National Government, 25 August 1931

GEORGE LANSBURY

I would close every recruiting station, disband the Army and disarm the Air Force. I would abolish the whole dreadful equipment of war and say to the world: 'Do your worst'

CLEMENT ATTLEE

Democracy means government by discussion, but it is only effective if you can stop people talking.

The House of Lords is like a glass of champagne that has stood for five days.

I think the British have the distinction above all other nations of being able to put new wine into old bottles without bursting them.

The last of our enemies is laid low.

HUGH GAITSKELL

In the last few years we have learned to distinguish the means of Socialism from the ends.

There are some of us, Mr Chairman, who will fight, fight and fight again to save the Party we love.

You still hear some people speaking as though we could decide whether the Common Market existed or not.

GEORGE BROWN

In the last few years, employers have recognised the importance of branding their employment as something to be desired. It's become a way of life for them. It starts at the top and goes through the organisation. There is nowhere in the city with power.

HAROLD WILSON

He who rejects change is the architect of decay. The only human institution which rejects progress is the cemetery.

A week is a long time in politics.

I'm an optimist, but an optimist who carries a raincoat.

One man's wage increase is another man's price increase.

The Labour Party is like a stage-coach. If you rattle along at great speed everybody is too exhilarated or too seasick to cause any trouble. But if you stop everybody gets out and argues about where to go next.

If the Tories get in, in five years no one will be able to afford to buy an egg.

The only limits of power are the bounds of belief.

JAMES CALLAGHAN

The rule of law should be upheld by all political parties. They should neither advise others to break the law, nor encourage others to do so even when they strongly disagree with the legislation put forward by the government of the day.

You can never reach the promised land. You can march towards it.

A leader must have the courage to act against an expert's advice.

Never let me hear anyone say again that a Socialist State cannot provide outlets for those with initiative. The rewards given to ability in the USSR at all levels are far greater than those given to the employed in capitalist Britain. I have seen it and it works.

We used to think that you could spend your way out of a recession and increase employment by cutting taxes and boosting government spending. I tell you in all candour that that option no longer exists, and in so far as it ever did exist, it only worked on each occasion since the war by injecting a bigger dose of inflation into the economy, followed by a higher level of unemployment as the next step.

I hate putting up taxes.

MICHAEL FOOT

Is the Labour Party to remain a democratic party in which the right of free criticism and free debate is not merely tolerated but encouraged? Or are the rank and file of the party to be bludgeoned or cowed into an uncritical subservience towards the leadership?

Socialism without public ownership is nothing but a fantastic apology.

A Britain which denounced the insanity of the nuclear strategy would be in a position to direct its influence at the United Nations and in the world at large, in a manner at present denied us.

NEIL KINNOCK

I warn you not to be ordinary, I warn you not to be young, I warn you not to fall ill, and I warn you not to grow old.

I'm the guy everybody wanted to live next door. They just didn't want me to be Prime Minister.

Margaret Thatcher was not a malicious person. She was a person who couldn't see, or didn't want to see, the unfairness and disadvantaging consequences of the application of what she thought to be a renewing ideology.

JOHN SMITH

The opportunity to serve our country – that is all we ask.

If it is the case that one Department of this Government deliberately organised a leak to frustrate a Minister in the same Government, that is not only dirty tricks but a habit that is inimical to the practice of good government in this country.

MARGARET BECKETT

You have to make your choice and live with your choice.

I don't join or leave things lightly.

TONY BLAIR

The art of leadership is saying no, not yes. It is very easy to say yes.

Sometimes it is better to lose and do the right thing than to win and do the wrong thing.

I cannot think of any circumstances in which a government can go to war without the support of parliament.

GORDON BROWN

Take, therefore, what modern technology is capable of: the power of our moral sense allied to the power of communications and our ability to organise internationally. That, in my view, gives us the first opportunity as a community to fundamentally change the world.

You need in the long run for stability, for economic growth, for jobs, as well as for financial stability, global economic institutions that make sure that growth to be sustained has to be shared, and are built on the principle that the prosperity of this world is indivisible.

We spend more on cows than the poor.

I believe there is a moral sense and a global ethic that commands attention from people of every religion and every faith, and people of no faith. But I think what's new is that we now have the capacity to communicate instantaneously across frontiers right across the world.

HARRIET HARMAN

There are many women with children under five who want to work and who lack affordable, high-quality child care.

I think a balanced team of men and women makes better decisions. That's one of the reasons why I was prepared to run for deputy leader.

Actually, I don't ever think there will be a men-only team of leadership in the Labour Party again. People would look at it and say, 'What? Are there no women in the Party to be part of the leadership? Do men want to do it all themselves?' It just won't happen again.

ED MILIBAND

My beliefs will run through everything I do. My beliefs, my values, are my anchor and when people try to drag me, as I know they will, it is to that sense of right and wrong, that sense of who I am and what I believe, to which I will always hold.

I come from a generation that suffered school lessons in portacabins and crumbling hospitals. I tell you one thing, for the 18 years they were in power the Tories did nothing to fix the roof when the sun was shining.

The new generation of Labour is different. Different attitudes, different ideas, different ways of doing politics.

JEREMY CORBYN

Are super-rich people actually happy with being super-rich? I would want the super rich to pay properly their share of the needs of the rest of the community.

He was a fascinating figure who observed a great deal and from whom we can learn a great deal. (on Karl Marx to the BBC's Andrew Marr)

Without exception, the majority electricity, gas, water and railway infra-structures of Britain were built through public investment since the end of WWII and were all privatised at knock-down prices for the benefit of greedy asset-strippers by the Thatcher and Major-led Tory governments.

Some people say to me, are we still worried about Hiroshima. My reply is that the weapons were used specifically against civilians and while 'fireworks' compared to what is now available, killed and have killed for the past 59 years. Nuclear weapons have saved no lives, killed thousands and maimed many more and impoverished the poor nations who have them.

It was an illegal war and therefore [Tony Blair] has to explain to that. Is he going to be tried for it? I don't know. Could he be tried for it? Possibly. (on the Iraq war)

We have grown enormously because of the hopes of so many ordinary people for a different Britain, a better Britain, a more equal Britain, a more decent Britain.

We go forward now as a movement and a party, bigger than we have ever been for a very, very long time, stronger than we have ever been for a very long time, more determined than we have been for a long time, to show to everyone that the objectives of our party are intact.

APPENDIX 4

Labour Votes at General Elections

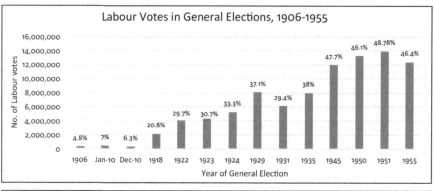

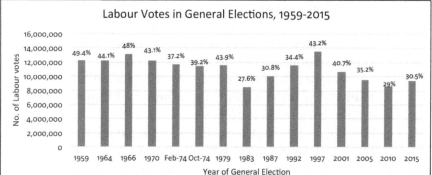

ELECTION RESULTS – NO. OF LABOUR VOTES

1906	254,202	1964	12,205,808
Jan 1910	435,770	1966	13,096,629
Dec 1910	309,963	1970	12,208,758
1918	2,171,230	Feb 1974	11,645,616
1922	4,076,665	Oct 1974	11,457,079
1924	5,281,626	1979	11,532,218
1929	8,048,968	1983	8,456,934
1931	6,081,826	1987	10,029,270
1935	7,984,988	1992	11,560,484
1945	11,967,746	1997	13,518,167
1950	13,266,176	2001	10,724,953
1951	13,948,883	2005	9,552,436
1955	12,405,254	2010	8,609,527
1959	12,216,172	2015	9,347,324

APPENDIX 5

Campaign Chronology

14/3/15   Labour launch their election pledges in Birmingham.

16/3/15   Ed Miliband rules out a coalition with the SNP – at an event in Pudsey.

26/3/15   'Hell, Yes!' – Miliband tells Jeremy Paxman he is tough enough to be PM.

27/3/15   Labour launch their election campaign at London's Olympic Park – 'Britain Succeeds When Working People Succeed'.

30/3/15   David Cameron goes to the Palace to begin the formal election campaign.
Ed Miliband and Ed Balls unveil their 'business manifesto' in the City of London.

2/4/15   Ed Miliband clashes with David Cameron on the ITV debate in Salford – their only head-to-head encounter of the campaign.

8/4/15   Labour announce plans to ban 'non-doms'.

9/4/15   Conservative defence secretary Michael Fallon accuses Ed Miliband of being willing to stab his own brother – and the UK – in the back to get in to power.

10/4/15   Ed Miliband, Ed Balls and Jim Murphy attack SNP plans for Full Fiscal Autonomy in Edinburgh – but shift very few votes.

13/4/15   Ed Miliband launches Labour's election manifesto in Manchester and puts fiscal responsibility on a hastily-added front page.

14/4/15   The Conservative manifesto is launched in Swindon.

16/4/15   Nicola Sturgeon wounds Ed Miliband in the 'challenger's debate' in London by saying 'there isn't enough of a difference' between Labour and Conservatives. David Cameron and Nick Clegg don't take part.

20/4/15   Ed Miliband addresses the STUC conference in Ayr, but doesn't mention the key line of attack – that the SNP might back a second referendum. Nicola Sturgeon unveils her party's manifesto in Edinburgh, stressing SNP opposition to austerity.

26/4/15   In a BBC interview, the Labour leader rules out post-election deals, short of a coalition, with the SNP.

27/4/15   Labour unveils an additional, sixth pledge, on housing at a rally in Stockton.
Later, Ed Miliband meets Russell Brand at the comedian's Shoreditch home.

30/4/15 On a special edition of BBC Question Time from Leeds, Ed Miliband indicates he would rather not be in government than do a deal with the SNP. He faces hostile questioning when he says Labour didn't overspend in office.

1/5/15 Ed Miliband narrowly avoids the 'Scottish Resistance' in Glasgow.

3/5/15 The 'Edstone' of campaign pledges is unveiled to mirth and derision.

6/5/15 Ed Miliband announces in Colne that his activists have had 'five million conversations' with voters.

7/5/15 Polling day – Labour insiders are predicting they will finish 'a good second' and could be in Downing Street.

8/5/15 Labour holds fewer seats than in 2010 and Ed Miliband resigns.

10/5/15 Liz Kendall declares she will run for Labour leader on the BBC's Sunday Politics.

12/5/15 Chuka Umunna declares his candidacy, only to withdraw three days later.

13/5/15 Labour's ruling NEC draws up a timetable for the leadership contest – and confirms Miliband's successor will be announced on 12 September. Registered supporters who pay £3 will have a vote.
Yvette Cooper and Andy Burnham say they will join the race.

16/5/15 Hustings hosted by the Blairite Progress group. All potential candidates agree that Labour wasn't pro-business enough.
Two of the potential contenders who take part – Mary Creagh and Tristram Hunt – don't have enough support from fellow MPs to make the ballot and later withdraw.

3/6/15 Jeremy Corbyn tells his local paper, the *Islington Tribune*, that he will stand for the Labour leadership, and criticises what's on offer from the other candidates:
'They are not offering a clear enough alternative on the economic strategy and austerity, and our attitude to welfare expenditure'.

15/6/15 Jeremy Corbyn meets the deadline for getting the necessary support of 35 MPs to get on the leadership ballot with less than two minutes to spare. Fourteen of those who nominated him say publicly that they will subsequently vote for other candidates.

12/7/15 Harriet Harman indicates, on BBC's Sunday Politics, that Labour will abstain on the welfare bill.

13/7/15   Harriet Harman faces a backlash at a meeting of her own MPs
          – and criticism from supporters of Yvette Cooper and Andy
          Burnham, who want to oppose the bill.

16/7/15   Harriet Harman announces that she will now attempt to
          amend the welfare bill but expects Labour MPs to abstain if
          this fails.

20/7/15   Forty-eight Labour MPs defy the party line and vote against
          the welfare bill – including Jeremy Corbyn. Yvette Cooper and
          Andy Burnham accept 'collective responsibility' and abstain.
          Burnham says he would oppose as leader but thinks the vote
          marks a 'turning point' in Corbyn's fortunes.

21/7/15   On BBC *Newsnight*, Kirsty Wark reads out the results of a
          YouGov poll which suggests that Jeremy Corbyn is leading in
          the race to become Labour leader. Her guest – Jim Murphy's
          former chief of staff, John McTernan – describes the Labour
          MPs who nominated him as 'morons'.

22/7/15   Tony Blair tells the modernising Progress group: 'I wouldn't
          want to win on an old fashioned leftist platform. Even if I
          thought it was the route to victory, I wouldn't take it' – and
          suggests those voting with the hearts not their heads 'need a
          transplant'. Meanwhile Jeremy Corbyn attends a central
          London seminar behind closed doors to discuss an anti-
          austerity economic programme.

16/8/15   Without naming him, Gordon Brown warns against Jeremy
          Corbyn winning his party's leadership by attacking his foreign
          policy positions and saying Labour must remain 'relevant'. He
          later makes it clear he would back Yvette Cooper.

19/8/15   Reports emerge about a backroom Labour row on whether to
          do further background checks – 'verification' – on some of
          those applying to join Labour as supporters to ensure they
          share the party's values.

25/8/15   Harriet Harman meets the candidates – initially at a secret
          location in Stevenage – to discuss accusations of 'infiltration'
          into Labour by opponents, and potential voting irregularities
          in the leadership contest. She says the process is 'robust'.

10/9/15   Voting closes in the Labour leadership contest.

12/9/15   Jeremy Corbyn is elected Labour leader with 59.5% of the
          vote – nearly 40 points ahead of his nearest opponent, Andy
          Burnham. Tom Watson is elected as his deputy.

16/9/15   Jeremy Corbyn's first PMQs – he breaks tradition by asking
          questions sent to him by voters.

APPENDIX 6

Labour Party Leadership results announced 12 September 2015

Results 1st Stage	Members	Registered Supporters	Affiliated Supporters	Total	% of Valid Vote	MP nomina-tions	% of nomina-tions
BURNHAM, Andy	55,698	6,160	18,604	80,462	19.0%	68	33%
COOPER, Yvette	54,470	8,415	9,043	71,928	17.0%	59	29%
CORBYN, Jeremy	121,751	88,449	41,217	251,417	59.5%	36*	18%
KENDALL, Liz	13,601	2,574	2,682	18,857	4.5%	41	20%
TOTAL	245,520	105,598	71,546	422,664	100%	204**	100%

**28 Labour MPs chose not to nominate any of the candidates prior to the deadline of 15 June 2015 including Ed Miliband, Harriet Harman and Tom Watson.
*Comprises 20 Backers and 16 Non-backers

BACKERS:

Diane Abbott	Kelvin Hopkins	Grahame Morris
Richard Burgon	Imran Hussain	Kate Osamor
Ronnie Campbell	Clive Lewis	Dennis Skinner
Sarah Champion	Rebecca Long-Bailey	Cat Smith
Jeremy Corbyn	Michael Meacher	Jon Trickett
Clive Efford	John McDonnell	Catherine West

NOMINATING CORBYN BUT OPENLY BACKING OTHER CANDIDATES:

Rushanara Ali	Rupa Huq	Chi Onwarah
Margaret Beckett	Huw Irranca Davies	Tulip Siddiq
Jo Cox	Sadiq Khan	Andrew Smith
Neil Coyle	David Lammy	Gareth Thomas
Louise Haigh	Gordon Marsden	Emily Thornberry

NOMINATING CORBYN TO 'BROADEN THE DEBATE' BUT NOT BACKING HIM:

Dawn Butler
Jon Cruddas
Frank Field

APPENDIX 7

Miliband and Corbyn buzzwords

Miliband buzzwords

Britain succeeds when working people succeed	Responsible capitalism	Predistribution	Connect with the voters	Inequality	Tough decisions
Empathy	The race to the top	We are better than this	Not under my government	Individual working people	Extreme cuts
Fully funded	Cost of living crisis	Broken Britain	You can't fund the NHS from an IOU	Rich and powerful	Together

Corbyn buzzwords

Democratic collective	Arts for everyone	Stay together	Reducing inequality	Public good	Fairer society
Collective aspirations	Support everybody	Interest of the people	Inclusive	Affordability	Better world
Humanitarian response	Common endeavour	21st century democracy	Gender equality	No to austerity	10-point plan

What Would Keir Hardie Say?: Exploring Hardie's vision and relevance to 21st Century politics

Pauline Bryan (ed.)
ISBN 978-1-910745-15-1 PBK £9.99

My work has consisted of trying to stir up a divine discontent with wrong
KEIR HARDIE

Founder and first leader of the Labour Party, Keir Hardie was a passionate campaigner for social justice. A socialist and a trade unionist, he described himself as 'above all anagitator'. Hardie gave unstinting commitment to women's suffrage, building the labour movement and the fight against imperialism. Now, 100 years after Hardie's death, Pauline Bryan gathers together essays from writers, trade unionists, academics and politicians reflecting on Hardie's contribution and what it means today.

Has Hardie left a lasting legacy of socialist ideals and vision?

Why is Hardie still relevant to present day politics?

What would Keir Hardie say about: attacks on welfare • trade union rights • immigration • privatisation • globalisation • the economy?

Hardie's life remains exemplary today... because he embodied one of the enduring laws about politics: that it is largely popular pressure that brings about change.
MELISSA BENN, Honorary President of the Keir Hardie Society

The great lesson from Hardie is the crying need to unite people of very different cultures and traditions in a quest for peace.
JEREMY CORBYN, MP

Dave Does The Right Thing

Introduced by Owen Dudley Edwards
ISBN: 978-1-910021-63-7 PBK £6.99

Meet Dave. Dave is Prime Minister. Dave really wants to do the right thing. He keeps telling us he wants to do the right thing. Again and again and again. One afternoon he told us four times in half an hour.

Then he went off and did the right thing. Every morning when he wakes up, he reminds himself to remind us that he's doing the right thing.

But what is the right thing? And what is the wrong thing? And is doing the right thing the right thing or the wrong thing to do? Or is doing the wrong thing the right thing to do when doing the right thing might turn out to be the wrong thing, and doing the wrong thing might turn out to be the right thing?

Next to doing the right thing, the most important thing is to let people know you are doing the right thing.
JOHN D. ROCKEFELLER

Luath Press Limited
committed to publishing well written books worth reading

LUATH PRESS takes its name from Robert Burns, whose little collie Luath (*Gael.*, swift or nimble) tripped up Jean Armour at a wedding and gave him the chance to speak to the woman who was to be his wife and the abiding love of his life. Burns called one of 'The Twa Dogs' Luath after Cuchullin's hunting dog in Ossian's *Fingal*. Luath Press was established in 1981 in the heart of Burns country, and now resides a few steps up the road from Burns' first lodgings on Edinburgh's Royal Mile. Luath offers you distinctive writing with a hint of unexpected pleasures.

Most bookshops in the UK, the US, Canada, Australia, New Zealand and parts of Europe either carry our books in stock or can order them for you. To order direct from us, please send a £sterling cheque, postal order, international money order or your credit card details (number, address of cardholder and expiry date) to us at the address below. Please add post and packing as follows: UK – £1.00 per delivery address; overseas surface mail – £2.50 per delivery address; overseas airmail – £3.50 for the first book to each delivery address, plus £1.00 for each additional book by airmail to the same address. If your order is a gift, we will happily enclose your card or message at no extra charge.

Luath Press Limited
543/2 Castlehill
The Royal Mile
Edinburgh EH1 2ND
Scotland
Telephone: 0131 225 4326 (24 hours)
email: sales@luath.co.uk
Website: www.luath.co.uk